EXPERT **RESUMES** for
Career Changers

Wendy S. Enelow and
Louise M. Kursmark

JIST Works
America's Career Publisher

Expert Resumes for Career Changers

© 2005 by Wendy S. Enelow and Louise M. Kursmark

Published by JIST Works, an imprint of JIST Publishing, Inc.
8902 Otis Avenue
Indianapolis, IN 46216-1033
Phone: 1-800-648-JIST   Fax: 1-800-JIST-FAX   E-mail: info@jist.com

Visit our Web site at **www.jist.com** for information on JIST, free job search tips, book chapters, and how to order our many products! For free information on 14,000 job titles, visit **www.careeroink.com**.

Quantity discounts are available for JIST books. Please call our Sales Department at 1-800-648-5478 for a free catalog and more information.

Acquisitions and Development Editor: Lori Cates Hand
Cover Designer: Katy Bodenmiller
Interior Designer and Page Layout: Trudy Coler
Proofreader: Jeanne Clark
Indexer: Tina Trettin

Printed in the United States of America
08 07 06 05   9 8 7 6 5 4 3

Library of Congress Cataloging-in-Publication Data

Enelow, Wendy S.
    Expert resumes for career changers / Wendy S. Enelow and Louise M. Kursmark.
        p. cm.
    Includes index.
    ISBN 1-59357-092-9 (alk. paper)
    1. Résumés (Employment) 2. Career changes. I. Kursmark, Louise. II. Title.
    HF5383.E47875   2005
    650.14'2--dc22   2004023589

We have been careful to provide accurate information in this book, but it is possible that errors and omissions have been introduced. Please consider this in making any career plans or other important decisions. Trust your own judgment above all else and in all things.

Trademarks: All brand names and product names used in this book are trade names, service marks, trademarks, or registered trademarks of their respective owners.

ISBN 1-59357-092-9

TABLE OF CONTENTS

ABOUT THIS BOOK

If you're reading this book, you're most likely one of tens of thousands of people who are considering a career change—either a change in position or a change in industry. You might have made this decision because of any one of the following reasons:

- Your current industry has been hard hit by the recent economic recession.

- The position that you currently hold has been eliminated in your company and also in many similar companies.

- You're bored in your current position and ready for a change.

- You want to pursue your true passion as your new career.

- Your personal situation has changed and you're now able to pursue a career of real interest to you.

- You're relocating and need to explore new opportunities in your new geographic area.

- You want greater opportunities for increased compensation and advancement.

- You're frustrated and ready for a change.

- You're tired of all the responsibilities of your career and ready to downsize.

These are just a few of the reasons you might be considering a career change. There are many other reasons, and you'll find resumes in this book that are relevant to them all.

Now, here's the good news: You've selected a great time to make a career change! Despite the economic concerns that we are facing, believe it or not, it's a great time to look for a new job or a new career. According to the Bureau of Labor Statistics of the U.S. Department of Labor, the employment outlook is optimistic. Consider these findings:

- Total U.S. employment is projected to increase 15 percent between 2000 and 2010.

- Service-producing industries will continue to be the dominant employment generator, adding more than 20 million jobs by 2010.

- Goods-producing industries will also experience gains in employment, although not as significant as those in the service sector.

In chapter 1, you can read more interesting statistics, all of which will reinforce the fact that you've made the right decision to launch your search campaign today.

To take advantage of all of these opportunities, you must first develop a powerful, performance-based resume. To be a successful job seeker, you must know how to communicate your qualifications in a strong and effective written presentation. Sure, it's important to let employers know essential details, but a resume is more than just your job history and academic credentials. A winning resume is a concise yet comprehensive document that gives you a competitive edge in the job market. Creating such a powerful document is what this book is all about.

We'll explore the changes in resume presentation that have arisen over the past decade. In the past, resumes were almost always printed on paper and mailed. Today, e-mail has become the chosen method for resume distribution in many industries and professions. In turn, many of the traditional methods for "typing" and presenting resumes have changed dramatically. This book will instruct you in the methods for preparing resumes for e-mail, scanning, and Web site posting, as well as the traditional printed resume.

By using *Expert Resumes for Career Changers* as your professional guide, you will succeed in developing a powerful and effective resume that opens doors, gets interviews, and helps you land your next great opportunity!

INTRODUCTION

This book, the seventh in the *Expert Resumes* series, has been one of the most challenging to write because it covers such a large and diverse audience. There are, however, several common denominators facing every individual who is interested in making a career change, either within their profession or to another industry. In summary, the fact that you are seeking to change careers will dictate almost everything that you write in your resume, how you write it, and where it is positioned. Your goal is to paint a picture of the "new" you and not simply reiterate what you have done in the past, expecting a prospective employer to figure out that you can do the "new" thing just as well. It simply does not work that way!

If you fall into the career-changer category, the critical questions you must ask yourself about your resume and your job search are the following:

- *How* **are you going to paint a picture of the "new" you?** What are you going to highlight about your past experience that ties directly to your current objectives? What accomplishments, skills, and qualifications are you going to "sell" in your resume to support your "new" career objective?

- *What* **resume format are you going to use?** Is a chronological, functional, or hybrid resume format going to work best for you? Which format will give you the greatest flexibility to highlight the skills you want to bring to the forefront in support of your career change?

- *Where* **are you going to look for a job?** Assuming you know the type of position and industry you want to enter at this point in your career, how are you going to identify and approach those companies?

When you can answer the how, what, and where, you'll be prepared to write your resume and launch your search campaign. Use chapters 1 through 3 to guide you in developing the content for your resume and selecting the appropriate design and layout. Your resume should focus on your skills, achievements, and qualifications, demonstrating the value and benefit you bring to a prospective employer as they relate to your current career goals. The focus is on the "new" you and not necessarily what you have done professionally in the past.

Review the sample resumes in chapters 4 through 12 to see what other people have done—people in similar situations to yours and facing similar challenges. You'll find interesting formats, unique skills presentations, achievement-focused resumes, project-focused resumes, and much more. Most importantly, you'll see samples written by the top resume writers in the U.S., Canada, and Australia.

These are real resumes that got interviews and generated job offers. They're the "best of the best" from us to you.

What Are Your Career Objectives?

Before you proceed any further with writing your resume, you'll need to begin by defining your career or job objectives–specifically, the types of positions, companies, and industries in which you are interested. This is critical, because a haphazard, unfocused job search will lead you nowhere.

KNOW THE EMPLOYMENT TRENDS

One of the best ways to begin identifying your career objectives is to look at what opportunities are available today, in the immediate future, and in the longer-term future. Two of the most useful tools for this type of research and information collection are the U.S. Department of Labor's Bureau of Labor Statistics Web site (www.bls.gov) and the Bureau's *Occupational Outlook Handbook* (www.bls.gov/oco).

Some of the most interesting findings that you'll discover when investigating potential industry and job targets are these:

- Total employment is projected to increase 14.8 percent between 2002 and 2012.

- Service-producing companies will continue to be the dominant employment generator, adding 20.8 million jobs by 2012, a gain of 19.2 percent.

- Goods-producing companies (manufacturing and construction) will contribute modest employment gains of only 3.5 percent.

- Computer- and health-related occupations account for 21 of the 30 fastest-growing occupations.

- Computer- and health-related occupations account for all of the top 10 fastest-growing occupations (health care with six; computer with four).

- The 10 fastest-growing industries are in the service sector and include software publishing, computer systems design, management and technical consulting, employment, social assistance, child day care, professional and business services, motion picture and video, health services, and arts/entertainment and recreation.

- Of all goods-producing industries, only four were projected to demonstrate growth. They are pharmaceutical and medicine manufacturing, construction, food manufacturing, and motor vehicle and parts manufacturing.

These facts and statistics clearly demonstrate that there are numerous employment opportunities across diverse sectors within our economy, from advanced technology positions to hourly wage jobs in construction and home health care. Although most industries may not be growing at double-digit percentages as in years past, companies continue to expand and new companies emerge every day. The opportunities are out there; your challenge is to find them and position yourself as the "right" candidate.

MANAGE YOUR JOB SEARCH AND YOUR CAREER

To take advantage of these opportunities, you must be an educated job seeker. That means you must know what you want in your career, where the hiring action is, what qualifications and credentials you need to attain your desired career goals, and how best to market your qualifications. It is no longer enough to have a specific talent or set of skills. Whether you're a teacher seeking a position in public relations, a nurse wanting to transfer into pharmaceutical sales, an engineer seeking new opportunities as a financial manager, or a person with any one of hundreds of other career-change goals, you must also be a strategic marketer, able to package and promote your experience to take advantage of this wave of employment opportunity.

There's no doubt that the employment market has changed dramatically from only a few years ago. According to the U.S. Department of Labor, you should expect to hold between 10 and 20 different jobs during your career. No longer is stability the status quo. Today, the norm is movement, onward and upward, in a fast-paced and intense employment market where there are many, many opportunities for career changers. And to take advantage of all of the opportunities, every job seeker—no matter the profession, no matter the industry, no matter the job goal—must proactively control and manage his career.

You are also faced with the additional challenge of positioning yourself for a successful career change. In fact, in many instances, you may be competing against other candidates who have experience within the industry or profession you are attempting to enter. This can make your job search even more difficult than that of the more "traditional" job seeker who moves from one position to another similar position without having to make a career change.

And that is precisely why this book is so important to you. We'll outline the strategies and techniques that you can use to effectively position yourself against other candidates, creating a resume that highlights your skills and qualifications, while effectively minimizing the fact that you're seeking a career change.

Job Search Questions and Answers

Before we get to the core of this book—resume writing and design—we'd like to offer some practical job search advice that is valuable to virtually every career changer.

WHAT IS THE MOST IMPORTANT CONSIDERATION FOR A CAREER CHANGER?

As outlined previously, the single most important consideration for any career-change candidate is how you're going to highlight your skills, qualifications, and achievements as they relate to and support your current career objectives. Remember, your career-change resume is not a historical document that simply lists where you've worked and what you've done. Rather, a truly effective career-change resume is one that takes all of the skills and experience you have that are relevant to your new career goal and brings them to the forefront to create a picture of the "new" you.

Sometimes, this can be a relatively easy process. Let's use a nurse transitioning into the field of medical equipment sales as an example. Sheila Barnes already has extensive experience in the medical and health-care fields, has worked closely with physicians and other health-care providers so she is comfortable interacting with them, and most likely has a wealth of experience working with a diversity of medical equipment and perhaps with vendors. This is the type of information that will be highlighted in her career-change resume and *not* her daily nursing and patient-care responsibilities.

In other situations, the parallels between past experience and current objectives might not be so closely aligned. Consider John Mackam who, after 20 years in the construction industry, has now decided to seek a position in the field of accounting and finance, an area that has *not* been one of his primary responsibilities. Writing this resume will take more creativity to identify any and all relevant skills he might have (for example, setting project budgets, estimating project costs, writing reports, keeping records, and administering projects). The concept is the same as with the previous nursing example. The stretch to identify transferable skills might be more difficult, but it's certainly not impossible.

Whatever your situation or objectives, when preparing your resume you should keep in mind one critical fact:

Your resume is a marketing tool written to sell YOU!

How Do You Enter a New Career?

Your success in entering a new career field relies on two important factors:

- Highlighting any relevant skills, qualifications, accomplishments, experiences, education, credentials, volunteer work, involvement with professional or civic associations, and more that tie directly into your current career objective.

- Using an integrated job search campaign that will get you in front of decision makers at a wide array of companies in your field of interest. You can read much more about job search strategy in the next few pages of this chapter in the section titled "How Do You Get the Jobs?"

What Is the Best Resume Strategy for Making a Successful Career Change?

The single most important factor in making a career change is to remember that your resume must *sell* what you have to offer:

- If you're a teacher seeking to transition into a position in corporate training and development, *sell* the fact that you created new curricula, designed new instructional programs, acquired innovative teaching materials, and trained new faculty.

- If you're a hands-on computer technician now seeking a position marketing new technology products, *highlight* the wealth of your technical expertise, your success in working with and supporting end-users, your ability to manage projects, and your strong communication skills.

- If you're an accountant pursuing opportunities in general management, *sell* your experience in policy and procedure development, business management, team building and leadership, strategic planning, and organizational development.

When writing your resume, your challenge is to create a picture of knowledge, action, and results. In essence, you're stating "This is what I know, this is how I've used it, and this is how well I've performed." Success sells, so be sure to highlight yours. If you don't, no one else will.

WHERE ARE THE JOBS?

The jobs are everywhere—from multinational manufacturing conglomerates to the small retail sales companies in your neighborhood; from high-tech electronics firms in Silicon Valley to 100-year-old farming operations in rural communities; from banks and financial institutions to hospitals and health-care facilities in every city and town. The jobs are everywhere.

HOW DO YOU GET THE JOBS?

To answer this question, we need to review the basic principle underlying job search:

Job search is marketing!

You have a product to sell—yourself—and the best way to sell it is to use all appropriate *marketing channels* just as you would for any other product.

Suppose you wanted to sell televisions. What would you do? You'd market your products using newspaper, magazine, and radio advertisements. You might develop a company Web site to build your e-business, and perhaps you'd hire a field sales representative to market to major retail chains. Each of these is a different *marketing channel* through which you're attempting to reach your audience.

The same approach applies to job search. You must use every marketing channel that's right for you. Unfortunately, there is no exact formula that works for everyone. What's right for you depends on your specific career objectives—the type of position you want, the industry you're targeting, your geographic restrictions (if you have any), your salary requirements, and more.

Following are the most valuable marketing channels for a successful job search. These are ordered from most effective to least effective.

1. **Referrals.** There is nothing better than a personal referral to a company, either in general or for a specific position. Referrals can open doors that, in most instances, would never be accessible any other way. If you know anyone who could possibly refer you to a specific organization, contact that person immediately and ask for his or her assistance. This is particularly critical for career changers and will be, by far, your single best marketing strategy to land a new position.

2. **Networking.** Networking is the backbone of every successful job search. Although you might consider it an unpleasant or difficult task, it is essential that you network effectively with your professional colleagues and associates, past employers, past co-workers, suppliers, neighbors, friends, and others who might know of opportunities that are right for you. Another good strategy is to attend meetings of trade or professional associations in your area that are for professions in occupations like those you're seeking to enter. This is a wonderful strategy to make new contacts and start building your network in your new career field. And particularly in today's nomadic job market—where you're likely to change jobs every few years—the best strategy is to keep your network "alive" even when you're *not* searching for a new position.

3. **Responding to newspaper, magazine, and periodical advertisements.** Although the opportunity to post job opportunities online has reduced the overall number of print advertisements, they still abound. Do not forget about this "tried-and-true" marketing strategy. If they've got the job and you have the qualifications–even if you are a career changer, it can be a perfect fit.

4. **Responding to online job postings.** One of the most advantageous results of the technology revolution is an employer's ability to post job announcements online and a job seeker's ability to respond immediately via e-mail. It's a wonder! In most (but not all) instances, these are bona fide opportunities, and it's well worth your while to spend time searching for and responding to appropriate postings. However, don't make the mistake of devoting *too* much time to searching the Internet. It can consume a huge amount of your time that you should spend on other job-search efforts.

   To expedite your search, here are the largest and most widely used online job-posting sites—presented alphabetically, not necessarily in order of effectiveness or value:

http://careers.msn.com	www.hirediversity.com
http://careers.yahoo.com	www.hotjobs.com
www.americanjobs.com	www.hotresumes.yahoo.com
www.careerbuilder.com	www.monster.com
www.employmentguide.com	www.net-temps.com
www.dice.com	www.sixfigurejobs.com
www.flipdog.monster.com	

5. **Posting your resume online.** The Net is swarming with reasonably priced (if not free) Web sites where you can post your resume. It's quick, easy, and the only *passive* thing you can do in your search. All of the other marketing channels require action on your part. With online resume postings, once you've posted, you're done. You then just wait (and hope!) for some response. Again, it's important not to invest too much time, energy, or anticipation in this approach. Your chances of landing a job this way are slim. But because it is quick, easy, and low- or no-cost, it is certainly a worthwhile activity.

6. **Targeted e-mail campaigns (resumes and cover letters) to recruiters.** Recruiters have jobs, and you want one. It's pretty straightforward. The only catch is to find the "right" recruiters who have the "right" jobs. Therefore, you must devote the time and effort to preparing the "right" list of recruiters. There are many resources on the Internet where you can access information about recruiters (for a fee), sort that information by industry (such as banking, sales, manufacturing, purchasing, transportation, finance, public relations, or telecommunications), and then cross-reference it with position specialization (such as management, technical, or administration). This allows you to identify the recruiters who would be interested in a candidate with your qualifications. Because these campaigns are transmitted electronically, they are easy and inexpensive to produce. Here are some sites to help with this activity:

   www.profileresearch.com

   www.kennedyinfo.com

   When working with recruiters, it's important to realize that they *do not* work for you! Their clients are the hiring companies that pay their fees. They are not in business to "find a job" for you, but rather to fill a specific position with a qualified candidate, either you or someone else. To maximize your chances of finding a position through a recruiter or agency, don't rely on just one or two, but distribute your resume to many that meet your specific criteria.

   A word of caution: Most recruiters are looking to fill specific positions with individuals with very specific qualifications. As a career changer, you are likely to find that recruiters are not your best source of job opportunities because they are not paid to "think outside the box." If their client (the hiring company) has requested a candidate with experience in x, y, and z, recruiters are going to present only those job seekers with precisely that experience. Knowing that you're attempting to change careers and might not have precisely the background that the company is looking for, recruiters might simply pass you by. Don't be alarmed; it's their job! But what this means for you as a career changer is that you should invest minimal effort toward recruiter searches and certainly shouldn't think that it will be "the" approach for you. Quite likely, it will not.

7. **Targeted e-mail and print resume-mailing campaigns to employers.** Just as with campaigns to recruiters (see item 6), you must be extremely careful to select just the right employers that would be interested in a candidate with your qualifications. The closer you stick to "where you belong" in relation to your specific experience, the better your response rate will be. Just as with recruiters, human resources professionals and hiring managers might have

difficulty appreciating the unique set of skills and qualifications career changers bring to a position.

If you are targeting companies in a technology industry, we recommend that you use e-mail as your preferred method for resume submission. However, if the companies you are contacting are not in the technology industry, we believe that print campaigns (paper and envelopes mailed the old-fashioned way) are a more suitable and effective presentation—particularly if you are a management or executive candidate.

8. **In-person "cold calls" to companies and recruiters.** We consider this the least effective and most time-consuming marketing strategy. It is extremely difficult to just walk in the door and get in front of the right person, or any person who can take hiring action. You'll be much better off focusing your time and energy on other, more productive channels.

WHAT ABOUT OPPORTUNITIES IN CONSULTING AND CONTRACTING?

Are you familiar with the term "free agent"? It's the latest buzzword for an independent contractor or consultant who moves from project to project and company to company as the workload dictates. If you have particular expertise (for example, new product development, business turnaround, corporate relocation, ad campaign design, or project management), this is an avenue that you might want to consider. For many career changers, this will not be a viable career alternative because it calls on specific expertise and experience that you might not want to use in your new career. But it is important enough that it does warrant a brief discussion.

According to an article in *Quality Progress* magazine, 10 years ago less than 10 percent of the U.S. workforce was employed as free agents. Currently, that number is greater than 20 percent and is expected to increase to 40 percent over the next 10 years. The demand for free agents is vast, and the market offers excellent career opportunities.

The reason for this growth is directly related to the manner in which companies are now hiring—or not hiring—their workforces. The opportunity now exists for companies to hire on a "per-project" basis and avoid the costs associated with full-time, permanent employees. Companies hire the staff they need just when they need them—and when they no longer need them, they're gone.

The newest revolution in online job search has risen in response to this demand: job-auction sites where employers bid on prospective employees. Individuals post their resumes and qualifications for review by prospective employers. The employers then competitively bid to hire or contract with each candidate. Also, employers can post projects that they want to outsource and prospective employees can bid on them. One well-established job-auction Web site is www.freeagent.com. Check it out. It's quite interesting, particularly if you're pursuing a career in consulting or contracting. Another good Web resource is www.freeagentnation.com, a support and information site for people pursuing this career path.

Conclusion

Career opportunities abound today, even for the career changer. It has never been easier to learn about and apply for jobs than it is now with all the Internet resources available to us. Your challenge is to arm yourself with a powerful resume and cover letter, identify the best ways to get yourself and your resume into the market, and shine during every interview. If you're committed and focused, we can almost guarantee that you'll make a smooth transition into your new career field and find yourself happily employed.

PART I

Resume Writing, Strategy, and Formats

CHAPTER 1

Resume-Writing Strategies for Career Changers

If you're reading this book, chances are you have decided to change your career direction; enter a new industry; or pursue a new, more fulfilling profession. Regardless of the underlying reasons for your career change, you are faced with some unique challenges in your job search and, more specifically, in how you write your resume. What can you do to capture employers' attention, impress them with your qualifications and achievements, and not be put "out of the running" because you do not have experience in a particular industry or profession?

Before we answer those questions and many others, let's talk about who this book was written for—people representing just about every profession and industry imaginable. The *only* thing that our readers have in common is that each one has decided to make a career change for any one of a host of personal or professional reasons. Consider this book an excellent resource for tips, strategies, and techniques on resume writing if you are making a career change because of any of the following reasons:

- Your original industry or profession has been extremely hard hit by economic recession or "offshoring," and opportunities have virtually dried up.

- You have always wanted to pursue a different career track but were unable to do so because of family, financial, or other personal obligations.

- You fell into a position right out of college and pursued that career for years, and then woke up one day and realized it was time to do what you wanted to do and not what you were "supposed" to do.

- You are now in a position to pursue the lifelong dream or hobby that has been burning inside of you since your early days.

- You are relocating to a new area where opportunities for individuals with your experience are quite limited and you need to open yourself to new opportunities and career challenges.

- You have decided you want to pursue a career that will offer greater opportunities for career progression.

- You are driven to make more money, and the best strategy to achieve this goal is to leave your current, low-paying industry or profession.

- Your volunteer work has become increasingly important and you want to pursue professional opportunities with an association, a not-for-profit organization, or a similar entity.

- You are frustrated by the lack of opportunities and the tremendous volatility in the corporate marketplace and have decided to pursue a career with federal, state, or local government where you believe your job will be more stable.

- You retired from your original career and have now decided to return to work in a different, yet more personally rewarding, position.

- You are tired of the tremendous responsibilities associated with your position and want to downsize your career into a less-stressful job.

For every job seeker—those currently employed and those not currently working—a powerful resume is an essential component of the job search campaign. In fact, it is virtually impossible to conduct a search without a resume. It is your calling card that briefly, yet powerfully, communicates the skills, qualifications, experience, and value you bring to a prospective employer. It is the document that will open doors and generate interviews. It is the first thing people will learn about you when you forward it in response to an advertisement, and it is the last thing they'll remember when they're reviewing your qualifications after an interview.

Your resume is a sales document, and you are the product! You must identify the *features (what you know* and *what you can do)* and *benefits (how you can help an employer)* of that product, and then communicate them in a concise and hard-hitting written presentation. Remind yourself over and over, as you work your way through the resume process, that you are writing marketing literature designed to sell a new product—YOU—into a new position.

Your resume can have tremendous power and a phenomenal impact on your job search. So don't take it lightly. Rather, devote the time, energy, and resources that are essential to developing a resume that is well written, visually attractive, and effective in communicating *who* you are and *how* you want to be perceived.

The Top Nine Strategies for an Effective Resume

Following are the nine core strategies for writing effective and successful resumes.

RESUME STRATEGY #1: WHO ARE YOU AND HOW DO YOU WANT TO BE PERCEIVED?

Now that you've decided to change your career direction, the very first step is to identify your career interests, goals, and objectives. *This task is critical* because it is the underlying foundation for *what* you include in your resume, *how* you include it, and *where* you include it. Knowing that you want to make a career change is not enough. To write a powerful and effective resume, you must know—to some degree of certainty—the type or types of position you will be seeking.

There are two concepts to consider here:

- **Who you are:** This relates to what you have done professionally and/or academically. Are you a sales representative, contract administrator, training professional, engineer, banker, scientist, technologist, or management executive? What is it that you have done for a living all these years? Who are you?

- **How you want to be perceived:** This is critical and relates to your current career objectives. Consider the following scenario: You're a customer service representative in the telecommunications industry and you've decided to pursue opportunities in personnel training and development, where you believe you will be more personally rewarded. Rather than focus your resume on your customer service career, focus it on the skills you've acquired in that career track that relate to a position in training and development. Specifically, you'll want to include information about employee training programs that you've helped to create and deliver, one-on-one training that you've provided, consultations with management about internal training needs, any experience you have in developing and designing training materials, any other personnel experience you may have (for example, hiring, orientation, employee development planning), your public-speaking experience, and, of course, your outstanding communication skills.

   Here's another example: You're a successful insurance sales associate, but you've had enough of that career: you're bored, you're unfulfilled, and you're ready for new challenges. You're somewhat uncertain as to your specific career objective at this point, but you do know you want an "inside" job that will use your strong planning, analytical, financial-reporting, and related skills. Rather than focus on your chronological work experience that will put tremendous emphasis on your insurance experience, prepare a resume that highlights all the relevant skills you bring to the position—the skills we outlined previously, along with any relevant achievements. Allow the beginning of your resume to focus on all that you've accomplished and the value you bring to a new employer as you want them to perceive it; then, just briefly list your work history at the end.

The strategy is to connect these two concepts by using the *who you are* information that ties directly to the *how you want to be perceived* message to determine what information to include in your resume. By following this strategy, you're painting a picture that allows a prospective employer to see you as you want to be seen—as an individual with the qualifications for the type of position you are pursuing.

WARNING: If you prepare a resume without first clearly identifying what your objectives are and how you want to be perceived, your resume will have no focus and no direction. Without the underlying knowledge of "This is what I want to be," you do not know what to highlight in your resume. As a result, the document becomes a historical overview of your career and not the sales document it should be in order to facilitate your successful career change.

RESUME STRATEGY #2: SELL IT TO ME...DON'T TELL IT TO ME

We've already established the fact that resume writing is sales. You are the product, and you must create a document that powerfully communicates the value of that product. One particularly effective strategy for accomplishing this is the "Sell It to Me...Don't Tell It to Me" strategy, which impacts virtually every word you write on your resume.

If you "tell it," you are simply stating facts. If you "sell it," you promote it, advertise it, and draw attention to it. Look at the difference in impact between these examples:

> **Tell It Strategy:** Managed start-up of a new 100-employee teleclass center.

> **Sell It Strategy:** Directed team of 12 in the successful start-up, staffing, policy/procedure development, budgeting, and operations design for a new $1.4 million teleclass center.

> **Tell It Strategy:** Coordinated all secretarial, clerical, and administrative functions for large commodities export company.

> **Tell It Strategy:** Implemented a series of process improvements that reduced staffing requirements 20%, increased daily productivity 30%, and reduced billing errors 14% for a large commodities export company. Full responsibility for all secretarial, clerical, and administrative functions.

> **Tell It Strategy:** Set up PCs for newly hired sales and service staff.

> **Sell It Strategy:** Installed more than 100 PCs and implemented customized applications to support nationwide network of sales and service staff for one of the world's largest insurance companies. Provided ongoing troubleshooting and technical support that reduced PC downtime by 38% over a 6-month period.

What's the difference between "telling it" and "selling it"? In a nutshell…

Telling It	Selling It
Describes features.	Describes benefits.
Tells what and how.	Sells why the "what" and "how" are important.
Details activities.	Includes results.
Focuses on what you did.	Details how what you did benefited your employer, department, team members, students, and so on.

RESUME STRATEGY #3: USE KEYWORDS

No matter what you read or who you talk to about searching for jobs, the concept of keywords is sure to come up. Keywords (or, as they were previously known, buzz words) are words and phrases that are specific to a particular industry or profession. For example, keywords for the manufacturing industry include *production-line operations, production planning and scheduling, materials management, inventory control, quality, process engineering, robotics, systems automation, integrated logistics, product specifications, project management,* and many, many more.

When you use these words and phrases—in your resume, in your cover letter, or during an interview—you are communicating a very specific message. For example, when you include the word "merchandising" in your resume, your reader will most likely assume that you have experience in the retail industry—in product selection, vendor/manufacturing relations, in-store product display, inventory management, mark-downs, product promotions, and more. As you can see, people will make inferences about your skills based on the use of just one or two specific words.

Here are a few other examples:

- When you use the words **investment finance,** people will assume you have experience with risk management, mergers, acquisitions, initial public offerings, debt/equity management, asset allocation, portfolio management, and more.

- When you mention **sales,** readers and listeners will infer that you have experience in product presentations, pricing, contract negotiations, customer relationship management, new product introduction, competitive product positioning, and more.

- By referencing **Internet technology** in your resume, you convey that you most likely have experience with Web site design, Web site marketing, metatags, HTML, search-engine registration, e-learning, and more.

- When you use the words **human resources,** most people will assume that you are familiar with recruitment, hiring, placement, compensation, benefits, training and development, employee relations, human resources information systems (HRIS), and more.

Keywords are also an integral component of the resume-scanning process, whereby employers and recruiters electronically search resumes for specific terms to find candidates with the skills, qualifications, and credentials for their particular hiring needs. Over the past several years, keyword scanning has dramatically increased in its popularity because of its ease of use and efficiency in identifying prime candidates. Every job seeker today must stay on top of the latest trends in technology-based hiring and employment to ensure that their resumes and other job-search materials contain the "right" keywords to capture the interest of prospective employers.

In organizations where it has been implemented, electronic scanning has replaced the more traditional method of an actual person reading your resume (at least initially). Therefore, to some degree, the *only* thing that matters in this instance is that you have included the "right" keywords to match the company's or the recruiter's needs. Without them, you will most certainly be passed over.

Of course, in virtually every instance your resume will be read at some point by human eyes, so it's not enough just to throw together a list of keywords and leave it at that. In fact, it's not even necessary to include a separate "keyword summary" on your resume. A better strategy is to incorporate keywords naturally into the text within the appropriate sections of your resume.

For career changers, keywords are particularly relevant and require a good deal of thought, because you do not necessarily want to include keywords that are descriptive of your past experiences. Rather, you want to include keywords that reflect your current career goals so that those words are the ones that will get your resume noticed and not passed over. There are basically two ways to accomplish this:

- **In sections throughout your resume, integrate keywords from your past experiences that directly relate to your current career goals.** Referring back to the example we gave of a customer service representative seeking to transition into a position in personnel training and development, that individual did have experience in personnel training, new employee orientation, training program design, and the like. Those are the keywords that should be highlighted on the resume. Even though these tasks might have been a minor part of the career changer's experience, they are relevant to their current goals and, therefore, should be highlighted on the resume.

- **Include an "Objective" section on your resume that states the type of position that you are seeking and the associated responsibilities.** For example, "Seeking a position in purchasing management where I can utilize my strong skills in research, analysis, negotiations, and product management." This is the recommended strategy if you do *not* have the appropriate experience (keywords) in your background to include in the career summary and experience sections on your resume that will support your current career goals.

Keep in mind, too, that keywords are arbitrary; there is no defined set of keywords for a secretary, production laborer, police officer, teacher, electrical engineer, construction superintendent, finance officer, sales manager, or chief executive officer. Employers searching to fill these positions develop a list of terms that reflect the specifics they desire in a qualified candidate. These might be a combination of professional qualifications, skills, education, length of experience, and other easily defined criteria, along with "soft skills," such as organization, time management, team building, leadership, problem-solving, and communication.

> **NOTE:** Because of the complex and arbitrary nature of keyword selection, we cannot overemphasize how vital it is to be certain that you include in your resume *all* of the keywords that summarize your skills *as they relate to your current career-change objectives.*

How can you be sure that you are including all the keywords, and the *right* keywords? Just by describing your work experience, achievements, educational credentials, technical qualifications, objective, and the like, you might naturally include most of the terms that are important in your new career field. To cross-check what you've written, review online or newspaper job postings for positions that are of interest to you. Look at the precise terms used in the ads and be sure you have included them in your resume (as appropriate to your skills and qualifications).

Another great benefit of today's technology revolution is our ability to find instant information, even information as specific as keywords for hundreds of different industries and professions. Refer to the appendix for a listing of Web sites that list thousands of keywords, complete with descriptions. These are outstanding resources.

RESUME STRATEGY #4: USE THE "BIG" AND SAVE THE "LITTLE"

When deciding what to include in your resume, try to focus on the "big" things—new programs, special projects, cost savings, productivity and efficiency improvements, new products, technology implementations, and more. Give a good, broad-based picture of what you were responsible for and how well you did it. Here's an example:

> Supervised daily sales, customer service, and maintenance-shop operations for a privately owned automotive repair facility. Managed a crew of 12 and an annual operating budget of $300,000 for supplies and materials. Consistently achieved/surpassed all revenue, profit, quality, and production objectives.

Then, save the "little" stuff—the details—for the interview. With this strategy, you will accomplish two things:

- You'll keep your resume readable and of a reasonable length (while still selling your achievements).

- You'll have new and interesting information to share during the interview, instead of merely repeating what is already on your resume.

Using the preceding example, when discussing this experience during an interview you could elaborate on your specific achievements—namely, improving productivity and efficiency ratings, reducing annual operating and material costs, improving employee training, strengthening customer relations, increasing sales volume, and managing facility upgrades.

RESUME STRATEGY #5: MAKE YOUR RESUME "INTERVIEWABLE"

One of your greatest challenges is to make your resume a useful interview tool. Once the employer has determined that you meet the primary qualifications for a position (you've passed the keyword scanning test or initial review) and you are contacted for a telephone or in-person interview, your resume becomes all-important in leading and prompting your interviewer during your conversation.

Your job, then, is to make sure the resume leads the reader where you want to go and presents just the right organization, content, and appearance to stimulate a productive discussion. To improve the "interviewability" of your resume, consider these tactics:

- Make good use of Resume Strategy #4 (Use the "Big" and Save the "Little") to invite further discussion about your experiences.

- Be sure your greatest "selling points" are featured prominently, not buried within the resume.

- Conversely, don't devote lots of space and attention to areas of your background that are irrelevant or about which you feel less than positive; you'll only invite questions about things you really don't want to discuss. This is particularly true for career changers who want their resumes to focus on the skills that will be needed in their new profession and not necessarily on skills they acquired in past positions.

- Make sure your resume is highly readable—this means plenty of white space, an adequate font size, and a logical flow from start to finish.

RESUME STRATEGY #6: ELIMINATE CONFUSION WITH STRUCTURE AND CONTEXT

Keep in mind that your resume will be read *very quickly* by hiring authorities! You might agonize over every word and spend hours working on content and design, but the average reader will skim quickly through your masterpiece and expect to pick up important facts in just a few seconds. Try to make it as easy as possible for readers to grasp the essential facts:

- **Be consistent.** For example, put job titles, company names, and dates in the same place for each position.

- **Make information easy to find** by clearly defining different sections of your resume with large, highly visible headings.

- If relevant to your new career path, **define the context in which you worked** (for example, the organization, your department, and the specific challenges you faced) before you start describing your activities and accomplishments.

RESUME STRATEGY #7: USE FUNCTION TO DEMONSTRATE ACHIEVEMENT

When you write a resume that focuses only on your job functions, it can be dry and uninteresting, and it will say very little about your unique activities and contributions. Consider the following example:

> Responsible for all aspects of consumer lending at the branch level.

Now, consider using that same function to demonstrate achievement and see what happens to the tone and energy of the sentence. It becomes alive and clearly communicates that you deliver results:

> Processed and approved more than $30 million in secured and unsecured consumer loans for Wachovia's largest branch operation in Memphis, Tennessee. Achieved and maintained a less than 2% write-off for unrecoverable loans (18% less than the industry average).

Try to translate your functions into achievements and you'll create a more powerful resume presentation.

RESUME STRATEGY #8: REMAIN IN THE REALM OF REALITY

We've already established that resume writing is sales. And, as any good salesperson does, one feels somewhat inclined to stretch the truth, just a bit. However, be forewarned that you must stay within the realm of reality. Do not push your skills and qualifications outside the bounds of what is truthful. You never want to be in a position where you have to defend something that you've written on your resume. If that's the case, you'll lose the job opportunity before you ever get the offer.

RESUME STRATEGY #9: BE CONFIDENT

You are unique. There is only one individual with the specific combination of employment experience, qualifications, achievements, education, and special skills that you have. In turn, this positions you as a unique commodity within the competitive job search market. To succeed, you must prepare a resume that is written to sell *you* and highlight *your* qualifications and *your* successes as they relate to your current career-change goals. If you can accomplish this, you will have won the job search game by generating interest, interviews, and offers.

There Are No Resume-Writing Rules

One of the greatest challenges in resume writing is that there are no rules to the game. There are certain expectations about information that you will include: principally, your primary skills, employment history, and educational qualifications. Beyond that, what you include is entirely up to you and what you have done in your career. You have tremendous flexibility in determining how to include the information you have selected. In chapter 2, you'll find a wealth of information on each possible category you might include in your resume, the type of information to be placed in each category, preferred formats for presentation, and lots of other information and samples that will help you formulate *your* best resume.

Although there are no rules, there are a few standards to live by as you write your resume. The following sections discuss these standards in detail.

CONTENT STANDARDS

Content is, of course, the text that goes into your resume. Content standards cover the writing style you should use, items you should be sure to include, items you should avoid including, and the order and format in which you list your qualifications.

Writing Style

Always write in the first person, dropping the word "I" from the front of each sentence. This style gives your resume a more aggressive and more professional tone than the passive third-person voice. Here are some examples:

First Person

> Manage 22-person team responsible for design and market commercialization of a new portfolio of PC-based applications for Marley's $100 million consumer-sales division.

Third Person

> Mr. Reynolds manages a 22-person team responsible for the design and market commercialization of a new portfolio of PC-based applications for Marley's $100 million consumer-sales division.

By using the first-person voice, you are assuming "ownership" of that statement. You did such-and-such. When you use the third-person voice, "someone else" did it. Can you see the difference?

Phrases to Stay Away From

Try *not* to use phrases such as "responsible for" and "duties included." These words create a passive tone and style. Instead, use active verbs to describe what you did.

Compare these two ways of conveying the same information:

> Responsible for all marketing and special events for the store, including direct mailing, in-store fashion shows, and new-product introductions and promotions.

OR

> Orchestrated a series of marketing and special-event programs for Macy's Reston, one of the company's largest and most profitable operating locations. Managed direct-mail campaigns, in-store fashion shows, and new-product introductions and promotions.

Resume Style

The traditional **chronological** resume lists your work experience in reverse-chronological order (starting with your current or most recent position). The **functional** style deemphasizes the "where" and "when" of your career and instead groups similar experience, talents, and qualifications regardless of when they occurred.

Today, however, most resumes follow neither a strictly chronological nor strictly functional format; rather, they are an effective mixture of the two styles usually known as a "combination" or "hybrid" format.

Like the chronological format, the hybrid format includes specifics about where you worked, when you worked there, and what your job titles were. Like a functional resume, a hybrid emphasizes your most relevant qualifications—perhaps within chronological job descriptions, in an expanded summary section, in several "career highlights" bullet points at the top of your resume, or in project summaries. Most of the examples in this book are hybrids and show a wide diversity of organizational formats that you can use as inspiration for designing your own resume.

We strongly recommend hybrid-format resumes for career changers. They allow you to begin your resume with an intense focus on skills, competencies, experience, accomplishments, and more that are directly related to your new career objective. Then, to substantiate a solid work experience, employment history is briefly listed with a focus on specific achievements, responsibilities, and projects that again relate to that individual's current career goals.

Resume Formats

Resumes, which are principally career summaries and job descriptions, are most often written in a paragraph format, a bulleted format, or a combination of both. Following are three job descriptions, all very similar in content, yet presented in each of the three different writing formats. The advantages and disadvantages of each format are also addressed.

Paragraph Format

Business Manager   1989 to 2005

Smith Ag Production Company, Garnerville, Arkansas

Purchased run-down, debt-ridden farming operation and transformed it into a near showplace, honored as one of the best commercial Angus operations in southern Arkansas. Developed a far-reaching network throughout the agricultural industry and with leaders in state government, banking, and commercial lending.

Held full management authority for cattle and alfalfa production generating 2,500+ tons of hay per year and running up to 500 stock cows. Hired, trained, and supervised all employees. Managed budgets of $750,000 annually and more than $2 million in operating lines of credit. Directed the sale/purchase of all commodities to support business operations. Gained an in-depth knowledge of the commercial agricultural industry and its unique financial, economic, and operating challenges.

Advantages

Requires the least amount of space on the page. Brief, succinct, and to the point.

Disadvantages

Achievements get lost in the text of the paragraphs. They are not visually distinctive, nor do they stand alone to draw attention to them.

Bulleted Format

Business Manager   1989 to 2005

Smith Ag Production Company, Garnerville, Arkansas

- Purchased run-down, debt-ridden farming operation and transformed it into a near showplace, honored as one of the best commercial Angus operations in southern Arkansas.

- Developed a far-reaching network throughout the agricultural industry and with leaders in state government, banking, and commercial lending.

- Held full management authority for cattle and alfalfa production generating 2,500+ tons of hay per year and running up to 500 stock cows.

- Hired, trained, and supervised all employees.

- Managed budgets of $750,000 annually and more than $2 million in operating lines of credit.

- Directed the sale/purchase of all commodities to support business operations.

- Gained an in-depth knowledge of the commercial agricultural industry and its unique financial, economic, and operating challenges.

Advantages

Quick and easy to peruse.

Disadvantages

Responsibilities and achievements are lumped together, with everything given equal value. In turn, the achievements get lost and are not immediately recognizable.

Combination Format

Business Manager   1989 to 2005

Smith Ag Production Company, Garnerville, Arkansas

Held full management authority for cattle and alfalfa production generating 2,500+ tons of hay per year and running up to 500 stock cows. Hired, trained, and supervised all employees. Managed budgets of $750,000 annually and more than $2 million in operating lines of credit. Directed the sale/purchase of all commodities to support business operations.

- Purchased run-down, debt-ridden farming operation and transformed it into a near showplace, honored as one of the best commercial Angus operations in southern Arkansas.

- Developed a far-reaching network throughout the agricultural industry and with leaders in state government, banking, and commercial lending.

- Gained an in-depth knowledge of the commercial agricultural industry and its unique financial, economic, and operating challenges.

Advantages

Our recommended format. Clearly presents overall responsibilities in the introductory paragraph and then accentuates each achievement as a separate bullet.

Disadvantages

If you don't have clearly identifiable accomplishments, this format is not effective. It also may shine a glaring light on the positions where your accomplishments were less notable. For career changers, past accomplishments might not be relevant to current career objectives, and therefore this format might be less appropriate.

You'll find numerous other examples of how to best present your employment experience in the resume samples that follow in chapters 4 through 12. Chapter 2 discusses formats you can use to highlight your skills and achievements more prominently than your work history. In many career-change situations, this approach is critical to get yourself noticed and not passed over.

E-Mail Address and URL

Be sure to include your e-mail address prominently at the top of your resume. As we all know, e-mail has become one of the most preferred methods of communication between employers and job seekers. If you don't yet have an e-mail address, visit www.yahoo.com, www.hotmail.com, or www.netzero.com, where you can get a free e-mail address that you can access through the Web on any computer with an Internet connection.

In addition to your e-mail address, if you have a URL (Web site address) where you have posted your Web resume, be sure to also display that prominently at the top of your resume. For more information on Web resumes, refer to chapter 3.

PRESENTATION STANDARDS

Presentation focuses on the way your resume looks. It relates to the fonts you use, the paper you print it on, any graphics you might include, and how many pages your resume should be.

Typestyle

Use a typestyle (font) that is clean, conservative, and easy to read. Stay away from anything that is too fancy, glitzy, curly, and the like. Here are a few recommended typestyles:

Tahoma	Times New Roman
Arial	Bookman
Krone	Book Antiqua
Soutane	Garamond
CG Omega	Century Schoolbook
Century Gothic	Lucida Sans
Gill Sans	Verdana

Although it is extremely popular, Times New Roman is our least preferred type-style simply because it is overused. More than 90 percent of the resumes we see are printed in Times New Roman. Your goal is to create a competitive-distinctive document, and, to achieve that, we recommend an alternative typestyle.

Your choice of typestyle should be dictated by the content, format, and length of your resume. Some fonts look better than others at smaller or larger sizes; some have "bolder" boldface type; some require more white space to make them read-able. Once you've written your resume, experiment with a few different typestyles to see which one best enhances your document.

Type Size

Readability is everything! If the type size is too small, your resume will be difficult to read and difficult to skim for essential information. Interestingly, a too-large type size, particularly for senior-level professionals, can also give a negative impres-sion by conveying a juvenile or unprofessional image.

As a general rule, select type from 10 to 12 points in size. However, there's no hard-and-fast rule, and a lot depends on the typestyle you choose. Take a look at the following examples:

Very readable in 9-point Verdana:

Won the 1999 "Employee of the Year" award at Chrysler's Indianapolis plant. Honored for innovative contributions to the design and manufacturability of the Zodiac product line.

Difficult to read in too-small 9-point Gill Sans:

Won the 1999 "Employee of the Year" award at Chrysler's Indianapolis plant. Honored for innovative contributions to the design and manufacturability of the Zodiac product line.

Concise and readable in 12-point Times New Roman:

Training & Development Consultant specializing in the design, development, and presentation of multimedia training programs for hourly workers, skilled labor, and craftsmen.

A bit overwhelming in too-large 12-point Bookman Old Style:

Training & Development Consultant specializing in the design, development, and presentation of multimedia training programs for hourly workers, skilled labor, and craftsmen.

Type Enhancements

Bold, *italics*, <u>underlining</u>, and CAPITALIZATION are ideal to highlight certain words, phrases, achievements, projects, numbers, and other information to which you want to draw special attention. However, do not overuse these enhancements. If your resume becomes too cluttered with special formatting, nothing stands out.

> **NOTE:** Resumes intended for electronic transmission and computer scanning have specific restrictions on typestyle, type size, and type enhancements. We discuss these details in chapter 3.

Page Length

For most industries and professions, the "one- to two-page rule" for resume writing still holds true. Keep it short and succinct, giving just enough information to pique your readers' interest. However, there are many instances when a resume can be longer than two pages. For example:

- **You have an extensive list of technical qualifications that are relevant to the position for which you are applying.** You might consider including these on a separate page as an addendum to your resume.

- **You have extensive educational training and numerous credentials/certifications, all of which are important to include.** You might consider including these on a separate page as an addendum to your resume.

- **You have an extensive list of special projects, task forces, and committees to include that are important to your current career objectives.** You might consider including these on a separate page as an addendum to your resume.

- **You have an extensive list of professional honors, awards, and commendations.** This list is tremendously valuable in validating your credibility and distinguishing you from the competition, and deleting it from your resume would be a disadvantage. It might be best to let your resume run to three, four, or even five pages to include this information. Just be sure that what you are including is relevant to your new career direction.

If you create a resume that's longer than two pages, make it more reader-friendly by carefully segmenting the information into separate sections. Your sections might include a career summary, work experience, education, professional or industry credentials, honors and awards, technology and equipment skills, publications, public-speaking engagements, professional affiliations, civic affiliations, volunteer experience, foreign-language skills, and other relevant information you want to include. Put each into a separate category so that your resume is easy to peruse and your reader can quickly see the highlights. You'll read more about each of these sections in chapter 2.

Paper Color

Be conservative. White, ivory, and light gray are ideal. Other "flashier" colors are inappropriate for most individuals unless you are in a highly creative industry and your paper choice is part of the overall design and presentation of a creative resume.

Graphics

An attractive, relevant graphic can really enhance your resume. When you look through the sample resumes in chapters 4 through 12, you'll see some excellent examples of the effective use of graphics to enhance the visual presentation of a resume. Just be sure not to get carried away; be tasteful and relatively conservative.

White Space

We'll say it again—readability is everything! If people have to struggle to read your resume, they simply won't make the effort. Therefore, be sure to leave plenty of white space. It really does make a difference.

ACCURACY AND PERFECTION

The very final step, and one of the most critical in resume writing, is the proof-reading stage. It is essential that your resume be well written; visually pleasing; and free of any errors, typographical mistakes, misspellings, and the like. We recommend that you carefully proofread your resume a minimum of three times, and then have two or three other people also proofread it. Consider your resume an example of the quality of work you will produce on a company's behalf. Is your work product going to have errors and inconsistencies? If your resume does, it communicates to a prospective employer that you are careless, and this is the "kiss of death" in job search.

Take the time to make sure that your resume is perfect in all the little details that do, in fact, make a big difference to those who read it.

CHAPTER 2

Writing Your Resume

For many job seekers, resume writing is *not* at the top of the list of fun and exciting activities! How can it compare to landing a new account, cutting costs, introducing new technology, streamlining operations, or starting a new production plant? In your perception, we're sure that it cannot.

However, resume writing can be an enjoyable and rewarding task. When your resume is complete, you can look at it proudly, reminding yourself of all that you have achieved. It is a snapshot of your career and your success. When it's complete, we guarantee you'll look back with tremendous self-satisfaction as you launch and successfully manage your job search.

As the very first step in finding a new position or advancing your career, resume writing can be the most daunting of all tasks in your job search. If writing is not one of your primary skills or a past job function, it might have been years since you've actually sat down and written anything other than e-mail or notes to yourself. Even for those of you who write on a regular basis, resume writing is unique. It has its own style and a number of peculiarities, as with any specialty document.

Recommended Resume-Writing Strategy and Formats for Career Changers

Writing career-change resumes is a unique challenge, and many of the strategies and formats that the more "typical" job seeker uses are generally not applicable for career changers. Standard formats most often put an emphasis on past work experience, along with the responsibilities and achievements of each of those positions. If you're a career changer, most likely your goal is to downplay your specific work experience and job titles on your resume while highlighting your skills and core competencies as they relate to your current objectives.

CAREER-CHANGER STRATEGIES

In chapter 1 we provided an overview of strategies; here we get down to the nuts and bolts of deciding what to include in your resume (the strategies) and how to organize and present it (the format). As with every good resume, it's important to start out with a clear understanding of your ultimate target so that your resume is a clear and sharply focused presentation of qualifications for that target.

Know Your Career Goal

Before you even begin to start writing your career-change resume, you must know the specific type(s) of position(s) you are going after. This will give your resume a "theme" around which you can build the entire document. Your "theme" (or objective) should dictate everything that you include in your resume, how you include it, and where. Writing a career-change resume is all about creating a picture of how you want to be perceived by a prospective employer—a picture that closely mirrors the types of people who are hired in that career field.

From researching the type of career you want to pursue, you will have collected a great deal of information about the duties and responsibilities for positions in that field. You should then carefully review your past employment experience, educational background, volunteer work, professional affiliations, civic affiliations, and more to identify skills you've acquired that are transferable to your new career. These, then, are the items that become the foundation of your resume.

> **WARNING**: If you don't know what your objective is—you only know that you want to change careers—we strongly urge that you spend some time investigating potential career tracks to determine your overall areas of interest. Without this knowledge, you cannot focus your resume in any one particular direction and, as a result, it simply becomes a recitation of your past work experience. To effectively position you for new career opportunities, your resume must have a theme and a focus. If you're having difficulty determining your objective, you might want to consider hiring a career coach who can help you critically evaluate your skills and qualifications, match them to potential career opportunities, explore new professions, and guide you in setting your direction.

Identify Your Transferable Skills

Transferable skills are the foundation for every successful career-change resume. If you're not sure how to identify your transferable skills, here's an easy way to do just that. First, review advertisements for positions that are of interest. You can get this information from newspapers, professional journals, and hundreds of online resources. You can also talk to and network with people who are already working in your new career field and ask them to give you feedback regarding their specific responsibilities, the challenges they face, the opportunities that are available, how to get into the field, and so much more.

Once you've collected this information, make a detailed list of the specific requirements for these jobs (for example, budgeting, staff training, staff supervision, project management, statistical analysis, and customer relationship management). Be as comprehensive as possible, even if the list goes on and on for pages. Then, go through the list and highlight each of the skills in which you have some experience from your work, education, or outside activities. Finally, take some time to think of specific examples of how you've used those skills. Used in your resume, these "success stories" will be powerful proof that you already possess the very skills and competencies you want to use in your new job.

> **NOTE:** There is no need to describe these skills as "transferable" in your resume, cover letter, or conversations during your job search. Why highlight the fact that your skills are not directly related to the field you want to pursue? Quite simply, these are skills you possess, experience you own, and activities you have accomplished. They are the foundation of your performance in past experiences and in your new role.

It is important to remember that your *entire* background counts—everything that you've ever done—from your 10-year sales career to your 6-year volunteer position coordinating your local Special Olympics. Just think of the great skills you acquired in event planning, logistics, volunteer training, fund raising, media affairs, and contract negotiations. Those skills are just as important to include in your career-change resume as any other skills you acquired in a paid position.

SAMPLE FORMATS AND SITUATIONS FOR CAREER-CHANGE RESUMES

Following are three excellent examples of career-change resumes, all of which focus on transferable skills, but each of which uses a different format and structure to highlight those skills. Think about which of these formats and styles is most appropriate for you, based on your particular situation and career objectives. It is very unlikely that you will find a format that exactly "matches" your life, experience, and educational credentials. Use the following examples as the foundation for your resume, customizing and reformatting as necessary to create your own winning resume.

Charles: A New Career After Additional Education

Charles was a most interesting job seeker. After a successful career in building maintenance, he returned to college to earn a graduate degree in Counseling Psychology in preparation for changing his career track. He had always had a passion for counseling and knew that to successfully change careers, he would have to get the requisite academic training.

Charles's resume begins with a brief, yet hard-hitting listing of his core skills and competencies as they relate to the field of counseling. The headline format that was used ("COUNSELING/HUMAN RELATIONS") clearly identifies "who" Charles is and "what" he wants. Then, at the top of the list is his master's degree, a necessity for anyone pursuing a professional career in counseling. The other items highlight his core skills, the types of clients he has worked with, and professional credentials. This format is particularly effective because the reader can simply glance and "get it all," rather than having to read through paragraphs of text.

Immediately following his summary is detailed information about Charles's educational qualifications. Note that specific coursework is included as a great strategy to highlight his specific areas of training while being sure to include all the buzz words (or keywords) that are relevant to a career in counseling. Although Charles cannot say that he necessarily has "hands-on" experience in each of these areas, he can include them as areas of training. Not only will these catch a reader's attention, but they will also get Charles's resume selected if it is run through scanning technology that is searching for those specific terms.

The next section is detailed information about Charles's eight-month counseling internship. The job description is comprehensive and clearly creates the perception that Charles is an experienced counseling professional, despite the fact that this job was an internship.

Most important to note about this resume is that all of page 1 focuses on counseling and relevant skills. You never realize that Charles is a maintenance supervisor until you turn to page 2.

The writer was also very clever in how she formulated Charles's job description. Of course, it is obvious that he's a maintenance supervisor—we can't change the facts. However, much of the job description focuses on skills, responsibilities, projects, and more that required strong counseling, communication, and interpersonal skills. All of a sudden the maintenance man begins to disappear and the counselor begins to emerge.

CHARLES M. SUGARMANN

608 Covington Lane
Newtown, PA 18940

(267) 291-4866
csugarmann@dotresume.com

COUNSELING / HUMAN RELATIONS

Master's Degree
Adolescents & Adults
Drug & Alcohol Abuse
EAP & HMO Precertification
Assessments & Treatment Plans
Group, Individual, and Family Counseling
Supervision, Administration, Coordination

EDUCATION

M.A., Counseling Psychology, Immaculata University, Immaculata, PA, 1/2004
Maintained **3.7 GPA** while working full-time and taking an average of 6 credits per semester.

Courses: Adolescent Counseling, Appraisal in Counseling, Brief Strategic Therapy, Counseling Theory & Practice, Crisis Interventions, Ethical & Legal Issues in Counseling, Family Interventions, Gestalt Approach—Counseling, Group Counseling Theory & Practice, Human Growth & Development, Lifestyle & Career Development, Psychopathology, Research & Evaluation, Strategies for "At-Risk" Students, Substance Abuse Counseling

Labs: Counseling Diverse Populations, Counseling Skills, Group Dynamics

B.B.A., Temple University, Philadelphia, PA, 1/1994

EXPERIENCE

REHAB CENTER AT ARDMORE, PA, 5/2003–12/2003
A drug and alcohol outpatient rehabilitation facility for adults, adolescents, and families

Counselor Intern

Counseled adult and adolescent substance abusers in group, individual, and family sessions using education, psychodrama, psychotherapy, solution-focused counseling, cognitive-behavioral therapy, and person-centered counseling. Performed psychosocial assessments, developed treatment plans, and documented case activity. Precertified clients for HMO and EAP coverage. Recruited AA (Alcoholics Anonymous) and NA (Narcotics Anonymous) members to chair 12-step meetings for adolescents.

- Helped family members move from a state of powerlessness to active participation in client's therapy and life through education and awareness of family dynamics.

- Achieved numerous individual successes; for example, helped client gain acceptance by peers upon return to work, enabled counseling to proceed smoothly by helping to resolve medication problem of dual MH/D&A client, and counseled former drug dealer who is now a scholarship student.

- Commended by supervisor for relating well with clients and establishing an excellent rapport.

continued

Resume for Charles M. Sugarmann (written and designed by Jan Holliday, MA, NCRW, of Arbridge Communications).

CHARLES M. SUGARMANN

page 2

EXPERIENCE
continued

ST. MARK'S ACADEMY, Norristown, PA, 3/1996–present
A Catholic high school with 950 students and 100 staff members

Maintenance Supervisor, 2/1998–present
Head Groundskeeper, 1/1997–2/1998
Maintenance Man, 3/1996–1/1997

As maintenance supervisor, oversee staff of 10 to maintain school building and grounds. Serve as liaison to organizations that rent school facilities and to archdiocesan headquarters for special capital projects. Work with Delaware County Community Service to coordinate tasks for adolescents and adults performing work at the school in lieu of jail time—teach skills, where necessary, and apply counseling principles to make program run smoothly and to the benefit of all. Review grant proposals to advise on jobs that can be delegated to community-service workers.

- Praised by school president for success of community-service program.

- Sought out by students and maintenance staff for help with daily problems.

- Served as junior varsity softball coach for 5 years and as freshman basketball coach for 1 year.

- Ensured completion of work in all classrooms and restored amicable relationship between teachers and maintenance department by reinstituting use of service request form.

- Averted building fire through quick response; placed on list of national fire heroes by Curt Weldon, a member of the United States House of Representatives.

PRIOR EXPERIENCE in construction/home improvement, real estate sales, and tourism.

COMPUTER SKILLS

Experience with Microsoft Word and specialized spreadsheet applications.

Peter: From Attorney to Educator

Peter was a practicing attorney with more than 20 years of experience. Now he wanted to make a change and, since teaching had always been his passion, he decided to pursue that career on a full-time basis. His primary objective was a position teaching legal studies to junior and senior high school students, but he would also look at other related teaching opportunities.

Peter's resume begins with a comprehensive career summary that clearly identifies his two areas of expertise—teaching and the law. The resume then follows with a strong summary of his relevant teaching, program-development, classroom-management, and public-speaking skills, with concurrent emphasis on his areas of teaching specialization (for example, accounting, business law, and professional legal liability). The summary creates the perception of an individual with a wealth of teaching experience in a variety of professional settings.

The second section is Peter's education. As you can see, this section clearly demonstrates that he has the academic credentials to support his teaching specializations.

The next and most substantial section is Peter's employment history. Rather than focus on his actual legal practice, however, the resume highlights Peter's teaching, mentoring, and public-speaking experience—his transferable skills related to his current objective. People will review this resume and see someone who was an attorney but devoted a tremendous amount of his professional time to teaching. As such, he has positioned himself as a well-qualified candidate for an appropriate teaching position. When reviewing this resume, the reader does not "see" an attorney, but rather "sees" a teacher.

The writer used a highly effective strategy of creating a new hierarchy of skills, where teaching became the primary emphasis in the resume and Peter's law career became secondary.

PETER JONES, JR.

98 Ben Franklin Drive
Unit 5B, The Esplanade
Pensacola Beach, FL 32561   peterjones@midway.net

Home (850) 222-3333
Work: (850) 222-4444
Home Fax: (850) 222-7777

EDUCATOR/ATTORNEY AT LAW

Accomplished trainer and facilitator, experienced in the design and implementation of dynamic, state-of-the-art education and training programs for colleges, public educational organizations, small businesses, and large corporations. Encourage active student participation and engagement in learning, instilling in students a sense of self-direction by extending and enhancing the learning process. Creative and intuitive problem solver, cheerfully meeting challenges. *Core Competencies include*

- ☑ Training & Development
- ☑ Classroom Motivation Techniques
- ☑ Instructional Design & Development
- ☑ Adult Education Training & Facilitation
- ☑ College & Corporate Educational Course Design

- ☑ Accounting
- ☑ Business Law
- ☑ Professional Legal Liability
- ☑ Corporate & Individual Income Tax
- ☑ Mediation/Alternative Dispute Resolution

EDUCATION

J.D., Juris Doctor
FLORIDA STATE UNIVERSITY COLLEGE OF LAW, Tallahassee, FL

B.S., Accounting
FLORIDA STATE UNIVERSITY, Tallahassee, FL

CERTIFICATIONS: Supreme Court of Florida Certified Family Law Mediator

PROFESSIONAL LICENSES: Attorney At Law — Florida
Certified Public Accountant — Florida

PROFESSIONAL EXPERIENCE

PETER JONES, ATTORNEY AT LAW — Pensacola, FL   JAN 1990–PRESENT
Attorney At Law
Direct operations with full responsibility for P&L, business development, client relationship management, case management, staff recruitment, and training.
Key Achievements:

- ➤ Professional presenter/spokesperson at numerous continuing-education seminars in Tampa, Miami, and Pensacola, Florida. Areas of discussion included taxation, qualified retirement plans, accountants' legal liability, family law, mediation/alternative dispute resolution, and estate planning.
- ➤ Outstanding mentor and coach: Educated, trained, mentored, and motivated employees, stimulating them to higher levels of performance.
- ➤ Successfully created Peter Jones, Attorney At Law, as a financially viable start-up business, demonstrating decisive, proactive, and action-driven entrepreneurial leadership.

Resume for Peter Jones, Jr. (written and designed by Jennifer Rushton, CRW, of Keraijen).

PETER JONES, JR. Page 2

Professional Experience, Continued

➢ Established and maintained excellent business relationships with clients from diverse backgrounds through consistent demonstration of professionalism, preparedness, and good business ethics.

STEWARTS, BROOKS, MATTHEWS & TRENT — Pensacola, FL   OCT 1977–DEC 1990

Attorney/ Shareholder

Key Achievements:

➢ Facilitated continuing-education seminars, conducting instructor-led training to 25–100 attorney and CPA participants.
➢ Pioneered the development of numerous educational training programs in income tax and accounting for non-business majors as an adjunct professor at The University of West Florida.
➢ Initiated efforts to continually improve operations by developing the first legal assistant (paralegal) pool for use by the firm members.
➢ Key player in the development of a "structured settlement" approach to financial settlements in personal injury and wrongful death cases, resulting in favorable tax treatments for plaintiffs.

SMITH, WALLACE & COLLINS — Pensacola, FL   JUN 1975– OCT 1977

Associate Attorney

Key Achievements:

➢ Collaborated with associates in developing the condominium ownership concept in Florida; contributed to the taxation issues concerning the evolving concept of condominium ownership.

COOPERS & LYBRAND — Pensacola, FL   MAR 1973–JUN 1975

Taxation Specialist

Key Achievements:

➢ Designed and taught educational lessons to enhance student knowledge in taxation and accounting as an adjunct professor at The University of South Florida.
➢ Instrumental in developing and presenting continuing-education courses on tax law changes to members and guests of the firm.

PROFESSIONAL AFFILIATIONS

Member, Estate Planning Councils of Tampa

Member, Florida State & Local Bar Associations

Member, Florida Institute of Certified Public Accountants

COMMUNITY ACTIVITIES

Legal Member, Ombudsman Committee

Speaker, High School 'Life Sciences' classes

Mike: A Functional Resume to Support His Transition from Educator to Top Business Executive

Although, as we discussed in chapter 1, combination or hybrid resume formats are preferred style, there are instances when a functional resume can be the best presentation of skills. As you review Mike Burns' resume, you will see that is certainly the case. After 13 years as a teacher and elementary school principal, Mike wanted to transfer his skills and qualifications into a corporate career track where he felt greater opportunities would exist for career growth and compensation.

Just like Charles's resume, Mike's begins with a headline format ("SEASONED MANAGER AND ADMINISTRATOR...Developing Strategic Plans/Managing Projects/Leading Operations and People"). This is one of our favorite formats because it allows the reader to quickly identify "who" the job seeker is.

Mike's Executive Profile is just that—a profile of an accomplished executive who has experience in virtually all key management disciplines. As you'll note, this section highlights finance, critical thinking, leadership, decision making, process management, relationship building, and many other skills, all of which are essential characteristics of a senior-level business manager. This section creates just the right perception of Mike without mentioning that he's an elementary principal.

The third section of this resume is exceptionally strong and is the bulk of the remaining information that Mike shares about his background. Although Mike's actual employment experience is very briefly listed at the bottom of page 2, it is not the focus on this document. Rather, the third section highlights his particular areas of expertise and related projects, accomplishments, and responsibilities. Again, it's not until you get halfway through page 2 that you are aware that Mike is an elementary principal.

Note that in the short section that lists Mike's employment, no job descriptions are used. The only information included in that section, beyond employers and job titles, is his list of professional honors and awards. This clearly communicates that Mike is a producer who delivers results and wins recognition from his employer.

Mike's education is included at the end of this resume because it is related to education and, therefore, the writer did not want to draw attention to it. And, finally, the resume ends with a great quote that highlights his management competencies and not his teaching competency.

MIKE BURNS

77002 Borgert Avenue
Anoka, MN 55304

Home: (763) 555-3789
Office: (763) 555-0562

mikeburns@anok.net

SEASONED MANAGER AND ADMINISTRATOR

Developing Strategic Plans / Managing Projects / Leading Operations and People

EXECUTIVE PROFILE

➢ More than seven years of senior-level experience in the administration of fiscally challenged organizations. Organized, take-charge professional with exceptional follow-through abilities and excellent management skills; able to plan and oversee projects/programs from concept to successful conclusion.

➢ A hands-on manager and critical thinker who can learn quickly, develop expertise, and produce immediate contributions in systems, analysis, business operations, and motivational team management. Possess a valuable blending of leadership, creative, and analytical abilities that combine efficiency with imagination to produce bottom-line results.

Core Strengths & Capabilities
Shared Decision Making ▪ Budget Development & Administration ▪ Staff / Team Training & Development
Operations Management ▪ Goal Setting & Strategic Planning ▪ Human Resources Leadership
Customer Care ▪ Cross-Functional Relationship Building ▪ Process Management ▪ Ideas & Opportunities
Consensus Building ▪ Productivity & Efficiency Improvement ▪ Service Design & Delivery Systems
Analysis & Assessment ▪ Organizational Communications ▪ Grant Writing ▪ Public Speaking ▪ "Can-Do" Mindset

RELEVANT CAREER SUCCESSES

STAFF TRAINING & DEVELOPMENT / HUMAN RESOURCES MANAGEMENT
➢ Directed human resource activities for two facilities with yearly budgets of $2 million and $4 million, respectively.

- Established a successful Staff Mentoring Program in Plymouth. Collaborated with tenured staff to develop a three-year plan toward easing new staff's transitions into the field. Paired tenured and new staff one-to-one.

- Led staff training opportunities with an average yearly budget of $40,000, providing much of the training myself.

- Hired professional, support, and all other staff. Directly supervised more than 70 employees.

- Proactively hired and teamed 20 new staff members within budget, accommodating Anoka's 300-student increase.

BUDGET & FISCAL MANAGEMENT / CAPITAL DEVELOPMENT
➢ Individually managed an average annual building budget of $4 million. Served on an administrative team managing a yearly $25 million budget (faced with an average $1 million in cuts each year).

- Weathered student population **increase from 550 to 850 in three years** by streamlining operations, cutting costs, and creatively raising funds, including co-authoring a successful $30,000 grant to hire a Behavior Planning Specialist.

- Played a key leadership and support role under the acting superintendent to lead a successful 2000 Building Bond Referendum Campaign. Results included a balanced budget and $6 million in new building construction. Also served on a team that successfully passed a $4 million referendum in 2001.

Resume for Mike Burns (written and designed by Barbara Poole, CPRW, CRW, of Hire Imaging).

MIKE BURNS / RELEVANT CAREER SUCCESSES CONTINUED

RELATIONSHIP BUILDING & COMMUNICATIONS
➢ Excelled at establishing and nurturing collaborative relationships with staff, parents, administrators, students, and other community members to clarify goals and communicate progress.
- Rallied community and parental support in school districts by sharing with them a vision based on the belief that all children are gifted and talented in their own way.
- Frequently served as public speaker to small and large groups: Graduation Emcee, Banquet Emcee, and University of Minnesota Educational Administration Class Presenter.
- Led monthly "Fun Night" recognition for volunteers, increasing attendance by 300+ per event.
- Acted as liaison with staff, families, and the school board. Commended for leading unified decision-making efforts.
- Directed the production of a school newsletter to foster school/community communications and connections.

OPERATIONS MANAGEMENT
➢ Directed food service, custodial and maintenance, computer and media services, front office, and bussing operations as well as teaching/non-teaching staff activities for two community schools.
- Scheduled and coordinated facility utilization.
- Supervised maintenance and custodial staff; redefined performance standards to streamline operations.
- Handled all repair and maintenance requests, and supervised staff in their implementation.
- Headed the integration and upkeep of technology applications including voice mail, computer, and Internet.

EVENT MANAGEMENT
➢ Initiated and/or coordinated numerous programs and events.
- Initiated Spanish, science, and language arts curriculum; a knowledge bowl; and a goal-setting conference.
- Spearheaded and coordinated career events, holiday events, school-wide enrichment themes, and other activities.

LEADERSHIP & TEAM ROLES
Graduation Standards ▪ Leadership Team ▪ District Strategic Planning ▪ Building President
Advisory Board ▪ Co-Op Mentor Board ▪ Title I Coordinator ▪ Student Council Advisor
Parent Involvement Council ▪ Curriculum Committees ▪ Staff Development Coordinator ▪ Construction Leadership

CAREER PATH

ANOKA PUBLIC SCHOOLS—Anoka, MN   1999– present
Elementary Principal
➢ Honored in 2001 as "Outstanding Service Award" recipient, a distinguished award given to only 5 out of 450 statewide employees annually.
- First administrator to ever receive the award.
- Second first-year employee to be honored with this award.

PLYMOUTH PUBLIC SCHOOLS—Plymouth, MN   1991–1999
Elementary Principal (1996–1999)
Superintendent Intern (Superintendent) (1998)
Fifth-Grade Teacher (1992–1996)
➢ At the age of 29, based on my performance, was hired in 1996 as the youngest principal in the state of Minnesota.

EDUCATION

UNIVERSITY OF MINNESOTA—Minneapolis, MN
Specialist's Degree, Educational Leadership and Administration   2000
Master's Degree, Educational Leadership and Administration   1996
Bachelor's Degree, Elementary Education   1992

> *"I was immensely impressed with Mike's performance from my very first contact with him ... he has strong communication skills, an excellent background, and intelligence that provides him with a quick perception of most situations ... he was quickly recognized for his sincerity, genuine interest in others, and leadership qualities ... he has enriched the entire community."*
> Sam Johnson, Superintendent, Plymouth Public Schools

WHY FORMAT IS SO IMPORTANT

To see how important the right format is to the success of your resume and job search, carefully review the following two resumes. They are prime examples of how critical it is for career changers to bring their transferable skills to the forefront of the resume and let other, non-related experience become secondary (even if that experience is where they've spent the majority of their careers).

Both resumes are for the same job seeker but use a different format and strategy. When you read the first resume, which follows the traditional chronological format, you're instantly drawn to the fact that Mary is a classroom teacher. Her teaching career has been solid but is certainly not supportive of her current objective to transition into an outside sales position.

Now look at Mary's second resume. What you see is a talented sales professional with experience in sales, relationship building, customer service, communications, organization, planning, and follow-through. Two-thirds of this resume is devoted to her sales skills, accomplishments, and experience, while the remainder briefly summarizes her teaching background. This format instantly changes the perception of who Mary is. She's no longer "just a classroom teacher." Rather, she's an experienced sales professional who will bring value to any sales position. The writer (Louise Garver, MA, JCTC, CMP, CPRW, MCDP, CEIP, of Career Directions in Connecticut) did an excellent job of changing the perception of "who" Mary is to closely align with her current career objectives.

MARY A. DANVERS

466 Forester Drive
Baltimore, MD 21099

Tel: (415) 877-9976
E-mail: danvers@earthlink.net

CAREER FOCUS: SALES

PROFILE

Outgoing, energetic professional with a successful record in challenging positions. Currently employed as a full-time classroom teacher with previous experience in sales, customer relationship management, customer service, and fund raising. Excellent communication and interpersonal relationship skills. Proven ability to establish and achieve professional and business objectives. Experienced presenter/trainer with excellent listening skills and a positive demeanor. Adept in identifying customer needs and creatively solving problems. Seeking new professional challenges and opportunities.

Computer proficient with MS Word and Excel, Lotus 1-2-3, and Internet research.
Foreign-language fluency in Spanish.

EMPLOYMENT EXPERIENCE

ARLINGTON PUBLIC SCHOOLS, Baltimore, MD • 1998 to present
Spanish Teacher

- Design and present curriculum in level 1 and 2 Spanish-language courses at a middle school and high school; effectively manage classes comprised of 30 students.
- Develop and implement innovative lesson plans that stimulate students' interest in the learning process.
- Combine lecture and demonstration with audiovisuals and other materials to enhance presentations.
- Demonstrate effective leadership and encourage team concepts to accomplish organizational goals.
- Initiated, created, and provide guidance to the Spanish Club.

HARRINGTON STORES, Baltimore, MD • 1998 to 1992
Sales Associate

WALLACE UNIVERSITY 2000 CAMPAIGN, Baltimore, MD • 1989 to 1991
Fund-raiser

LANCER ESTATES, Baltimore, MD • 1990
Sales Assistant

MARRIETTA & ASSOCIATES, Baltimore, MD • 1987 to 1989
Staff Accountant & Auditor

EDUCATION

B.S., Business Administration
Major in Accounting and Minor in Spanish
WALLACE UNIVERSITY, Baltimore, MD, 1993

Mary's resume in chronological format.

MARY A. DANVERS

466 Forester Drive
Baltimore, MD 21099

Tel: (415) 877-9976
E-mail: danvers@earthlink.net

CAREER FOCUS: SALES

Contributing to a company's success through application of key skills: Sales, Relationship Building, Customer Service, Persuasive Communications, Organization, Planning, and Follow-Through.

PROFILE

Outgoing, energetic professional with a successful record in challenging positions involving extensive communications with management, the general public, and peers. Proven ability to establish and achieve professional and business objectives. Experienced presenter/trainer with excellent listening skills and a positive demeanor. Adept in identifying customer needs and creatively solving problems. Computer proficient with MS Word and Excel, Lotus 1-2-3, and Internet research. Foreign-language fluency in Spanish.

SELECTED ACCOMPLISHMENTS

- Consistently ranked among the top 3 sales producers at Harrington Stores, exceeding weekly quotas. Effective in promoting products and creating displays that attracted customer attention.
- Cultivated long-term customer relationships that resulted in 80% referral/repeat business, contributing to business growth at Harrington Stores.
- Recognized as one of the top 3 fund-raisers in generating $75,000 for Wallace University's 2000 Campaign. Contacted and persuaded physicians and other professionals to contribute.
- Generated prospective buyers' interest by effectively describing property features; provided referrals to real estate agents at Lancer Estates.
- Contributed to successful fund-raising activities for the Special Olympics and Variety Club that benefited handicapped children.

SALES EXPERIENCE

Sales Associate • HARRINGTON STORES, Baltimore, MD • 1988 to 1992
Fund-raiser • WALLACE UNIVERSITY 2000 CAMPAIGN, Baltimore, MD • 1989 to 1991
Sales Assistant • LANCER ESTATES, Baltimore, MD • 1990

CURRENT EMPLOYMENT

ARLINGTON PUBLIC SCHOOLS, Baltimore, MD • 1998 to present
Spanish Teacher

Design and present curriculum in level 1 and 2 Spanish-language courses at a middle school and high school; effectively manage 30-student classes. Develop and implement innovative lesson plans that stimulate students' interest in the learning process. Combine lecture and demonstration with audiovisuals and other materials to enhance presentations. Demonstrate effective leadership and encourage team concepts to accomplish organizational goals. Initiated, created, and provide guidance to the Spanish Club.

Prior Experience: Staff Accountant and Auditor, MARRIETTA & ASSOCIATES, Baltimore, MD

EDUCATION

B.S., Business Administration
Major in Accounting and Minor in Spanish
WALLACE UNIVERSITY, Baltimore, MD, 1993

Mary's new resume, which emphasizes her sales and customer relationship management skills while effectively downplaying her teaching background.

Step-by-Step: Writing the Perfect Resume

This section is a detailed discussion of the various sections that you might include in your resume (for example, Career Summary, Professional Experience, Education, Technical Qualifications, Professional Memberships, Public Speaking, Publications, Honors and Awards, and Volunteer Experience), what each section should include, and where to include it.

CONTACT INFORMATION

Before we get into the major sections of the resume, let's briefly address the very top section: your name and contact information.

Name

You'd think writing your name would be the easiest part of writing your resume! But there are several factors you might want to consider:

- Although most people choose to use their full, formal name at the top of a resume, it has become increasingly more acceptable to use the name by which you prefer to be called.

- Bear in mind that it's to your advantage when readers feel comfortable calling you for an interview. Their comfort level may decrease if your name is gender-neutral, difficult to pronounce, or very unusual; they don't know how to ask for you. You can make it easier for them by following these examples:

> Lynn T. Cowles (Mr.)
>
> (Ms.) Michael Murray
>
> Tzirina (Irene) Kahn
>
> Ndege "Nick" Vernon

Address

You should always include your home address on your resume. If you use a post-office box for mail, include both your mailing address and your physical residence address if possible.

An exception to this guideline is when you are posting your resume on the Internet. For security purposes, it is a good idea to include just your phone and e-mail contact as well as possibly your city and state with no street address.

Telephone Number(s)

Your home telephone number must be included so that people can pick up the phone and call you immediately. In addition, you can also include a mobile phone number (refer to it as "mobile" rather than "cellular," to keep up with current terminology) or a pager number (however, this is less desirable because you must call back to speak to the person who called you). You can include a private home fax number, if it can be accessed automatically.

E-mail Address

Without question, if you have an e-mail address, include it on your resume. E-mail is now often the preferred method of communication in job search, particularly in the early stages of each contact. If you do not have an e-mail account, you can obtain a free, accessible-anywhere address from a provider such as www.yahoo.com, www.hotmail.com, or www.netzero.com.

As you look through the samples in this book, you'll see how resume writers have arranged the many bits of contact information at the top of a resume. You can use these as models for presenting your own information. The point is to make it as easy as possible for employers to contact you!

Page Two

We strongly recommend that you include your name, phone number, and e-mail address at the top of the second page of your resume and any additional pages. If, by chance, the pages get separated, you want to be sure that people can still contact you, even if they have only page 2 of your resume.

Now, let's get into the nitty-gritty of the core content sections of your resume.

CAREER SUMMARY

The Career Summary is the section at the top of your resume that summarizes and highlights your knowledge and expertise. You might be thinking, "But shouldn't my resume start with an Objective?" Although many job seekers still use Objective statements, we believe that a Career Summary is a much more powerful introduction. The problem with Objectives is that they are either too specific (limiting you to an "Electrical Engineering position") or too vague (doesn't everyone want "a challenging opportunity with a progressive organization offering the opportunity for growth and advancement"?). In addition, objective statements can be read as self-serving because they describe what *you* want rather than suggesting what you have to offer an employer.

In contrast, an effective Career Summary allows you to position yourself as you want to be perceived, and this is particularly important for people changing careers. A Career Summary allows you to immediately "paint a picture" of yourself that directly supports your current career objective.

It is critical that this section focus on the specific skills, qualifications, and achievements of your career that are related to your objectives. Your summary is *not* a historical overview of your career. Rather, it is a concise, well-written, and sharp presentation of information designed to *sell* you into your next position.

This section can have various titles, such as the following:

Career Summary	**Management Profile**
Career Achievements	**Professional Qualifications**
Career Highlights	**Professional Summary**
Career Synopsis	**Profile**
Executive Profile	**Summary**
Expertise	**Summary of Achievement**
Highlights of Experience	**Summary of Qualifications**

Or, as you will see in the Headline Format example shown later, your summary does not have to have any title at all.

The Career Summary section can be the single most important section on any career-changer's resume because of its content—the skills, qualifications, achievements, technical competencies, and other facts that you offer that are in line with your current career objectives. Your goal is to capture your reader's attention and immediately communicate the value you bring to their organization. If you are able to bring your relevant skills to the forefront, you will have favorably positioned yourself before a prospective employer; the fact that your prior work experience is in a different profession or industry becomes much less significant.

A Career Summary is a great thing because it allows you to include skills and competencies that you've acquired through volunteer work, training, internships, sabbaticals, association memberships, and other activities. The skills you include in your Summary *do not* have to be as a direct result of paid work experience. This is wonderful news for career changers! Remember, a summary is just that—a summary of the things that you do best—and it doesn't matter where you learned to do them.

The Career Summary probably will be the focal point of your resume. Be sure to package and sell all of your qualifications as they relate to your current career goals. Don't be concerned if your Career Summary is longer than normal. This section is the foundation for your entire resume, so be thorough so you're sure to sell yourself into your next job.

Here are five sample Career Summaries. Consider using one of these as the template for developing your Career Summary, or use them as the foundation to create your own presentation. You will also find some type of Career Summary in just about every resume included in chapters 4 through 12. Closely review them as well to find a format and style that's in line with your specific needs.

Bullet Format

Career Change: Government employee with diverse work experience seeking new career as manager of administrative affairs in "corporate" America.

HIGHLIGHTS

- 15 years of increasingly responsible experience at various administrative levels.
- Numerous college-level business courses and in-house training programs.
- Outstanding follow-up skills; goal-driven; always seek to bring projects to completion on time and within budget.
- Self-starter who sees what has to be done and then does it.
- Recipient of many Outstanding Service Awards.

RELEVANT SKILLS AND EXPERIENCE

Office Technology

- Mastery of MS Office Suite (Word, Excel, Access) and Windows 2002 environment.
- Expertise in other software packages (SAS, WordPerfect, CODAP, SPSS, PROFS, CorelDRAW, Lotus 1-2-3).
- Keyboarding skills of 50 wpm.

Administration

- Developed and managed operating budgets.
- Scheduled and taught training classes.
- Served on personnel screening and selection panels.
- Organized nationwide management conferences.

Leadership

- Supervised 7 to 9 employees as Team Leader for the Special Projects Task Force.
- Coordinated development, implementation, and operation of an advanced information systems application supporting employees worldwide.
- Honored with an Outstanding Leadership Award—Administrative Division.

Writing

- Wrote policy statements, procedures manuals, and programs of instruction.
- Wrote user manuals for 6 new system implementations.
- Wrote comprehensive personnel, asset, and resource analysis reports.

This career changer had a wealth of experience working for the federal government in a variety of administrative, training, and project support positions. Knowing that she wanted to transition out of the government, her core skills and qualifications were presented in a "skills-based" format with no mention of her government background. In turn, her skills are precisely the skills one would need for a position in corporate administration.

Headline Format

Career Change: Telecommunications engineering manager seeking new career in international telecommunications sales.

INTERNATIONAL BUSINESS PROFESSIONAL
Telecommunications Products, Solutions & Technologies
MBA, Executive Management, Harvard University
Cornell University Executive Sales Leadership

Although this individual's background was principally in managing the design and development of telecommunications products and technologies, the summary was written to downplay his technical expertise while highlighting his strong general management, international, and industry-related experience.

Paragraph Format

Career Change: Corporate sales and service manager seeking new career in corporate training and development.

CAREER SUMMARY

TRAINING & DEVELOPMENT PROFESSIONAL with proven expertise in the design and implementation of cost-effective staff training, e-learning, customer service, sales management, and marketing programs. Recognized for innovation and creativity in designing real-world training programs that focus on the development of core skills and competencies. Talented speaker, motivator, and group facilitator. Skilled in seminar and conference planning/logistics.

Although this individual's primary job responsibilities have been in sales and service, he also had years of experience in training his own staff. As such, and based on his current career goal, the summary was used to highlight his relevant training and development experience.

Core Competencies Summary Format

Career Change: Entrepreneur/owner of a small retail business now seeking a career in corporate finance and accounting.

PROFESSIONAL QUALIFICATIONS SUMMARY
CORPORATE FINANCE & ACCOUNTING
Manufacturing / Retail / Food Service

- Budget Development & Administration
- Profit & Loss Reporting
- Cash Flow Planning & Control
- Capital Expenditures
- Benefits Administration

- Revenue & Expense Forecasting
- Long-Range Fiscal Planning
- ROI, ROA & ROE Analysis
- Contract Negotiations
- Policy & Procedure Development

After 20 years as a self-employed business owner, this individual had acquired a wealth of experience in finance and accounting. Rather than focus his resume on the diversity of his management and entrepreneurial experience, all of the skills and qualifications listed focus on his current career goals and clearly position him as a well-qualified financial executive.

Project Format

Career Change: Business manager of a small bookkeeping-supply company now seeking a career as a computer programmer and applications developer.

PROFESSIONAL QUALIFICATIONS

Programmer / Technologist with 5+ years of experience with C/C++, Java (JDK 1.2), Visual Basic 5, Oracle (SQL, SQL*Plus, PL/SQL), DataEase, Windows 2000, and UNIX. Major projects have included

- ▶ ▶ **Point-of-Sale (POS) System** for The Tech Corner, Inc. Created a normalized relational database (using DataEase on a Windows 2000 network) to provide complete invoicing, billing, accounts receivable, and accounts payable management for a $2 million company with 200 active accounts.

- ▶ ▶ **Client-Service Sales Module in Java** for Sounds Systems LLC. Using TCP/IP sockets, connected GUI front end to console application, allowing user to query server for price, availability, and credit status.

- ▶ ▶ **Sales Module in Visual Basic** for class project. Created GUI front end to Access database, allowing input of customer information, parts numbers, and quantities and automatically generating orders, invoices, and sales summaries.

- ▶ ▶ **Billing System in Oracle** for class project. Generated users, tables, views, sequences, and triggers using SQL, SQL*Plus, and PL/SQL to create Oracle database. Imported data and used Developer 2000 to create forms.

During this job seeker's 12-year career, he had risen through the ranks to hold a relatively senior-level management position directing daily business, sales, and personnel operations. During the past five years, he had also spearheaded all technology development and implementation projects for the company (as well as several projects at a technical school he was attending). These projects became the cornerstone of his new career-change resume to create the perception that he is a skilled programmer and technologist.

PROFESSIONAL EXPERIENCE

As a career changer, how much information you include in your Professional Experience section will depend entirely on how relevant that experience is to your current career objectives. If relevant (or if just parts of it are relevant), you'll want to be sure to highlight that information—in detail—on your resume. If irrelevant, you'll want to be very brief with your job descriptions, if you include them at all. As discussed previously, the best strategy for a career changer might be a functional or hybrid format focusing on skills and qualifications while downplaying work experience. Read further and you'll understand why.

Writing your Professional Experience section might take you the longest of any section of your resume. Suppose, for example, that you had the same position for 10 years. How can you consolidate all that you have done into one short section? If, on the opposite end of the spectrum, you've had several short-term jobs over the past several years, how can you make your experience seem substantial, noteworthy, and relevant? And, for all of you whose experience is in between, what do you include, how, where, and why?

These are not easy questions to answer. In fact, the most truthful response to each question is, "it depends." It depends on you, your experience, your achievements and successes, your current career objectives, and how closely your past experience ties into and supports those objectives.

Here are five samples of Professional Experience sections. Review how each individual's unique background is organized and emphasized, and consider your own background when using one of these as the template or foundation for developing your Professional Experience section. And be sure to review the resume samples in chapters 4 through 12 to get even more ideas.

Achievement Format

Career Change: Director of emergency medical services seeking a new career as a college instructor. Format emphasizes rapid promotion through each position, overall scope of responsibility, and resulting achievements particularly relevant to his new career objective.

PROFESSIONAL EXPERIENCE

ALBANY COUNTY FIRE DEPARTMENT, Colonie, NY   1990 to 2004

DIRECTOR OF EMERGENCY MEDICAL SERVICES (1998 to 2004)
SHIFT COMMANDER—CAPTAIN (1994 to 1998)
ENGINE COMPANY OFFICER—LIEUTENANT (1992 to 1994)
EMERGENCY MEDICAL TECHNICIAN—ENGINEER (1990 to 1992)

Supervised Emergency Medical Services comprising 45 EMTs and paramedics at three fire stations. Participated in the direction of all aspects of personnel relations, including training, hiring, new-employee orientation, staff development, and performance evaluations. Served as Incident Commander at medical emergencies and structure fires. Coordinated all phases of EMS and served as Chairman of EMS Operations Committee. Wrote and implemented EMS protocols.

Achievements:

- Served as Emergency Medical Services Training Officer with responsibility for planning, organizing, and delivering EMS training, testing, and recertification for 63 EMTs.

- Catalyst in the conceptualization of an innovative paramedic training program for Albany County Fire Department.

- Created the model for state licensure for other fire departments based on stringent training and performance requirements.

- Established and launched Fire Cadet Program (paid internship) to allow 17- to 21-year-olds to participate in fire service through a comprehensive training and mentoring opportunity.

- Reduced annual material costs by 50% through more efficient vendor sourcing and purchasing processes.

Challenge, Action, and Results (CAR) Format

Career Change: Corporate sales manager seeking a career change to a position as a general manager, division vice president, or other senior-level operating management position. Format emphasizes the challenge of each position, the action taken, and the results delivered.

EXPERIENCE AND ACHIEVEMENTS————————————————

Corporate Sales Manager   1998 to Present
DOLINVEST CORPORATION   Chicago, Illinois

Challenge: To plan and execute a complete turnaround, revitalization, and return to profitability of the non-performing Chicago metro region for this $20 million specialty gift products manufacturer.

Action: Revitalized relationships with more than 300 accounts, negotiated credit line to support corporate cash requirements, recruited talented staff and management teams, and launched a massive cost-reduction initiative. Rewrote corporate policies and procedures, introduced advanced technologies, and eliminated reliance on third-party consultants.

Results: ➤ Achieved/surpassed all turnaround objectives and returned the operation to profitability in first year. Delivered strong and sustainable gains:
  - 128% increase in sales revenues over 12 months.
  - 8.5% increase in bottom-line profitability.
  - $1.8 million in sales from new products.
  - 100% on-time customer delivery.

➤ Won the company's 2001 Leadership Achievement Award.

➤ Quoted in the National Management Association's annual publication as one of 1999's *"Turnaround Specialists."*

➤ Developed and taught the corporation's flagship Leadership Development program.

➤ Eliminated more than $2.8 million in excess spending and reduced annual contractor fees by more than 30%.

➤ Invested $800,000 in new technology to automate and streamline all core business functions. Delivered an additional 4% to bottom-line profit contribution.

Functional Format

Career Change: Director of day-care center seeking a new career in outside sales in the toy, pharmaceutical, consumer products, or cosmetics industries. Format emphasizes the functional areas of responsibility within her job and her associated achievements.

EMPLOYMENT EXPERIENCE

Center Director   ARNOLD'S LEARNING CENTER, Minneapolis, MN   1998–Present

Member of three-person management team directing the operations of a large-scale day-care facility with more than 200 children and more than 40 full-time and part-time staff. Scope of responsibility is extensive and includes the following:

SALES/MARKETING

- ☑ Attracted potential customers through print advertising, tours, referrals, open houses, and outreach to area schools. Utilized guest registration forms to grow prospect list, and conducted follow-up mail and callback campaigns.

- ☑ Personally credited with delivering 25%+ annual growth, year-over-year, for seven consecutive years.

- ☑ Wrote, designed, and directed production of the first-ever brochure and accompanying marketing literature.

- ☑ Positioned center as the fastest-growing and most-profitable operation of its kind in a 200-mile radius.

CUSTOMER RELATIONSHIP MANAGEMENT & CUSTOMER SERVICE

- ☑ Introduced the center's first formal customer service program to ensure that parents had easy access to information and to decision makers.

- ☑ Created a customer satisfaction survey and administered it annually. Utilized collected data to expand and strengthen existing service operations.

- ☑ Trained newly hired staff in effective communication and service strategies.

FUND RAISING & SPECIAL EVENTS MANAGEMENT

- ☑ Planned, staffed, and coordinated an average of 10 special events each year (for example, open houses, talent shows, orientations, competitive sporting events).

- ☑ Managed all event promotions, publicity, media relations, and marketing. Demonstrated excellent oral and written communication skills.

- ☑ Acted as emcee at numerous events, speaking to groups of more than 200 at a time.

Project Highlights Format

Career Change: An experienced media sales representative seeking a new career as a graphic designer and illustrator. This format highlights her special projects and activities as they relate to graphic design although this was a very small component of her overall position.

Sales Representative, December 2000 to September 2004

THE DALLAS CENTURION NEWS, Dallas, Texas

High-profile position working with companies throughout the Dallas metro region to provide expert leadership in the creative design, development, and execution of media advertising campaigns. Expanded scope of client relationships to include a portfolio of graphic design and illustration services.

- **Dallas County Arts Commission.** Commissioned by DCAC to design artwork for mural and footpath for the Buck Henry Theater.

- **Oodles & Oodles.** Designed and painted mural for one of Dallas's hottest night spots.

- **Transventure Insurance.** Created graphics for a 200-page investor report.

- **Dallas Regional Broadcasting Company.** Guided design of 3-D animation, characters, and designs for new television series.

- **Toy Crazy.** Designed corporate logo, letterhead, brochure, and sales documentation.

- **National Speakers Association.** Illustrated 252-page book written and published by NSA.

Experience Summary Format

Career Change: Site remediation superintendent seeking new career working in environmental regulatory affairs. Format briefly emphasizes relevant highlights of each position because the bulk of this individual's experience in remediation will have been summarized—at length—in the Career Summary.

EXPERIENCE SUMMARY

Site Superintendent, ABX REMEDIATION SERVICES, Cincinnati, OH—1999 to 2004

- Investigated, analyzed, and identified objectives for remedial actions/cleanups throughout the Midwest.
- Negotiated with state and federal regulators to establish plans for the remediation of specific sites nationwide.
- Independently handled the filing of all regulatory documents, reports, and other submissions mandated by local, state, and federal officials.
- Coordinated remediation of 50,000 tons of lead-contaminated soil from 150 residential sites two weeks ahead of schedule and $56,000 under budget.

Senior Electrician, ABX ELECTRICAL SERVICES, Cincinnati, OH—1994 to 1999

- Installed electrical, plumbing, and gas systems in decontamination, office, lab trailers, and project sites. Often worked at hazardous/EPA-controlled sites.
- Researched relevant regulations and trained other employees to meet regulatory standards.
- Filed regulatory documentation and met with regulators to resolve any potential field issues.

Electrician, MYERS ELECTRIC, Covington, KY—1992 to 1994

- Installed, maintained, and repaired residential electrical systems and service.

EDUCATION, CREDENTIALS, AND CERTIFICATIONS

Your Education section should include college, certifications, credentials, licenses, registrations, and continuing education. For career changers whose greatest selling point for their new career is education, this section is extremely important and will, most likely, be placed on your resume immediately following your Career Summary. Be sure to display your educational qualifications prominently if they are a key selling point in your transition into a new career track.

Here are five sample Education sections that illustrate a variety of ways to organize and format this information.

Academic Credentials Format

EDUCATION

M.S., Counseling Psychology, University of Akron, 1996
B.S., Psychology, University of Miami, 1994

Highlights of Continuing Professional Education:
- Organizational Management & Leadership, Ohio Leadership Association, 2001
- Industrial Relations, Purdue University, 2000
- Conflict Resolution & Violence Management in the Workplace, Institute for Workplace Safety, 1998

Licensed Clinical Psychologist, State of Ohio, 1996 to Present
Licensed Recreational Therapist, National Recreation Association, 1998 to Present

Executive Education Format

EDUCATION

Executive Leadership Program .... STANFORD UNIVERSITY

Executive Development Program .... NORTHWESTERN UNIVERSITY

Master of Business Administration (MBA) degree .... HARVARD UNIVERSITY GRADUATE SCHOOL

Bachelor of Science degree .... UNIVERSITY OF PENNSYLVANIA

Certifications Format

TECHNICAL CERTIFICATIONS & DEGREES

Registered Nurse, University of Maryland, 1988

Certified Nursing Assistant, University of Maryland, 1986

Certified Nursing Aide, State of Maryland, 1982

Bachelor of Science in Nursing (BSN), University of Maryland, 1988

Associate of Arts in General Studies, Byerstown Community College, Byerstown, Delaware, 1986

Specialized Training Format

Technical Licenses & Certifications

- Rhode Island Journeyman License #67382
- Vermont Journeyman License #LK3223839
- Licensed Electrician #8737262
- Construction Supervisor #99089
- Impact Training, Motor Control Seminar, 2001
- CAT-5 Certification, 2000
- Variable Speed Drive Certification, 1999
- Soars Grounding of Electrical Systems for Safety Certification, 1998
- Graduate, Jefferson Forest High School, Lynchburg, VA, 1995

Non-Degree Format

TRAINING & EDUCATION

UNIVERSITY OF FLORIDA, Tampa, Florida
B.S. Candidate—Business Administration (senior class status)

UNIVERSITY OF OREGON, Portland, Oregon
Dual Majors in Business Administration & Computer Science (2 years)

Completed 100+ hours of continuing professional education through the University of Miami, University of Georgia, and University of Phoenix. Topics included business administration, finance, strategic planning, organizational development, team building, and communications.

THE "EXTRAS"

The primary focus of your resume should be on information that is directly related to your career goals, whether from your paid work experience, volunteer experience, education and training, affiliations, or elsewhere. However, you also should include things that will distinguish you from other candidates and clearly demonstrate your value to a prospective employer. And, not too surprisingly, it is often the "extras" that get the interviews.

Following is a list of the other categories you might or might not include on your resume depending on your particular experience and your current career objectives. If one of these categories is pertinent to you, use the samples for formatting your own data. Remember, however, that if something is truly impressive, you might want to draw even more attention to it by including it in your Career Summary at the beginning of your resume. If this is the case, it's not necessary to repeat the information at the end of your resume.

Technology Skills and Qualifications

Many technology professionals will have a separate section on their resumes for technology skills and qualifications. It is here that you will summarize all the hardware, software, operating systems, applications, networks, and more that you know and that are relevant to your current career objectives.

You'll also have to consider placement of this section in your resume. If the positions for which you are applying require strong technical skills, we would recommend you insert this section immediately after your Career Summary (or as a part thereof). If, on the other hand, your technical skills are more of a plus than a specific requirement, the preferred placement is further down on your resume.

Either way, these skills are vital in virtually any technology-related position. As such, this is extremely important information to a prospective employer, so be sure to display it prominently.

Here are two different ways to format and present your technical qualifications:

TECHNOLOGY PROFILE

Operating Systems	Windows XP/2002/98/NT 4.0 Workstation; Novell NetWare 6.x; MS-DOS 6.22
Protocols/Networks	TCP/IP, NetBEUI, IPX/SPX, Gigabit Ethernet
Hardware	Hard drives, printers, scanners, fax/modems, CD-ROMs, Zip drives, Cat5 cables, hubs, NIC cards
Software	Microsoft Office Modules, FileMaker Pro, PC Anywhere, MS Exchange, ARCserve, Project Manager

TECHNOLOGY SKILLS SUMMARY

Windows XP/2000/98	SAP	TCP/IP
NT 4.0 Workstation	MRP	Gigabit Ethernet
Novell NetWare 6.x	DRP	IPX/SPX
Microsoft Office	MS Exchange	ARCserve
Project Manager	PC Anywhere	FileMaker Pro

If your goal is to simply mention the fact that you are proficient with specific PC software, a quick line at the end of your Career Summary should cover this information. For example:

PC Proficient with Word, Excel, Access, PageMaker, and WordPerfect.

Equipment Skills and Qualifications

People employed in manufacturing, construction, engineering, and related industries will have a unique portfolio of equipment skills and knowledge. If this information is relevant to your current career goals, it is critical that you communicate it in your resume, highlighting all the equipment with which you are proficient or familiar. Consider this format for an individual with extensive experience in pharmaceutical product packaging:

Trained in and worked on a diversity of packaging equipment and technology, including R.A. Jones, Hoppmann, Syntron, Lakso, Scandia, Westbrook, Wexxar, and Edson:

Leaflet Inserters	Cappers	Bottle Cleaners & Elevators
Fillers	Desiccants	Neckbanders
Heat Tunnels	Labelers	Cartoners
Case Packers & Sealers	Hoppers	Bundlers
Sorters	Carousels	Cottoners

Honors and Awards

If you have won honors and awards, you can either include them in a separate section near the end of your resume, or integrate them into the Education or Professional Experience section if they are particularly noteworthy or related to your current career objectives. If you choose to include them in a separate section, consider this format:

- Winner, 2003 **"Sales Performance"** award from the Bechtel Mortgage Company, Inc.

- Winner, 2000 **"Customer Service"** award for outstanding contributions to customer service and retention from Kraft Foods, Inc.

- Named **"Employee of the Year,"** Kraft Foods, Inc., 1999

- **Cum Laude Graduate,** Southern Illinois University, 1991

Public Speaking

Experts are the ones who are invited to give public presentations at conferences, seminars, workshops, training programs, symposia, and other events. So if you have public-speaking experience, others must consider you an expert. Be sure to include this very complimentary information in your resume. Here's one way to present it:

- Keynote Speaker, "Architectural Engineering & Design," AAI National Conference, New York City, 2004

- Panel Presenter, "Maximizing Space Design & Utilization," AAI National Conference, Dallas, 2002

- Session Leader, "Ergonomic Design," Ohio Society of Architects, Cleveland, 2000

Publications

If you're published, you must be an expert (or at least most people will think so). Just as with your public-speaking engagements, be sure to include your publications. They validate your knowledge, qualifications, and credibility. Publications can include books, articles, online Web site content, manuals, and other written documents. Here's an example:

- Co-Author, *Computer-Aided Design of Hybrid Microcircuits,* National Electronic Packaging Conference, 2003.

- Author, *Subtle Aspects of Micro-Packaging,* Product Assurance Conference, 2001.

- Author, *Micro-Packaging Practices, Policies, and Processes,* IBM Training Manual, 1999.

Teaching and Training Experience

Many professionals, regardless of their industry or profession, also teach or train at colleges, universities, technical schools, and other organizations, in addition to training that they may do "on the job." If this is applicable to you and your current objectives, you will want to include that experience on your resume. If someone hires you (paid or unpaid) to speak to an audience, it communicates a strong message about your skills, qualifications, knowledge, and expertise. Here's a format you might use to present that information:

- **Adjunct Faculty,** Department of Chemical Engineering, Texas A&M University, 1999 to 2003. Taught Introductory and Advanced Chemical Engineering.

- **Guest Lecturer,** Department of Statistics, Reynolds Community College, 1998 to 2002. Provided semiannual, day-long lecture series on the applications of statistics and statistical theory in the workplace.

- **Trainer,** Macmillan School of Engineering, 1995 to 1997. Taught Chemical Engineering 101 and Chemical Lab Analysis to first-year students.

Committees and Task Forces

Many professionals serve on committees, task forces, and other special project teams either as part of, or in addition to, their full-time job responsibilities. Again, this type of information further strengthens your credibility, qualifications, and perceived value to a prospective employer when it is related to your current objectives. Consider a format such as this:

- Member, 2003–04 Corporate Planning & Reorganization Task Force

- Member, 2002 Study Team on "Redesigning Corporate Training Systems to Maximize Employee Productivity"

- Chairperson, 2001–02 Committee on "Safety & Regulatory Compliance in the Workplace"

Professional Affiliations

If you are a member of any educational, professional, or leadership associations, be sure to include that information on your resume. It communicates a message of professionalism, a desire to stay current with the industry, and a strong professional network. If you have held leadership positions within these organizations, be sure to include them. Here's an example:

NATIONAL EDUCATION ASSOCIATION (NEA)

Professional Member (1995 to Present)

Fundraising Committee Member (2002 to 2004)

Curriculum Committee Member (2000 to 2002)

NATIONAL TEACHERS ASSOCIATION (NTA)

Professional Member (1998 to Present)

Instructional Materials Design Committee Member (2001 to 2004)

Technology Task Force Member (1999 to 2001)

LAFAYETTE TEACHERS ASSOCIATION (LTA)

President (2002 to 2004)

Vice President (2000 to 2002)

Member (1992 to Present)

Civic Affiliations

Civic affiliations are fine to include if they fit one of the following criteria:

- Are with a notable organization.

- Demonstrate leadership experience.

- May be of interest to a prospective employer.

However, things such as treasurer of your local condo association and singer with your church choir are not generally of value in marketing your qualifications unless, of course, that experience is directly relevant to your current career objectives. Here's an example of what to include and how:

- Volunteer Chairperson, United Way of America—Detroit Chapter, 2000 to Present

- President, Greenwood Environmental District, 1999 to Present

- Treasurer, Habitat for Humanity—Memphis Chapter, 1998 to 2000

Personal Information

We do not recommend that you include such personal information as birth date, marital status, number of children, and related data. However, there may be instances when personal information is appropriate. If this information will give you a competitive advantage or answer unspoken questions about your background, by all means include it. Here's an example:

- Born in Belgium. U.S. Permanent Residency Status since 1997.

- Fluent in English, French, German, Flemish, and Dutch.

- Competitive Triathlete. Top-5 finish, 1995 Midwest Triathlon and 1999 Des Moines Triathlon.

Note in the preceding example that the job seeker is multilingual. This is a particularly critical selling point. Although it's listed under Personal Information in this example, it is more appropriately highlighted in your Career Summary.

Consolidating the Extras

Sometimes you have so many extra categories at the end of your resume, each with only a handful of lines, that spacing becomes a problem. You certainly don't want to have to make your resume a page longer to accommodate five lines, nor do you want the "extras" to overwhelm the primary sections of your resume. Yet you believe the information is important and should be included. Or perhaps you have a few small bits of information that you think are important but don't merit an entire section. In these situations, consider consolidating the information using one of the following formats. You'll save space, avoid overemphasizing individual items, and present a professional, distinguished appearance. Here are two examples of how to consolidate and format your "extras":

PROFESSIONAL PROFILE

Technology Qualifications	IBM & HP Platforms Microsoft Office Suite, SAP R/3, ProjectPlanner, MRP, DRP, LAN, WAN, KPM, Lotus, Lotus Notes, Novell Networks
Affiliations	Association of Quality Control Institute of Electrical & Electronic Engineers American Electrical Association
Public Speaking	Speaker, IEEE Conference, Chicago, 2001 Presenter, AEA National Conference, Miami, 1998 Panelist, IEEE Conference, Detroit, 1996
Languages	Fluent in English, Spanish, and German

ADDITIONAL INFORMATION

- Co-Chair, Education Committee, Detroit Technology Association.
- PC literate with MRP, DRP, SAP, and Kaizen technologies.
- Available for relocation worldwide.
- Eagle Scout ... Boy Scout Troop Leader.

Writing Tips, Techniques, and Important Lessons

At this point, you've done a lot of reading, probably taken some notes, highlighted samples that appeal to you, and are ready to plunge into writing your resume. To make this task as easy as possible, we've compiled some "insider" techniques that we've used in our professional resume-writing practices. These techniques were learned the hard way through years of experience! We know they work; they will make the writing process easier, faster, and more enjoyable for you.

GET IT DOWN—THEN POLISH AND PERFECT IT

Don't be too concerned with making your resume "perfect" the first time around. It's far better to move fairly swiftly through the process, getting the basic information organized and on paper (or on screen), rather than agonizing about the perfect phrase or ideal formatting. When you've completed a draft, we think you'll be surprised at how close to "final" it is, and you'll be able to edit, tighten, and improve formatting fairly quickly.

WRITE YOUR RESUME FROM THE BOTTOM UP

Here's the system:

1. **Start with the easy things**—Education, Technology, Professional Affiliations, Public Speaking, Publications, and any other extras you want to include. These items require little thought and can be completed in just a few minutes.

2. **Write short job descriptions for your older positions.** Be very brief and focus on highlights such as rapid promotion, achievements, innovations, professional honors, or employment with well-respected, well-known companies.

   NOTE: Even if you plan to create a functional resume that combines job achievements in one "front-and-center" location, we recommend that you first draft these descriptions in a chronological format. It will be easier to remember what you did if you take each of your jobs in turn. Later you can regroup your statements to emphasize related skills and abilities, and leave your employment history as a simple list or brief description to support your career-change objectives.

   Once you've completed this, look at how much you've written in a short period of time! Then move on to the next step.

3. **Write the job descriptions for your most recent positions.** If you're writing a chronological or combination resume, this will take a bit longer than the other sections you have written. Remember to focus on the overall scope of your responsibility, major projects and initiatives, and significant achievements as they relate directly to your current objectives. Tell your reader what you did and how well you did it. You can use any of the formats recommended earlier in this chapter, or you can create something that is unique to you and your career.

   Now, see how far along you are? Your resume is 90 percent complete with only one section left to do.

4. **Write your career summary.** Before you start writing, remember your objective for this section. The summary should not simply rehash your previous experience. Rather, it is designed to highlight the skills and qualifications you have that are most closely related to your current career objective(s). The summary is intended to capture the reader's attention and "sell" your expertise and is the *most important* section for any career-change resume.

That's it. You're done. We guarantee that the process of writing your resume will be much, much easier if you follow the "bottom-up" strategy. Now, on to the next tip.

INCLUDE NOTABLE OR PROMINENT "EXTRA" STUFF IN YOUR CAREER SUMMARY

Remember the "extra-credit sections" that are normally at the bottom of your resume? If this information is particularly significant or prominent—you won a notable award, spoke at an international conference, developed a new teaching methodology, designed a new product that generated tens of millions of dollars in new revenues, or slashed 60 percent from operating costs—you might want to include it at the top in your Career Summary. Remember, the summary section is written to distinguish you from the crowd of other qualified candidates. As such, if you've accomplished anything that clearly demonstrates your knowledge, expertise, and credibility, consider moving it to your Career Summary for added attention. Refer to the sample career summaries earlier in the chapter for examples.

Use Resume Samples to Get Ideas for Content, Format, and Organization

This book is just one of many resources where you can review sample resumes to help you in formulating your strategy, writing the text, and formatting your resume. You don't have to struggle alone. Rather, use all the available resources at your disposal.

Be forewarned, however, that it's unlikely you will find a resume that fits your life and career to a "t." It's more likely that you will use "some of this sample" and "some of that sample" to create a resume that is uniquely "you."

Include Dates or Not?

Unless you are over age 50, we recommend that you date your work experience and your education. Without dates, your resume becomes vague and difficult for the typical hiring manager or recruiter to interpret. It often communicates the message that you are trying to hide something. By including the dates of your education and your experience, you create a clean and concise picture that one can easily follow to track your career progression.

If you want the dates to be prominent, consider putting them at the right margin. Conversely, if you want to downplay the dates, put them in small type immediately after the name of your company or the title of your position, or even at the end of the descriptive paragraph for each position.

An Individual Decision

If you are over age 50, dating your early positions must be an individual decision. On one hand, you do not want to "date" yourself out of consideration by including dates from the 1960s and early 1970s. On the other hand, those positions might be worth including for any of a number of reasons. Further, if you omit those early dates, you might feel as though you are misrepresenting yourself (or lying) to a prospective employer.

Here is a strategy to overcome those concerns while still including your early experience: Create a separate category titled "Previous Professional Experience," in which you summarize your earliest employment. You can tailor this statement to emphasize just what is most important about that experience.

If you want to capitalize on the good reputation of your past employers, include a statement such as this:

- Previous experience includes supervisory positions with IBM, Dell, and Xerox.

If you want to focus on the rapid progression of your career, consider this example:

- Promoted rapidly through a series of increasingly responsible sales and marketing management positions with Hilton Hotels.

If you want to focus on your early career achievements, include a statement such as this:

> • Member of 6-person task force credited with the design and rollout of Davidson's first-generation videoconferencing technology.

By including any one of the preceding paragraphs, under the heading "Previous Professional Experience," you are clearly communicating to your reader that your employment history dates further back than the dates you have indicated on your resume. In turn, you are being 100 percent above-board and not misrepresenting yourself or your career. You're also focusing on the success, achievement, and prominence of your earliest assignments.

Include Dates in the Education Section?

If you are over age 50, we generally do not recommend that you date your education or college degrees. Simply include the degree and the university with no date. Why exclude yourself from consideration by immediately presenting the fact that you earned your college degree in 1968, 1972, or 1976—about the time the hiring manager was probably being born? Remember, the goal of your resume is to share the highlights of your career and open doors for interviews. It is *not* to give your entire life story. As such, it is not mandatory to date your college degree.

However, if you use this strategy, be aware that the reader is likely to assume there is *some* gap between when your education ended and your work experience started. Therefore, if you choose to begin your chronological work history with your first job out of college, omitting your graduation date could actually backfire, because the reader might assume that you have experience that predates your first job. In this case, it's best either to *include your graduation date* or *omit dates of earliest experience,* using the summary strategy discussed earlier.

ALWAYS SEND A COVER LETTER WHEN YOU FORWARD YOUR RESUME

Sending a cover letter every time you send a resume is expected and is appropriate job search etiquette. As a career changer, your cover letter is *vital* to the success of your job search campaign.

Consider the following: When you write a resume, you are writing a document that you can use for every position you apply for, assuming that the requirements for all of those positions will be similar. You invest a great deal of time and effort in crafting just the "right" resume for you, but once it's done, it's done.

Your cover letter, however, is a document that is constantly changing to meet the needs of each individual situation for which you apply. In essence, it is the tool that allows you to customize your presentation to each company or recruiter, addressing their specific hiring requirements. Use your cover letter to highlight the most important qualifications, experiences, and achievements you bring to that specific company so that a prospective employer doesn't have to search through your resume to find what is most important. It is also the appropriate place to include any specific information that has been requested, such as salary history or salary requirements (see the following section for more on including salaries).

Your cover letter will allow you to briefly address why you're making a career change. Some examples might include the following:

> After years of success in the health care industry, I have decided to transition my skills to the pharmaceutical sales industry, where I can continue to apply my medical and nursing knowledge while achieving new career milestones.

> Although my career with CBS News has been exceptional and presented me with opportunities I never imagined possible, my real passion has always been public relations. As such, I have given my notice to CBS and am now interviewing with PR firms throughout New York to identify professional opportunities where I can begin to learn the business and establish my new career track.

> When I graduated from college in 1988, I was immediately recruited by Federal Express, where I have continued to work since that date. Now, 15 years later, I wonder what happened to my dreams of being a commercial photographer. Somehow, between career and family, they were sidetracked. Well, no more! I've committed myself to making a career change and am approaching it with energy, enthusiasm, and a real commitment to success.

> My 14-year career with ExPeTe International was an extraordinary experience, highlighted by rapid promotions and numerous corporate commendations. However, the company fell on hard times in the late 1990s and my position was subsequently eliminated in April 2004. Knowing that the entire cable industry is undergoing remarkable change and reorganization, I have decided to now concentrate my purchasing career in the more stable telecommunications industry—thus, my interest in your company.

NEVER INCLUDE SALARY HISTORY OR SALARY REQUIREMENTS ON YOUR RESUME

Your resume is *not* the correct forum for a salary discussion. First of all, you should never provide salary information unless a company has requested that information and you choose to comply. (Studies show that employers will look at your resume anyway, so you might choose not to respond to this request, thereby avoiding pricing yourself out of the job or locking yourself into a lower salary than the job is worth.)

When contacting recruiters, however, we recommend that you do provide salary information, but again, only in your cover letter. With recruiters you want to "put all of your cards on the table" and help them make an appropriate placement by providing information about your current salary and salary objectives. For example, "Be advised that my most recent compensation was $55,000 annually and that I am interested in a position starting at a minimum of $65,000 per year." Or, if you would prefer to be a little less specific, you might write, "My annual compensation over the past three years has averaged $50,000+."

ALWAYS REMEMBER THAT YOU ARE SELLING

As we have discussed over and over throughout this book, resume writing is sales. Understand and appreciate the value you bring to a prospective employer, and then communicate that value by focusing on your achievements. Companies don't want to hire just anyone; they want to hire "the" someone who will make a difference. Show them that you are that candidate.

CHAPTER 3

Printed, Scannable, Electronic, and Web Resumes

After you've worked so tirelessly to write a winning resume, your next challenge is the resume's design, layout, and presentation. It's not enough for it to read well; your resume must also have just the right look for the right audience. And, just as with everything else in a job search, no specific answers exist. You must make a few decisions about what your final resume presentation will look like.

The Four Types of Resumes

In today's employment market, job seekers use four types of resume presentations:

- Printed
- Scannable
- Electronic (e-mail attachments and ASCII text files)
- Web

The following sections give details on when you would need each type, as well as how to prepare these types of resumes.

THE PRINTED RESUME

We know the printed resume as the "traditional resume," the one that you mail to a recruiter, take to an interview, and forward by mail or fax in response to an advertisement. When preparing a printed resume, you want to create a sharp, professional, and visually attractive presentation. Remember, that piece of paper conveys the very first impression of you to a potential employer, and that first impression goes a long, long way. Never be fooled into thinking that just because you have the best qualifications in your industry, the visual presentation of your resume does not matter. It does, a great deal.

THE SCANNABLE RESUME

The scannable resume can be referred to as the "plain-Jane" or "plain-vanilla" resume. All of the things that you would normally do to make your printed resume look attractive—bold print, italics, multiple columns, sharp-looking typestyle, and more—are stripped away in a scannable resume. You want to present a document that can be easily read and interpreted by scanning technology.

Although the technology continues to improve, and many scanning systems in fact can read a wide variety of type enhancements, it's sensible to appeal to the "lowest common denominator" when creating your scannable resume. Follow these formatting guidelines:

- Choose a commonly used, easily read font such as Arial or Times New Roman.

- Don't use bold, italic, or underlined type.

- Use a minimum of 11-point type size.

- Position your name, and nothing else, on the top line of the resume.

- Keep text left-justified, with a "ragged" right margin.

- It's okay to use common abbreviations (for instance, scanning software will recognize "B.S." as a Bachelor of Science degree). But, when in doubt, spell it out.

- Eliminate graphics, borders, and horizontal lines.

- Use plain, round bullets or asterisks.

- Avoid columns and tables, although a simple two-column listing can be read without difficulty.

- Spell out symbols such as % and &.

- If you divide words with slashes, add a space before and after the slash to be certain the scanner doesn't misread the letters.

- Print using a laser printer on smooth white paper.

- If your resume is longer than one page, be sure to print on only one side of the paper; put your name, telephone number, and e-mail address on the top of page two; and don't staple the pages together.

- For best possible results, mail your resume (don't fax it), and send it flat in a 9 × 12 envelope so that you won't have to fold it.

Of course, you can avoid scannability issues completely by sending your resume electronically, so that it will not have to pass through a scanner to enter the company's databank. Read the next section for electronic resume guidelines.

THE ELECTRONIC RESUME

Your electronic resume can take two forms: e-mail attachments and ASCII text files.

E-mail Attachments

When including your resume with an e-mail, simply attach the word-processing file of your printed resume. Because a vast majority of businesses use Microsoft Word, it is the most acceptable format and will present the fewest difficulties when attached.

However, given the tremendous variety in versions of software and operating systems, not to mention printer drivers, it's quite possible that your beautifully formatted resume will look quite different when viewed and printed at the other end. To minimize these glitches, use generous margins (at least 0.75 inch all around). Don't use unusual typefaces, and minimize fancy formatting effects.

Test your resume by e-mailing it to several friends or colleagues, and then having them view and print it on their systems. If you use WordPerfect, Microsoft Works, or another word-processing program, consider saving your resume in a more universally accepted format such as RTF or PDF. Again, try it out on friends before sending it to a potential employer.

ASCII Text Files

You'll find many uses for an ASCII text version of your resume:

- To avoid formatting problems, you can paste the text into the body of an e-mail message rather than send an attachment. Many employers actually prefer this method. Pasting text into an e-mail message lets you send your resume without the possibility of also sending a virus.

- You can readily copy and paste the text version into online job application and resume bank forms, with no worries that formatting glitches will cause confusion.

- Although it's unattractive, the text version is 100 percent scannable.

To create a text version of your resume, follow these simple steps:

1. Create a new version of your resume using the Save As feature of your word-processing program. Select "text only" or "ASCII" in the Save As option box.

2. Close the new file.

3. Reopen the file, and you'll find that your word processor has automatically reformatted your resume into Courier font, removed all formatting, and left-justified the text.

4. To promote maximum readability when sending your resume electronically, reset the margins to 2 inches left and right, so that you have a narrow column of text rather than a full-page width. (This margin setting will not be retained when you close the file, but in the meantime you can adjust the text formatting for best screen appearance. For instance, if you choose to include a horizontal line [perhaps something like this: ++++++++++++++++++++++++] to separate sections of the resume, by working with the narrow margins you won't make the mistake of creating a line that extends past the normal screen width. Plus, you won't add hard line breaks that create odd-length lines when seen at normal screen width.)

5. Review the resume and fix any "glitches" such as odd characters that may have been inserted to take the place of "curly" quotes, dashes, accents, or other nonstandard symbols.

6. If necessary, add extra blank lines to improve readability.

7. Consider adding horizontal dividers to break the resume into sections for improved skimmability. You can use any standard typewriter symbols such as *, -, (,), =, +, ^, or #.

To illustrate what you can expect when creating these versions of your resume, on the following pages are some examples of the same resume in traditional printed format, scannable version, and electronic (text) format.

THE WEB RESUME

This newest evolution in resumes combines the visually pleasing quality of the printed resume with the technological ease of the electronic resume. You host your Web resume on your own Web site (with your own URL), to which you refer prospective employers and recruiters. Now, instead of seeing just a "plain-Jane" version of your e-mailed resume, with just one click a viewer can access, download, and print your Web resume—an attractive, nicely formatted presentation of your qualifications.

What's more, because the Web resume is such an efficient and easy-to-manage tool, you can choose to include more information than you would in a printed, scannable, or electronic resume. Consider separate pages for achievements, technology qualifications, equipment skills, honors and awards, management skills, and more, if you believe they would improve your market position. Remember, you're working to sell yourself into your next job!

For those of you in technologically related professions, you can take it one step further and create a virtual multimedia presentation that not only tells someone how talented you are, but also visually and technologically demonstrates it. Web resumes are an outstanding tool for people seeking jobs in technology-based industries.

A simplified version of the Web resume is an online version of your Microsoft Word resume. Instead of attaching a file to an e-mail to an employer, you can include a link to the online version. This format is not as graphically dynamic as a full-fledged Web resume, but it can be a very useful tool for your job search. For instance, you can offer the simplicity of text in your e-mail, plus the instant availability of a printable, formatted word-processing document for the interested recruiter or hiring manager. For a demonstration of this format, go to www.e-resume-central.com and click on "SEE A SAMPLE."

SAMUEL FEINMAN
489 Smithfield Road
Salem, OR 97301
503.491.3033
samfine@earthlink.net

SALES PROFESSIONAL

Dynamic, motivated, award-winning sales professional with extensive experience. Troubleshooter and problem-solver. Team player who can motivate self and others. Excellent management and training skills.

RELATED EXPERIENCE

WetWater Pool Products, Salem, OR
Sales/Customer Service   1995–2000
- Advised customers to purchase products that best met their needs, while focusing attention on products more profitable to company.
- Troubleshot and solved customer problems, identifying rapid solutions and emphasizing customer satisfaction and retention.
- Oversaw shipping and receiving staff.

Afford-A-Ford, Albany, NY
General Manager   1990–1995
- Consistently in top five for sales in district; met or exceeded sales objectives.
- Supervised, hired, and trained staff of 90.
- Converted a consistently money-losing store into a profitable operation by end of first year.
- Focused on customer satisfaction through employee satisfaction and training.
- Built strong parts and service business, managing excellent interaction among parts, service, and sales.
- Instituted fleet-sales department, becoming top fleet-sales dealer three years running.
- Built lease portfolio from virtually none to 31% of retail.

Jack's Chevrolet, Springfield, MA
General Manager   1988–1990
- Reached top-ten volume dealer three years straight in New England.
- Managed all dealership operations including sales, parts, service, and administration.
- Profitably operated dealership through difficult economic times.
- Raised customer satisfaction to zone average.
- Met or exceeded parts, sales, and service objectives.
- Maintained high-profile used car operation.

ADDITIONAL EXPERIENCE

State of Oregon, Salem, OR
Computer Technician   2000–2002
- Built customized computers for state offices.

EDUCATION

AS, Hudson Valley Community College, Troy, NY   Major: Business Studies

The print version of the resume.

SAMUEL FEINMAN
489 Smithfield Road
Salem, OR 97301
503.491.3033
samfine@earthlink.net

SALES PROFESSIONAL

Dynamic, motivated, award-winning sales professional with extensive experience. Troubleshooter and problem-solver. Team player who can motivate self and others. Excellent management and training skills.

RELATED EXPERIENCE

WetWater Pool Products, Salem, OR
SALES/CUSTOMER SERVICE, 1995–2000
- Advised customers to purchase products that best met their needs, while focusing attention on products more profitable to company.
- Troubleshot and solved customer problems, identifying rapid solutions and emphasizing customer satisfaction and retention.
- Oversaw shipping and receiving staff.

Afford-A-Ford, Albany, NY
GENERAL MANAGER, 1990–1995
- Consistently in top five for sales in district; met or exceeded sales objectives.
- Supervised, hired, and trained staff of 90.
- Converted a consistently money-losing store into a profitable operation by end of first year.
- Focused on customer satisfaction through employee satisfaction and training.
- Built strong parts and service business, managing excellent interaction among parts, service, and sales.
- Instituted fleet-sales department and became top fleet-sales dealer three years running.
- Built lease portfolio from virtually none to 31% of retail.

Jack's Chevrolet, Springfield, MA
GENERAL MANAGER, 1988–1990
- Reached top-ten volume dealer three years straight in New England.
- Managed all dealership operations including sales, parts, service, and administration.
- Profitably operated dealership through difficult economic times.
- Raised customer satisfaction to zone average.
- Met or exceeded parts, sales, and service objectives.
- Maintained high-profile used car operation.

ADDITIONAL EXPERIENCE

State of Oregon, Salem, OR
COMPUTER TECHNICIAN, 2000–2002
- Built customized computers for state offices.

EDUCATION

AS, Hudson Valley Community College, Troy, NY
Major: Business Studies

The scannable version of the resume.

```
SAMUEL FEINMAN
489 Smithfield Road
Salem, OR 97301
503.491.3033
samfine@earthlink.net

=============================================
SALES PROFESSIONAL

Dynamic, motivated, award-winning sales professional with
extensive experience. Troubleshooter and problem-solver. Team
player who can motivate self and others. Excellent management and
training skills.

=============================================
RELATED EXPERIENCE

WetWater Pool Products, Salem, OR
SALES/CUSTOMER SERVICE, 1995-2000
* Advised customers to purchase products that best met their
needs, while focusing attention on products more profitable to
company.
* Troubleshot and solved customer problems, identifying rapid
solutions and emphasizing customer satisfaction and retention.
* Oversaw shipping and receiving staff.


Afford-A-Ford, Albany, NY
GENERAL MANAGER, 1990-1995
* Consistently in top five for sales in district; met or exceeded
sales objectives.
* Supervised, hired, and trained staff of 90.
* Converted a consistently money-losing store into a profitable
operation by end of first year.
* Focused on customer satisfaction through employee satisfaction
and training.
* Built strong parts and service business, managing excellent
interaction among parts, service, and sales.
* Instituted fleet-sales department and became top fleet-sales
dealer three years running.
* Built lease portfolio from virtually none to 31% of retail.

Jack's Chevrolet, Springfield, MA
GENERAL MANAGER, 1988-1990
* Reached top-ten volume dealer three years straight in New
England.
* Managed all dealership operations including sales, parts,
service, and administration.
* Profitably operated dealership through difficult economic
times.
* Raised customer satisfaction to zone average.
* Met or exceeded parts, sales, and service objectives.
* Maintained high-profile used car operation.

=============================================
ADDITIONAL EXPERIENCE

State of Oregon, Salem, OR
COMPUTER TECHNICIAN, 2000-2002
* Built customized computers for state offices.

=============================================
EDUCATION

AS, Hudson Valley Community College, Troy, NY
Major: Business Studies
```

The electronic/text version of the resume.

The Four Resume Types Compared

This chart quickly compares the similarities and differences between the four types of resumes we've discussed in this chapter.

	PRINTED RESUMES	**SCANNABLE RESUMES**
TYPESTYLE/ FONT	Sharp, conservative, and distinctive (see our recommendations in chapter 1).	Clean, concise, and machine-readable: Times New Roman, Arial, Helvetica.
TYPESTYLE ENHANCEMENTS	**Bold**, *italics*, and <u>underlining</u> for emphasis.	CAPITALIZATION is the only type enhancement you can be certain will transmit.
TYPE SIZE	10-, 11-, or 12-point preferred... larger type sizes (14, 18, 20, 22, and even larger, depending on typestyle) will effectively enhance your name and section headers.	11- or 12-point, or larger.
TEXT FORMAT	Use centering and indentations to optimize the visual presentation.	Type all information flush left.
PREFERRED LENGTH	1 to 2 pages; 3 if essential.	1 to 2 pages preferred, although length is not as much of a concern as with printed resumes.
PREFERRED PAPER COLOR	White, Ivory, Light Gray, Light Blue, or other conservative background.	White or very light with no prints, flecks, or other shading that might affect scannability.
WHITE SPACE	Use appropriately for best readability.	Use generously to maximize scannability.

ELECTRONIC RESUMES	WEB RESUMES
Courier.	Sharp, conservative, and distinctive... attractive onscreen and when printed from an online document.
CAPITALIZATION is the only enhancement available to you.	**Bold,** *italics,* and <u>underlining</u>, and color for emphasis.
12-point.	10-, 11-, or 12-point preferred... larger type sizes (14, 18, 20, 22, and even larger, depending on typestyle) will effectively enhance your name and section headers.
Type all information flush left.	Use centering and indentations to optimize the visual presentation.
Length is immaterial; almost definitely, converting your resume to text will make it longer.	Length is immaterial; just be sure your site is well organized so viewers can quickly find the material of greatest interest to them.
N/A.	Paper is not used, but do select your background carefully to maximize readability.
Use white space to break up dense text sections.	Use appropriately for best readability both onscreen and when printed.

Are You Ready to Write Your Resume?

To be sure that you're ready to write your resume, go through the following checklist. Each item is a critical step that you must take in the process of writing and designing your own winning resume.

❑ Clearly define "who you are" and how you want to be perceived.

❑ Document your key skills, qualifications, and knowledge.

❑ Document your notable career achievements and successes.

❑ Identify one or more specific job targets or positions.

❑ Identify one or more industries that you are targeting.

❑ Research and compile key words for your profession, industry, and specific job targets.

❑ Determine which resume format suits you and your career best.

❑ Select an attractive font.

❑ Determine whether you need a print resume, a scannable resume, an electronic resume, a Web resume, or all four.

❑ Secure a private e-mail address.

❑ Review resume samples for up-to-date ideas on resume styles, formats, organization, and language.

PART II

Sample Resumes for Career Changers

CHAPTER 4

Resumes for Career Changers Seeking Accounting, Finance, Banking, Administrative, Office Management, Business Management, and Insurance Positions

- Contract analyst to administrative assistant
- Pharmacy technician to medical office administration or insurance billing
- Law enforcement officer to administrative management
- Sales to administrative support
- Truck driver to insurance claims
- Researcher and fitness trainer to banking/finance professional
- Retail sales associate to bank teller
- Small business owner to financial planner
- Nursing to medical insurance professional
- Retail management to accounting
- Physician to accounting/finance professional
- Marketing manager to business analyst
- Auto service manager to corporate transportation manager
- Military to corporate supervisor or manager
- Elementary school teacher to business project manager
- Computer programmer to business process specialist
- Nightclub general manager to building/facilities manager
- Call-center manager to finance executive
- Research scientist to management consultant

JESSICA MANSFIELD

203 Willow Lane
Costa Mesa, CA 92627

Phone: 949-646-8149
E-mail: jmansfield@hotmail.com

ADMINISTRATIVE ASSISTANT

Energetic and competent office professional with more than 10 years of administrative assistant/ secretarial experience, recognized for dependable and detail-oriented work in support of top management. Excellent computer, communication, and office support skills. Well known by management as someone who "gets things done." Proven skills in

Database Management	Meeting/Travel Arrangements	Customer Relations
PowerPoint Presentations	Appointment Scheduling	Problem Solving
Computer Programs	Contract Analysis	Editing
Correspondence	Office Machines	Billing

Promoted to Administrative Assistant and Executive Secretary to President as a result of excellent and consistently dependable performance.

PROFESSIONAL EXPERIENCE

Administrative Assistant and Executive Secretary

- Managed calendar and daily schedule for President, coordinating multiple activities in a fast-paced environment. Scheduled appointments and recorded them on electronic calendar.
- Liaised with COO, corporate executives, management, and clients to coordinate meetings and confirm information for presentations and documents. Edited documents for COO and management.
- Maximized corporate information storage and retrieval systems by reorganizing and maintaining all major company files, contracts, patents, and secrecy agreements.
- Organized executive and client meetings/luncheons (in-house and off-site), planning all amenities.
- Arranged domestic and international travel itineraries for Chief Operating Officer, President, Vice Presidents, and Management.

Secretary

- Maintained and coordinated calendar, set appointments, screened telephone calls, sorted mail, and made travel arrangements for the President.
- Assisted in PowerPoint presentations—editing, coordinating, and integrating multiple facets to facilitate a smooth corporate presentation.
- Communicated directly with all clients by writing routine correspondence and responding to telephone requests. Translated correspondence from Dictaphone and shorthand, as requested.
- Edited reports, company proposals, government proposals, and contracts for clients and management.
- Monitored corporate website and wrote a monthly report on website activity, outlining and consolidating information about e-mail content, trends, and geographic activity.

Career Change: *From contract analyst in a technology industry to administrative assistant in the health care field.*

Jessica Mansfield   page 2   **949-646-8149**

Contract Analyst

- Managed the entire process of recording and receipting all incoming signed contracts, purchase orders, credits, and cancellations and entered contract information into database.
- Reorganized Billing Department by implementing new billing protocol and filing procedures. Results: Expedited billing process and increased employee effectiveness.
- Monitored accounts and billing process, generating 300–500 invoices and credit memos per week for client base of 2,000 transportation, 300 media, and 100 energy customers.
- Consistently updated and maintained customer and product database, providing corporate personnel with accurate and compatible information at all times.
- Interfaced with internal members of Operations and Customer Support staff, as well as clients, and oversaw all inquiries relating to the administration of contract terms and agreements.
- Researched billing problems with clients and Sales Department and determined appropriate corrective actions while continually optimizing customer satisfaction.

EMPLOYMENT HISTORY

Satellite Media Corporation, Costa Mesa, CA   1999–Present
    Contract Analyst, Finance Department
    Administrative Assistant to Chief Operating Officer

TransNational Engineering Corporation, Fullerton, CA   1988–1999
    Executive Secretary to President
    Secretary to Technical Director

EDUCATION

Mesa West Community College, Orange, CA   2001
Business Administration Courses

Fullerton Community College, Fullerton, CA   Graduated 1987
Secretarial Program

COMPUTER SKILLS

Microsoft Word, Excel, PowerPoint; PeopleSoft Billing; data entry

Strategy: Use functional format to highlight relevant experience from prior career in health care administration.

Janice J. James

513-249-0090   *2490 Alliance Drive, Cincinnati, OH 45242*   *jjj@cinci.rr.com*

Medical Billing—Medical Office Administration

PROFILE

Team-spirited professional, patient and resourceful. Positive, creative thinker/problem solver—effective in streamlining operations, improving productivity, and reducing costs.

Able to handle multiple responsibilities, set priorities, clearly communicate ideas to others, and respond positively to demanding situations. Recognized for speed, accuracy, quality of work, and outstanding customer service.

QUALIFICATIONS

- Insurance Billing—online and manual billing experience for all insurances including Medicare and Medicaid—detailed working knowledge of insurance plans, overrides, and billing codes.
- 11 years of pharmacy experience—drug formulary, ingredients, compounding, analyzing prescriptions, inventory management, and recordkeeping.
- Outstanding customer service—recipient of numerous "Mystery Shopper" Customer Service Awards.

Added Value:

- 10+ years of experience in hospitality industry—catering, staff management, and event planning.

CAREER SUMMARY

Pharmacy Technician Level A, Walgreens Pharmacy, Blue Ash, OH, 1994–12/2004
Completed training program to become PTLA while working as cashier.

Main source of flow for prescriptions—analyze prescriptions; type prescriptions; and count, compound, and dispense drugs. Order drugs and supplies. Provide extensive, caring, and informed customer service—established loyal customer base.

Access insurance company computers—set up prescriptions, calculate supply and quantity, and apply knowledge of limitation of different insurance plans. Cashier, send and receive faxes, and answer 5-line telephone. Maintain customer records and profiles on nationally linked proprietary computer system.

Assistant Manager, Five Seasons Country Club, Cincinnati, OH, 1991–1994
Answered to Board of Directors and General Manager of catering and fine-dining establishment.

Supervised up to 30 employees in all aspects of food and beverage area of Club. Assisted chef with menu planning and food costs control. Instrumental in bringing about modernization of service styles. Initiated systems to improve efficiency and food service.

Service Manager, Maple Grove Inn, Cincinnati, OH, 1987–1991
Catering and fine-dining restaurant

Oversaw all food and beverage staff, up to 30 people. Assisted in planning and executing functions for catering and full-service dining room. Purchased and maintained alcohol inventory for lounge. Assisted chef with menu planning and food costs control.

Food and Beverage/Catering Manager, Holiday Inn, Covington, KY, 1980–1987
(now Sunset Horizon Inn)

Oversaw staff of 60+ people—purchasing, scheduling, event planning, budgeting. Assisted chef with menu planning. Involved with entire remodel and re-imaging of hotel and lounge—participated in selecting and training staff, initiating new procedures, and implementing new computer system.

PROFESSIONAL DEVELOPMENT

Ohio State Pharmacy Technician License—current
Pharmacy Training, Walgreens Pharmacy
Coursework in Accounting/General Business, Raymond Walters College/University of Cincinnati

Career Change: *From pharmacy technician to medical office administration or insurance billing.*

Strategy: *Bring qualifications to the fore with a bold heading and identify "added value" of prior career experience.*

ADAM RHINEHART

1813 Buttonwood Trail, North Miami, FL 33179
305-934-3819 • ar1149@verizon.net

CAREER PROFILE

➢ Organizer with planning "know-how" and 16 years of supervisory and administrative experience.
➢ Team player with excellent problem-solving and analytical skills.
➢ Effective communicator (written and verbal).
➢ Master of multiple details with a talent for reducing administrative inefficiencies.
➢ Calm demeanor under stressful conditions.
➢ Consistently achieve or exceed organizational goals.

PROFESSIONAL EXPERIENCE

9/84–Present   Dade County Sheriff's Office, Miami, FL   **Sergeant /Administrative Officer**

➢ Supervise a staff of 20 deputies involved in executing court mandates. Involves securing inmates and safeguarding facilities, equipment, contained areas, and inter-facility communications, including phones, intercom, radio, and public address system.
➢ Schedule work assignments and deployment of human resources. Conduct administrative review of incident reports, medical leave requests, and worker compensation reports; includes periodic reviews of materials, equipment, personal appearance, and demeanor.
➢ Train, motivate, conduct performance evaluations, and assess suitability for assignment. As a Field Training Officer, planned, scheduled, and coordinated Career Development classes for recruits.
➢ Participate in complex departmental budget meetings; review cost proposals and expenditure forecasts.
➢ Prepare semi-annual analysis of operational activity to provide the Sheriff's Office with data on divisional manpower and other resource allocations. Includes anticipated personnel needs, anticipated capital equipment improvements, and equipment needs.
➢ Responsible for compliance and enforcement of organizational policies and practices.
➢ Compile and disseminate a comprehensive annual report of the department's goals and objectives.
➢ Provide computer support, analyze computer shutdowns, and apply corrective procedures and system upgrades.

2 Years   Bob Jones Golf Course, Sarasota, FL   **Accounting Assistant**

➢ Responsible for general ledger balances, bankcard receivables, discounts, and chargebacks. Analyzed card member accounts and established date payments on delinquent accounts. Accordingly, advised customers of suspended account status.

6 Years   U.S. Navy & Navy Reserve   **Administrative Supervisor**

➢ Assigned as Administrative Supervisor of the Maintenance Management System aboard the USS *Nimitz*. Primary responsibility was to oversee all computer operations and troubleshoot failures and shutdowns.
➢ Assigned to the Naval Intelligence Command (requiring Top-Secret Clearance) to perform operational maintenance on highly sophisticated electronic equipment. Acquired experience on system schematics and troubleshooting down to the equipment and signal-flow level.
➢ Assigned to the Construction Battalion Unit. Principal role was in the planning and budgeting of major building projects. Scope of budget upwards of $250,000. Led presentation team in promoting the need for re-allocating funding from other sources.

EDUCATION

➢ BA Business Administration, Florida Metropolitan University, Clearwater, FL, 1991, GPA: 3.64
➢ Courses in Supervisory Techniques, Models for Management, Advanced Writing Skills, and Positive Leadership

COMPUTER SKILLS

Advanced computer training in Windows 95/98/XP, MS Word, MS Excel, merges, macros, and forms.

Career Change: *From law enforcement officer to administrative management.*

Strategy: *Emphasize relevant administrative and personnel functions from his current position.*

RESUME 4: BY SUSAN GUARNERI, NCC, NCCC, CPRW, CCMC, CEIP, MCC

Annette Alstad
1775 Greene Avenue, Rockaway, NJ 07866
(973) 957-5555 Residence Phone/Fax ▪ annalstad@yahoo.net

Administrative Support/Customer Service—Medical/Clinical Setting

Dedicated, experienced professional with strong organizational, communications, and project management skills. Calm demeanor under stress; cooperative team leader. Recent training in medical billing, medical terminology, and ICD-9-CM coding. Proven multitasking/operations support skills. Adept in

☑ Client Relationship Management	☑ Medical Records Terminology	☑ Budget Controls
☑ Account/Territory Management	☑ Customer Needs Assessment	☑ Program Management

KEY SUPPORTING SKILLS

- **Administration:** Diverse administrative expertise includes directing nationwide SHARE (State Hospital Association Review & Evaluation) program for American Hospital Association; managing four-county sales territory in central California; and maintaining large, upscale apartment complexes.

- **Time Management:** Demonstrate top-notch organizational skills, with ability to prioritize and multitask. Developed records management systems to expedite back-office operations for sales generation, residential and retail property management, and meeting and event planning.

- **Communications:** Employ proactive problem-solving communications skills to generate "win-win" scenarios. Effectively communicated special situations and potential problem areas to management.

- **Personal Strengths:** Conscientious in following through on commitments and deadlines. Mature, discreet team player with experience interfacing with high-level executives and corporate clients.

EDUCATION

Medical Records Technician Program, Samuel Morris College, Morristown, NJ—2003
Courses: Medical Terminology, Advanced Medical Terminology, Medical Billing, ICD-9-CM Coding
Associate of Arts Degree, Fullerton Community College, Fullerton, CA

PROFESSIONAL EXPERIENCE

Estate and Health Care Management   2000–2003
✓ **Administrative Management.** Acted as prime interface with physicians, nurses, hospice, attorneys, CPA, stockbroker, and insurance companies for elderly parents with progressive, debilitating illnesses. Managed health care appointments and treatment as well as daily living arrangements on-site.

✓ **Records Management.** Submitted insurance claims and tracked insurance reimbursements. Oversaw distribution of $1 million estate. Arranged sale of house and distribution of all household goods.

Manufacturer's Representative   1994–2000
Kimball Associates, San Francisco, CA, and The Paper & Gift Center, Los Angeles, CA
Independent contractor representing fine gift, paper/stationery, and greeting-card lines for two businesses.

✓ **Account Management.** Grew accounts by 45% (from 175 to 250) and increased sales by 10% in four-county central California territory. Generated 20 new key accounts (such as Yosemite Park gift shops) through thorough market research, competitive market analysis, and persuasive prospect interaction.

✓ **Customer Relationship Management.** Developed strong client communications networks, building relationships with 250 buyers for retail stores, museums, hospital gift shops, and nurseries. Educated buyers in 60+ lines of merchandise, updating them on retail trends and demographics-driven marketing.

Career Change: From sales to administrative support.

Strategy: Create a strong profile that presents just the right skill set for an administrative professional. Support desire to enter health care field by citing relevant recent training.

Annette Alstad

(973) 957-5555 Residence Phone/Fax ▪ annalstad@yahoo.net   Page 2

PROFESSIONAL EXPERIENCE (continued)

Residential Property Management   1991–1994

Treadwell Properties, Inc., San Diego, CA (1993–1994), and Harmony Place, San Diego, CA (1991–1993)

✓ **Administrative Management.** Managed two upscale apartment communities (up to 516 units), with monthly rent collections of $432,000. Supervised on-site leasing as well as maintenance and grounds staff. Controlled expense budget, closely monitoring five vendor services. Oversaw renovation of 35 apartment units, coordinating workflow and scheduling of carpet, flooring, paint, and fixture vendors.

✓ **Customer Service.** Maintained 92% residency rate and achieved 98% on-time rent collection by developing proactive tenant relationship programs. Initiated educational newsletter for tenants and open-door policy for tenant complaints. Credited with stabilizing the tenant community through lawful evictions of known drug dealers.

Retail Property Management   1988–1991

The Andrus Company, Somerset, NJ; Highlands, Inc., Los Angeles, CA; Boltman & Graves, Boston, MA

✓ **Administrative Management.** Initiated and developed specialty leasing programs for three major developers (12 regional shopping centers) in high-profile metropolitan areas. Maintained high occupancy rates by actively recruiting retailers for year-round common area as well as developing long-term, favorable leases for in-line sales operations.

✓ **Program Management.** Supervised design projects for kiosks, store décor, and marketing communications (brochures, print advertising, and directories). Developed and met program budgets, generating in excess of $500,000 for each shopping center annually.

Meeting and Event Management   1985–1988

American Hospital Association, Highland Park, IL

✓ **Program Management.** Served as Director of SHARE (State Hospital Association Review & Evaluation) program. Traveled nationwide conducting peer-review meetings for 8 to 10 state hospital associations. Wrote comprehensive reports and recommendations based on participant feedback and critical observations and analysis of policies and procedures in place.

✓ **Customer Service.** Facilitated in-house discussions on-site of hospital personnel and management at all levels to increase quality assurance, strengthen employee relations, improve customer service, and streamline processes and procedures.

COMPUTER SKILLS

▪ Experienced in composing and editing letters, memos, marketing communications, and reports. Utilize Windows XP and 98, Microsoft Word XP and 2000, Internet Explorer, and email.

Richard G. Scanlon

129 Northgate ➤ Clear Spring, MD 21722

Residence: 301.555.0567   rgscanlon@aol.com   Cell: 240.555.2426

Career Target: Insurance Claims Representative

Offering 15+ Years of Transferable Experience

Logistics Management ➤ Motor Vehicle Maintenance ➤ Repair ➤ Military Leadership

Specialized Skills and Experience

Class "A CDL"/TPM Endorsements   Logistics Management
Qualified Road Tester Certification   Federal Contracts Management
Safety Inspections   Foreign Car Repair and Restoration
Petroleum Supply   Computer Literacy

Relevant Experience

Tractor Trailer Operator   1995–present
Sealy Mattress   Williamsport, MD

Established a reputation for reliability and efficiency in delivering company merchandise to warehouses and distribution centers throughout metro DC/Baltimore and surrounding areas. Work independently in planning and executing daily delivery routes while interfacing with warehouse supervisors, dispatchers, store managers, scale-house personnel, and state highway police. Accurately complete and record maintenance and safety inspections of the vehicle, adhering to all DOT standards.

Transportation Manager/Supervisor   1990-1994
Government Contracting Services   Alexandria, VA

Managed a three-year, $1.5M contract supplying comprehensive transportation services to the personnel and programs housed in Fort Ritchie, MD. Provided leadership and direction to a staff of 15-20 full- and part-time personnel; maintained oversight for a fleet of 125 motor vehicles. Established a vital link between the contractor and the federal government, earning high marks for efficiency and flexibility. Directed and controlled project resources to produce optimum results within the financial constraints of the contract. Held a federal security clearance.

- ➤ Collaborated with contract consultants in defining bid specifications regarding estimated man-hours and vehicle/machinery requirements.
- ➤ Hired and supervised military and non-military personnel, ensuring sufficient staffing levels for 24/7 operation coverage.
- ➤ Maintained a 95% vehicle readiness rate by establishing and maintaining effective maintenance schedules and seamless working relationships with numerous auto body and maintenance shops.
- ➤ Coordinated the logistics of transporting military and civilian personnel in and out of high-security sites.
- ➤ Collaborated with Military Police in motor accident follow-up, including review of accident reports; arranged for transport of accident vehicles for disposal or repair.
- ➤ Orchestrated the scheduling and instruction of driver safety and licensing training for personnel; made final recommendations for motor vehicle operators' license approval.
- ➤ Created and maintained an electronic spreadsheet to track employee hours for payroll.

Career Change: *From big-rig truck driver to insurance claims.*

Strategy: *Leverage prior experience as a transportation manager as well as knowledge of vehicles and maintenance to position him as a knowledgeable claims adjuster.*

Richard G. Scanlon   301.555.0567   **Page 2**

United States Army   1983-1990

Honorably Discharged Sergeant, with a diverse military career characterized by a record of "exceptionally meritorious service, dedication, and determination." Served in Germany, Korea, and Washington State. Scope of responsibility included supply and equipment records and parts; material storage and handling; vehicle repair and maintenance; and petroleum distribution.

➤ Earned leadership command of six subordinate personnel (Motor Sergeant) and 12 subordinate soldiers (Squad Leader); recognized for providing "superb guidance and leadership, which ensured optimum efficiency in the completion of tasks."

➤ Oversaw maintenance and use of 250 motor vehicles, consistently rendering outstanding achievement in procuring high-priority repair parts.

➤ Demonstrated technical expertise in repairing and replacing unserviceable parts on gas and diesel cars and trucks; interpreted work orders and determined intermediate maintenance operations for extending vehicle use.

➤ Completed military training in Defensive Driving, Small Engine Repair, Quality Management, and Quality Improvement Through Defect Prevention.

➤ Managed $20K building supply inventory, including procurement, storage, and distribution.

Additional Employment Experience

Correctional Officer   1994-1995
Cumberland Federal Correctional Institution   Cumberland, MD

Completed an eight-week training, prior to assuming responsibility for the supervision and security of 100 inmates in a newly opened maximum-security facility.

Carpenter/Mason   1986-1987
R F Kline   Frederick, MD

Interpreted drawings, blueprints, and plans to determine layout and material specifications for the construction of trestles, bridges, piers, and wharfs. Operated various hand tools and pieces of power equipment, including loaders, backhoes, mixers, and forklifts.

Education

Graduate, Williamsport High School, Williamsport, MD

College credits earned through Central Texas College and Big Bend Community College, Wiesbaden, Germany; Central Texas College, Korea

WILLIAM NEVADA

8917 Central Avenue
Agoura, California 91301

818-753-2548
w_nevada@aol.com

Mature, proactive, results-oriented young professional seeking to apply extensive research and data experience to the **loan** and **investment** industries. Resourceful, efficient, honest, and highly ethical, with a strong work ethic. Quick problem solver while dealing with new concepts, systems, and procedures. Decisive and self-starting in implementation. Conscientious application of policies and procedures. Professional and articulate; qualified for client / customer interaction at all levels. Committed. Recognized for

- Competency and thoroughness
- Going above and beyond requirements
- Analytical aptitude
- Organizational skills
- Being meticulous and detail oriented

- Strong communication skills
- Outstanding customer service skills
- Patience and composure
- Upbeat and positive attitude
- Working well under pressure

SKILLS

Computer Microsoft Office Applications (Word, Excel, PowerPoint, Access)
SPSS
Extensive Internet research experience

Personal Excellent one-on-one communication
Consistently exceed expectations
Basic conversational Spanish

EDUCATION

Bachelor of Science, Kinesiology, Exercise Science. California State University, Northridge, California, 2002 (Dean's List; GPA: 3.45)

EMPLOYMENT HISTORY

Forensic Biomechanics Assistant 2003
Gary Villareal • Pacific Palisades, CA
  Perform research on various cars relating to auto accident investigations. Prepare presentations using various Microsoft Office applications.

Personal Trainer 2001–Present
Training Center • Flintridge, CA (concurrently)
  Create personal and effective exercise programs for clients. Develop good professional relationships with clients.

Spinal Cord Injury Research Assistant 2002
Robert Sephears • CSUN, Northridge, CA
  Conducted literature reviews of prior related studies. Composed compilation reviews of research. Organized and entered collected data.

Career Change: From researcher and fitness trainer to banking/finance professional.

Strategy: Emphasize background in research, data analysis, and working with numbers.

RESUME 6, CONTINUED

WILLIAM NEVADA   Page 2

Research Assistant   2002
Richard Spencer ● CSUN, Northridge, CA
> Conducted independent research regarding aquatic exercise for adapted populations through
> various sources: Internet, library, medical reports, and peer-review journals. Selected relevant
> material.

Physical Therapy Aide   2000–2001
Providence Saint Joseph Medical Center ● Burbank, CA
> Supervised workout regimen for recovering surgery patients. Instructed patients in specific use of
> major muscle groups of lower extremities.

Day Camp Counselor   2000–2001
The Village Schools ● Sherman Oaks, CA
> Instructed and cared for middle-school students in various settings. Directed and supervised
> group and water games with aerobic benefit. Taught group lessons and led discussions.

COMMUNITY INVOLVEMENT
Middle and High School Youth Group Leader, Sun Valley, CA
Camp Counselor, Redlands, CA
Guitar Instructor, Sylmar, CA

CERTIFICATIONS
Red Cross Adult CPR Certification
Red Cross Water Safety Instructor Certification
Aerobics and Fitness Association of America: Personal Trainer Certification

CAROLINE SMITH

29 River Street, Norwalk, CT 06854
(203) 838-3052 • carolinesmith@snet.net

BANK TELLER

Superb customer-service skills honed by 15 years of retail experience to develop and maintain customer loyalty. Highly organized; keep all records with accuracy and thoroughness.

- Customer service
- Cashier transactions
- Strong communications skills
- Patience and humor

- Long-term customer relationships
- Team member
- Membership services, marketing
- Problem solving

PC proficiency in business applications, including MS Word, Excel, and Outlook.

PROFESSIONAL EXPERIENCE

Costless, Norwalk, CT
CASHIER / CUSTOMER SERVICE / MEMBERSHIP / MARKETING   2001–Present
- Control cash flow while ringing out customers. Keep lines of shoppers moving smoothly with courtesy and humor. Receive and direct patrons at the door.
- Work with security and loss-prevention issues.
- Develop customer relationships for long-term loyalty. Known for treating shoppers like family.
- Care for all client concerns: Sign up customers for Costless and American Express charge cards; communicate with main office; update membership accounts; offer general information and product availability by telephone and in person.
- Sell memberships to businesses and individuals in local-area towns. Upgrade current Members to Executive Membership for increased cash flow and customer loyalty.

PetPals, Norwalk, CT
JUNIOR MANAGER ON DUTY   1998–2001
- All aspects of opening and closing facility, including arming/disarming system, booting up computers, communicating with corporate office, counting store safe and register cash, and setting up the store.
- Created computer reports on sales, returns, and loss prevention for the corporate office.
- Motivated employees, developed customers, and oversaw animal care from ordering to sale.

Burger King, Norwalk, CT
JUNIOR MANAGER / SHIFT LEADER   1991–1998
- Opened kitchen and registers for breakfast. Observed strict food-service regulations. Met temperature and sanitizing standards.
- Supervised and motivated crew. Built solid relationships with patrons.

HealthDeli, Norwalk, CT
CASHIER   1988–1991
- Operated registers; assisted in deli; performed light stock work.
- Became knowledgeable about vitamins/supplements to advise shoppers. Worked to create trust with customers for lasting relationships.

Entrepreneurial Businesses, Norwalk, CT   Prior to 1991
HOUSE CLEANING SERVICE
OFFICE TEMPORARY WORK

EDUCATION

Psychology, Norwalk Community College, Norwalk, CT

Career Change: *From retail sales associate to bank teller.*

Strategy: *Highlight relevant skills in customer service, cash handling, and computer use; clearly show how her current position, though seemingly unrelated, requires extensive use of these skills.*

Thomas Owens

21 Revere Street
Westwood, NJ 07450

(845) 687-4499 (H)
(845) 535-3487 (W)
towens@aol.com

FINANCIAL PLANNER

PROFILE: Entrepreneurial, self-directed business professional with more than 20 years of experience running, growing, and developing a private business. Experienced in assessing risk for personal investments and for associates. Familiar with various financial products, including stocks, bonds, mutual funds, variable and fixed annuities, variable and term life insurance, disability insurance, and long-term-care insurance. Derive great satisfaction from assisting others in planning for their financial security.

STRENGTHS

- **Analyzed** and developed plan for disbursement of assets for two estates.
- **Managed all stages of sales cycle,** including identifying targets, qualifying leads, uncovering needs, overcoming objections, following through, and closing.
- **Seasoned, savvy** business professional with mature judgment.
- **Developed personal investment strategy** that yielded total portfolio return of 10.5% per year for 10-year period ending 12/31/01.
- **Adept at establishing rapport and trust** with individuals.
- **Irreproachable** business ethics, honesty, and integrity.

PROFESSIONAL EXPERIENCE

OWENS PHOTOGRAPHIC, INC.   Scarsdale, NY   1990–Present
Owner
Commercial photography studio serving advertising agencies and corporations in NYC–metro area. Organize, produce, and shoot various commercial projects for publication. Make frequent **sales** calls on prospective clients to **present** capabilities and examples of work. Identify prospective clients through **research** and **cold calling.** Conduct marketing campaigns through **direct mail** and **telemarketing.** Perform basic accounting functions such as paying and collecting bills and maintaining records.
- Built business from zero to more than $600,000 by providing quality products and service.
- Major clients included IBM, Pepsi, *Reader's Digest,* AGFA Gevaert, and Brown, Inc.
- Initially prepared corporate tax returns.

COLOR IMAGES   Teaneck, NJ   1985–89
Studio Manager
Commercial printing and photography studio. Managed four photographers. Scheduled and coordinated photography projects. Interacted with clients on status of work. Provided photographic support when needed.

MILITARY
- USAF, Honorable Discharge

EDUCATION & CERTIFICATION
- **CFP** course requirement completion by 01/04
- **BA,** Major in History, Muhlenberg College, Allentown, PA

Career Change: *From small business owner (photography shop) to financial planner.*

Strategy: *Focus on strengths that relate to financial planning, including his personal experience in this field.*

Maureen Welland

22398 Fox Lane • Little Rock, AR 72202 • (501) 380.6011 • moewelland@msn.com

PROFESSIONAL PROFILE

Medical Terminology • Medical Procedures • Healthcare Services • Medical Care • Insurance • Inventory/Ordering

Highly qualified medical professional with experience dealing with a multitude of medical-related administration procedures, products, and services.

- Empathetic and intuitive in client interactions; committed to providing quality care as an essential link in healing processes and pain management.

- Poised and confident contributing member of the healthcare team.

- Flexible in quickly mastering new terms, technologies, and systems.

- Demonstrated flexibility and resourcefulness in adapting to ever-changing complexity in the healthcare industry.

EXPERIENCE

HURON VALLEY OUTPATIENT SURGERY CENTER; Comanche, AR
Multi-specialty medical center providing expertise in orthopedic, plastic surgery, and ENT
Staff RN • 1987–93

- Promoted patient health through a comprehensive range of healthcare services.

- Identified patient care requirements; established a compassionate environment; assured quality of care; resolved patient problems and needs; protected patient and employee rights; documented patient care services; maintained continuity among nursing/physician/therapist teams; maintained medical supply inventory.

- Kept updated on professional and technical knowledge; managed a cooperative relationship among healthcare teams and contributed to the team effort.

SOUTHERN MEDICAL CENTER; Landsdale, AR
Multi-specialty trauma center
Staff RN • 1980–87

- Managed duties in both scrubbing and circulating for multi-specialty cases, including general, orthopedic, cardiovascular, ophthalmic, gynecologic, plastic, and urologic.

- Member of Trauma Team; dealt with life-threatening surgical conditions and critical medical conditions requiring surgical intervention.

- Managed orthopedic department (equipment, supplies); oversaw orthopedic cases throughout medical procedures.

EDUCATION & TRAINING

VATTEROTT COLLEGE; Joplin, MO
Bachelor of Science Degree in Nursing • 1980

Numerous in-service classes and medical-related courses

Basic understanding of MS Word and Excel

OTHER INFORMATION

Active in:
- School activities—room parent, lunch aide, member of several committees.

- Church committees—involved with various special events and programs.

Career Change: *From nursing to medical insurance professional (claims and administration).*

Strategy: *Create a strong Professional Profile that combines hard skills and medical knowledge with the attributes she will bring to her next position.*

GREGORY LAWRENCE, C.P.A.

445 Sunset Lane
Vernon, NY 60194

glawrence@yahoo.com

Mobile: (914) 962-7835
Home: (914) 918-3499

CORPORATE ACCOUNTING • PUBLIC ACCOUNTING • TAXATION

Certified Public Accountant with a master's degree in accounting and taxation, and business management experience. Proven analytical and financial management skills. Critical thinker and creative problem solver with excellent planning and organizational strengths. Technical skills: MS Office (Word, Excel, Access, and PowerPoint), JD Edwards, and Peachtree Accounting.

KEY SKILLS

General Accounting … Cost Accounting … Financial/Business Analysis … Asset and Liability Management
Cost/Benefit Analysis … Financial Modeling … Auditing … Risk Assessment … Working Capital

CAPABILITIES—ACCOUNTING/FINANCE
Education and training provided a solid foundation in:

- Setting up balance sheets, income statements, and cash-flow statements in compliance with GAAP.
- Analyzing financial performance of business operations, tracking and analyzing costs, and creating and implementing cost-control systems to achieve corporate objectives.
- Developing and administering budgets; familiar with capital budgeting process. Versed in the different types of corporations, consolidations, and tax advantages.
- Determining valuation of business assets, stock and bond prices, depreciation schedules, and pro forma statements. Creating capital asset pricing models and financial models.
- Calculating P/E ratios, DCF, EPS, discounted cash flow, and beta for equity security analysis.
- Devising portfolio asset allocation strategies and conducting risk assessments; developing business plans.
- Developing financial management and investment strategies for both individuals and companies.

EDUCATION

SIMMONS COLLEGE, NEW YORK, NEW YORK
M.S. in Accounting and Taxation, 2003
B.S. in Business Administration with concentration in **Finance,** 1994

Relevant Courses: Advanced Accounting, Intermediate Accounting, Managerial Accounting, Governmental
Accounting, Auditing, Finance, Business Law, Cost Accounting, Tax Accounting

Certified Public Accountant—State of New York, 2003

BUSINESS MANAGEMENT EXPERIENCE

Store Manager (1995–present) / **Assistant Manager** (1992–1995): **Value Stores, Inc., New York, New York**

Promoted to manage financial and day-to-day operations of $3 million business, including P&L, sales, merchandising, customer relations, inventory, security, human resources, and training. Scope of responsibility encompasses auditing financial records, processing payroll, managing cash, balancing drawers, entering inventory on computer system, adjusting inventory retail values, and preparing bank deposits and reconciliations.

Accomplishments:

- Significantly improved store's financial performance, bringing it from 10% under budget to 3% above budget within the first month as manager by
  - Assessing and realigning employee skills with appropriate tasks/functions.
  - Improving inventory levels and product mix on sales floor.
  - Reducing turnover, hiring and training quality candidates, and implementing a succession plan.
- Boosted profits 20% over prior year, sales by 4% annually, and budgeted profit forecasts by 6% per year.
- Winner of 3 Paragon Awards out of 15 managers in the district for achieving excellence in customer service and exceeding profitability/sales targets. Tapped as mentor, developing and training 25 new store managers.

Career Change: *From retail management to accounting.*

Strategy: *Lead off the resume with a concise summary of background, key skills, and new goal, followed by detailed information about his proven capabilities. In presenting work experience, emphasize financial skills related to his goal.*

Saul M. Lieb

113 Foster Road, Teaneck, NJ 07430
(201) 226-8745 • E-mail: Slieb@aol.com

ACCOUNTING / FINANCE / ADMINISTRATION

PERSONAL STATEMENT: After 13 years as a practicing physician, I'm changing career directions to follow my lifelong interest in finance and accounting. To that end, I am currently enrolled at the University of Maryland, where I am completing (12/04) my BS degree in Accounting. Following completion of this program, I plan to sit for my CPA exam and obtain my MBA from Rutgers State University and Master's in Accountancy from the University of Maryland.

My ultimate career goal is a senior-level corporate finance position. However, to achieve that level of position and responsibility, particularly considering my unique background in the health care arena, I realize that I need to start in a more junior position where I can gain practical, hands-on experience in corporate accounting and finance.

Key Qualifications:

- 3.8 GPA in accounting coursework.
- Completion of 150-credit course on Business of Medicine.
- Review and analysis of all financial and accounting statements of private practice.

EDUCATION AND TRAINING:

- **Bachelor of Science in Accounting,** University of Maryland, College Park, MD, 12/04—GPA 3.8
- **Business of Medicine Executive Certification Program,** Florida State University, Tallahassee, FL, 11/03
  - Marketing and the Management of Service Quality
  - Managing People/Development Strategies
  - The Business Environment of Health Care
  - Data-Driven Management
- **MBA** to be completed 6/06, Rutgers State University, New Brunswick, NJ
- **Master's of Accountancy** to be completed 11/06, University of Maryland
- **MD,** Northeastern Ohio School of Medicine, Rootstown, OH, 1985
- **Bachelor of Arts in Biology,** University of Rochester, Rochester, NY, 1979
- **Graduate Residency**—Family Practice, St. Thomas Hospital, Akron, OH, 1988

COMPUTER SKILLS:

- **Microsoft Excel Certification,** Career Blazers Computer Application Software Training
- **QuickBooks Pro Class,** 6/02

PROFESSIONAL EXPERIENCE:

RAMSEY MEDICAL GROUP   Ramsey, NJ   1987–Present
Partner / General Practitioner
Large family practice. One of three partners. Responsible for patient care and practice management. Review and analyze all financial and accounting statements. Monitor monthly statements for accuracy and timeliness.
- Implemented new computer system to allow for online billing.
- Negotiated with HMOs for competitive rates.

VALLEY MEMORIAL HOSPITAL   Ridgewood, NJ   1994–1998
Chairman—Department of Family Medicine

VALLEY MEMORIAL HOSPITAL   Ridgewood, NJ   1994
Member—Executive Committee

VALLEY MEMORIAL HOSPITAL   Ridgewood, NJ   1992
Member—Hospital Credentialing Committee

NEW JERSEY MEDICAL SCHOOL   Newark, NJ   1989–2001
Assistant Professor

Career Change: *From physician to accounting/finance professional.*

Strategy: *Lay out the rationale for the career change in an interesting "personal statement"; highlight the commitment to change by listing extensive relevant education, both completed and planned.*

RESUME 12: BY DIANE BURNS, CPRW, CCMC, CCM, CEIP, JCTC

JOHN P. MYLES, M.SC., M.L.I.S.

1246 Silver Path ▪ Columbia, MD 21045
(555) 884-0891 ▪ myles@yahoo.com

CAREER FOCUS

COMPETITIVE INTELLIGENCE/ INFORMATION RESEARCH

PROFILE

Successful leader with broad scope of management responsibilities in growth-oriented companies. Consistently maximized revenue and earning opportunities through cost containment and quality service delivery in competitive and very turbulent international markets. Proven communicator with refined interpersonal skills.

Design mechanisms to gather, identify, analyze, and disseminate *controlled* and *actionable* intelligence and research solutions from a variety of primary and secondary sources. Excel in developing information visualization to convey complex competitive dynamics in multivariate ways. Solid knowledge and understanding of retrieval techniques to effectively evaluate and extract accurate, reliable, and relevant information from commercial databases utilizing current technologies, methodologies, and research tools. Strong investigative market research and analytical skills to effectively retrieve, organize, catalog, synthesize, and evaluate information in response to diverse research requests utilizing current technologies, tools, and resources.

Combined expertise in the following:
**Corporate Profiling · Information Visualization · Online Search & Retrieval · Channel Development
Customer Service · Contracts · Strategic Business Planning · Training & Development
Production & Operations · Pricing & Budget Management · Team Management**

EDUCATION

❑ **Master's Degree in Library and Information Science,** University of Maryland, Baltimore, MD, 2003
   (GPA: 4.0/4.0)
   ▪ *Independent Study: Measurement of Social Capital of Competitive Intelligence (CI) Professionals: an exploration of networks, trust, and performance issues in organizations*
   ▪ *Recipient, Full Tuition Merit Scholarship, Department of Library and Information Sciences*
❑ **Master's Degree in Sound and Vibration Studies,** California State University, Fullerton, CA, 1990
❑ **Bachelor's Degree in Electrical & Electronics Engineering,** University of Texas, Dallas, TX, 1982

INTERNSHIPS, FIELD PLACEMENT & PROJECT WORK

❑ **Systems / Programmer II**   05/2003–Present
   Department of Otolaryngology, Johns Hopkins University Medical Center, MD
   Evaluated and recommended top-ranking software-configuration management tools. Designed, constructed, and implemented an Information Resource Center prototype utilizing the Perforce engine for the Medical Virtual Reality Center, a research laboratory for testing balance disorders in humans.
❑ **Reference Intern**   05/2002–Present
   Middleton Library, University of Maryland
   Research information requests from faculty, students, and the public. Deliver answers to complex reference questions using OPAC, subscription databases, print resources, and Internet research tools. Provide reference desk support.
❑ **Information Research Assistant (Practicum)**   08/2003–12/2003
   Hunt Library, Carnegie Mellon University, PA
   Compiled and organized Competitive Intelligence information resources on the pharmaceutical / biotechnology industries. Constructed an HTML-based business guide to support the academic research needs of CMU's faculty, students, and staff.

Career Change: *From marketing manager to business analyst.*

Strategy: *Focus the resume on recent education along with general management skills and research and analytical ability.*

John P. Myles, M.Sc., M.L.I.S., Page 2

PROFESSIONAL EXPERIENCE

Marketing Manager, Image Technologies, Baltimore, MD   1998–2000
Image Technologies is an IT solutions company (document management services).

- Provided leadership and established vision, strategy, and action to meet company's objectives. Implemented revenue and earnings growth initiatives. Devised positioning strategies of products and services for increased value creation and profitability. Re-engineered the sales and marketing organization. Directed all marketing communications.
- Prepared long-range, easily implemented strategic business and marketing plans for *integrated document management* (IDM) services.
- Implemented market research initiative and introduced competitive intelligence activities.

Technical Sales Executive—Government Market   1996–1998
Operations Executive—Imaging Centre   1994–1996
Channel Development Manager   1992–1994
Film Inc., Baltimore, MD (Document Imaging Division)

- Received the Camera Prize for Marketing Excellence & Fountain Pen Prize for Sales Achievement.
- Expanded and maintained relationships with channels network in assigned territories. Guided channels in identifying growth initiatives. Supervised six channel partners with operations team of 15, completing projects on time. Directed several *Digital Signatures* verification-system projects with multinational banks.
- Developed channel marketing communications, including competitive product pricing. Constructed and launched the Sales-Tool Kit, a first of its kind in the region for all channel partners.
- Negotiated, proposed, and closed the biggest order of microfilming equipment ($4 million in 1999).
- Increased the Annual Operating Plan (AOP) revenue target by 25% in 1997 and by 13% in 1998 for all assigned regions. Achieved an increase of 54% above the combined AOP earnings target in the assigned regions in 1998.

Executive Director, Documents R Us, Dallas, Texas   1982–1992
Built a local document imaging services company from the ground floor. Served on the Board of Directors.

- Directed sales and marketing functions, service bureau operations, staff training, and quality assurance.
- Orchestrated, implemented, and managed *computer-assisted* document conversion projects for insurance, manufacturing, and educational institutions with improvements in cost, efficiency, and turnaround time.

PROFESSIONAL AFFILIATIONS & DEVELOPMENT, LANGUAGES & TECHNICAL SKILLS

- Society of Competitive Intelligence Professionals (SCIP), Student Member, current
- Special Libraries Association (SLA), Student Member, current
- American Society for Information Science and Technology (ASIS&T), Student Member, current
- President, Student Chapter of the American Society for Information Science & Technology, 2001/2003
- Attended hundreds of hours of seminars, courses, and conferences in Information Management, specialized document imaging techniques, and general business administration, 1982–Present

~ Languages ~
Read, write, and speak fluent English. Speak fluent German. Conversational Spanish and Turkish.

~ Technical Skills ~
Operating Systems—MS-DOS; Windows 95, 98, 2000, NT & XP • MS Office Professional 97, 2000 & XP • MS Project • MS FrontPage 2002 • JASC Paint Shop Pro v7.0 • Adobe Acrobat & Photoshop v6.0 • UNIX • Lotus Notes v4.5 • Perforce Release 2002.1 • Proficient in Dialog (Classic and Web) • Lexis-Nexis & OCLC databases • Endeavor/Voyager v2000.1.3 OPAC • Other library bibliographic data and full-text search & retrieval systems • Web authoring using HTML, XHTML, PHP scripting, Ipswitch WS_FTP Pro v7.5, Telnet (Pine) & mySQL

RESUME 13: BY DON ORLANDO, MBA, CPRW, JCTC, CCM, CCMC

Stanton Kerry

222 Pine Drive   Coreyville, Alabama 36000   stantonk@bellsouth.net   ☎ 205.555.5555

PROFIT-BUILDING CAPABILITIES I CAN OFFER **TopLine** AS YOUR NEWEST
TRANSPORTATION MANAGER

❑ Building and maintaining teams that want to do well—as a point of honor

Matching the right person to the right job

Investing judiciously in training that produces a return on investment

Limiting liability

Keeping loyalty by showing each employee the tie between his job and his company's future

RECENT WORK HISTORY WITH EXAMPLES OF PROBLEMS SOLVED

❑ Sales Representative *promoted ahead of 10 more-experienced competitors to be*
Service Manager, Saturn of Centerville, Centerville, KY   90 to 02

Because we were one of Saturn's first service departments, my work was closely monitored not just by the dealership owner, but by some corporate levels at Saturn's headquarters. The shop I managed produced $700K in annual sales.

Served as direct reporting official for 21 service technicians, oil changers, and detailers; 2 service writers; and a cashier.

"Rescued" a top-performing employee whose work had deteriorated. Earned his trust by helping guide him through family problems. Gave him key tasks I knew he could do well. Then boosted his confidence by having him train others. *Payoffs:* His **morale and productivity soared.** He remains one of the company's **top-producing** technicians.

Redesigned our workload so employees saw their stake in doing a key job that had limited their earnings for years. My fix was ready in a week. *Payoffs:* **Costly repairs fell. People felt management cared** about them. That's why employees **worked on their own time** to do the job well.

Listened to my people and our customers well enough to design and execute new work schedules that helped everyone. Overcame owner's resistance with solid "homework." *Payoffs:* Generated **more money with fewer man hours.** Raised morale. Avoided overtime. My system became **the example for other dealerships.** All done **without extra funding.**

Helped transform a good policy into an excellent money maker. Worked closely with sales to match the right responsibilities with the right people. *Payoffs:* Customers liked our longer hours. Customer **complaints fell to their lowest point in 8 years.**

Changed the way we rewarded our workers by **transforming** customer service goals **from threats to rewards.** Overcame initial objections that centered on the cost of the celebration parties that were a key part of my plan. *Payoffs:* We **did so well,** corporate headquarters encouraged other dealers to copy our methods.

*More indicators of performance **TopLine** can use …*

Career Change: *From auto service manager to corporate transportation manager.*

Strategy: *Emphasize management skills and showcase ability to produce results.*

RESUME 13, CONTINUED

Stanton Kerry　　　　　　　**Transportation Manager**　　　　　　205.555.5555

❏ Mechanic and **Assistant Transportation Supervisor** *promoted to* Automotive Technology Instructor, Cross County Board of Education, Cross, AL　　85 to 90

Took full responsibility, as an instructor, for the performance of 48 students, many of whom were unskilled.

Ran, as an Assistant Transportation Supervisor, a fleet of 88 school buses and support vehicles.

Overcame a chronic funding problem by turning "junk" engines people usually throw away into classroom learning aids for our students. Used the success of that plan to persuade a local manufacturer to donate 6 brand-new engines for my kids to work on. *Payoffs:* When I told students the refurbished engines would be theirs if their work was excellent, **they became top candidates for jobs** in local industry.

Broke up a clique of disruptive students—just like the groups that sometimes hamper industry—by being ready to be "tested" by the ringleader. Saw beyond his bullying to let him grasp the greater rewards of performing well. *Payoffs:* Praised him when he did good work—and made sure others heard my words. **Not only won him over, but got the support of several more** good students at the same time.

❏ Previous employment includes night manager at a motel and 8 years of service with the United States Army.

RELEVANT EDUCATION AND PROFESSIONAL DEVELOPMENT

❏ MS, **Personnel Counseling,** Coreyville State University, Coreyville, AL　　Jun 84
   Earned this degree while working full time and carrying a full academic load.

❏ AS, Automotive, STRATTON COMMUNITY COLLEGE, STRATTON, AL　　MAY 81
   Worked full time while attending school full time.

❏ B.G.S., Psychology, ALOHA UNIVERSITY, KIHEI, HI　　JUN 77
   Completed this degree by attending night school and working full time.

❏ Comprehensive 2- to 5-day training in all phases of **managing skilled, semi-skilled, and unskilled work forces,** Saturn Corporation, Alcoa, TN　　90 to 02

COMPUTER SKILLS

❏ Near expert in proprietary work order and customer contact software suite; proficient in Internet search protocols; working knowledge of Word.

Page two

RESUME 14: BY JANE ROQUEPLOT, CPBA, CWDP

Keith R. Henderson, Jr.

3777 Kintuk Road, Madison, PA 15663   412-555-1212 ▶ krhenderson@hotmail.com

MANAGER ▶ SUPERVISOR ▶ TEAM LEADER

▶ Self-motivated individual with exceptional leadership, organizational, and supervisory skills, encompassing key values of integrity, honesty, appreciation, teamwork, growth, and results-orientation with an eye toward continuous improvement.

▶ Respected team leader with excellent interpersonal skills. Interact well with individuals from diverse cultures and all professional levels. Teach, train, mentor, motivate, and evaluate personnel to achieve the highest quality standards.

▶ Lead special projects and provide strategic insight into operations. Effectively manage and prioritize multiple responsibilities. Ensure adherence to policies and procedures to achieve objectives in safety, quality, production, good manufacturing practices, and cost.

▶ Knowledgeable in
   - Personnel Supervision
   - Human Relations
   - Organizational Management
   - Field Management
   - Records and Information Management
   - Problem Resolution
   - Mechanical Maintenance
   - Hazardous Materials Handling
   - Principles of Instruction
   - Office Administration
   - First Aid
   - Military Science

EXPERIENCE

United States Army   *1984–2004*
   Master Sergeant *(1995–2004)*   Specialist Fourth Class *(1985–1986)*
   Sergeant First Class *(1993–1995)*   Private First Class *(1985)*
   Staff Sergeant *(1988–1993)*   Private Second Class *(1984–1985)*
   Sergeant *(1986–1988)*   (Honorable Discharge, *2004*)

▶ Fast-track promotions in recognition of leadership, valor, discipline, and attainment of highest test scores.

Senior Military Science Instructor, Pebble University (ROTC)

▶ Managed ROTC program for 4 years. Trained cadets in military subjects with emphasis on land navigation, first aid, small unit tactics, marksmanship, physical fitness, drill, and ceremony. Coordinated and implemented all field training exercises. Led Pebble ROTC to top 10% ranking nationwide. Led Ranger Challenge Team to finish in the top 1 or 2 position in each of three years.

First Sergeant, Ft. Panera, North Dakota

▶ Served as senior enlisted soldier of Basic Combat Training Company consisting of 18 teams training approximately 240 Initial Entry Training Soldiers every 9-week cycle. Provided continuous guidance, counseling, and assistance to permanent-party and training soldiers. Served as Master Trainer; organized and directed Noncommissioned Officer Professional Development Program. Supervised all company personnel, logistics, and administration.

Senior First Sergeant, Drill Sergeant, Ft. Panera, North Dakota

▶ For 3 years, trained 55 initial-entry soldiers in each 8-week cycle to become highly motivated, skilled, and physically fit. Directed logistics and administrative support; monitored discipline and morale.

Platoon Sergeant, Ranger Squad Leader, Team Leader, 7 years, Ft. Haderus, Iowa

Instructor / Squad Leader, 4 years, Ft. Swanson, Missouri

Career Change: *From career in the military to corporate supervisor or manager.*

Strategy: *Use headline to call attention to career goals; include documented personal attributes that will make him an excellent leader and manager in the corporate world.*

Keith R. Henderson, Jr. 412-555-1212 Page 2

PERFORMANCE REMARKS

- Consummate team player
- Consistently sound judgment; works long, hard hours
- Highest degree of loyalty, integrity, and competence
- Instills skill, spirit to achieve, and a winning attitude
- Meticulous attention to detail
- Obtains maximum results in personnel's performance
- Makes safety decisions in best interest of personnel while maximizing training efforts

- Sets standard for personal and professional conduct
- A master at training and developing personnel
- Superior physical stamina and mental toughness
- Possesses diverse skill set: smart, hands-on, tough
- Prolific problem-solver; outstanding planner/organizer
- Accomplishes assigned tasks with superb results

CERTIFICATIONS / AWARDS

Emergency Medical Technician, National Registry of EMTs
HazMat Certification
Recipient of numerous performance awards, including Bronze Star for Valor and Purple Heart

EDUCATION / TRAINING

U.S. Army Training:

School of Cadet Command	Long-Range Surveillance Leader	Ranger / Airborne
Drill Sergeant	Basic Noncommissioned Officer	Infantryman / Pathfinder
Combat Lifesaver Training	Advanced Noncommissioned Officer	Primary Leadership Development
Military Freefall Jumpmaster	Packaging of Hazardous Materials	Outward Bound, Certified Trainer
Instructor / Trainer	for Transportation	(Group Training as well as One-on-One)

Graduate, 1984, Easton High School—Easton, PA

PERSONAL STRENGTHS

Descriptive terms of personal strengths in the workplace based on professional Personality Profiling

Competitive ▶ Pioneering ▶ Challenge-oriented ▶ Accomplishes goals through people ▶ Confident

RESUME 15: BY LOUISE KURSMARK, MRW, CPRW, JCTC, CEIP, CCM

Donna Mazzei

donna_mazzei@hotmail.com

Project Leader

Analysis • Creativity • Leadership • Communication • Presentation

Effective communicator, presenter, and project leader with strong planning, analysis, and implementation skills. Proven ability to lead teams, coordinate complex/detailed programs, and drive initiatives to successful conclusion. Exceptional skills as a presenter, influencer, and consensus builder; able to interact and build rapport with individuals of all ages and diverse cultures.

Relocating to Boston Spring/Summer 2005

Experience & Achievements

Instructor – Multicultural Classroom – U.S. Department of Defense, Illesheim, Germany, 2003–Present

- **Planning & Execution:** Strategically plan classroom activities and special projects to prepare students for next level of learning; design curriculum from the ground up and consistently above standards.

- **Communication:** Design and produce monthly newsletter; initiate regular formal and informal communication with students' families.

- **Project Management:** Selected as co-chair of annual fund-raising event, a community-wide talent show. Coordinated auditions, supervised team of 20–25 volunteers, negotiated hundreds of dollars worth of donated services, generated publicity (TV, radio, print), and managed all facets of high-visibility event.

- **Strategy & Analysis:** Participate on Improvement Committee, analyzing data and crafting reports and strategy recommendations for future direction in the areas of staffing, facilities, community relations, and administration.

- **Leadership:** Gain full support and cooperation of parents, achieving 100% participation in open house and conference evenings.

- **Creativity:** Successfully teach the scientific method to young children and incorporate all steps into diversified classroom projects and activities.

Instructor – U.S. Department of Defense School System, Ft. Bragg, NC, 1999–2003

- **Planning & Execution:** Created and implemented original lesson plans to ensure delivery of defined curriculum.

- **Project Management:** 1) Teamed with another staff member to write, direct, and produce an original play for African-American History Month; managed teams of adult volunteers and directed student actors. 2) Adapted and produced original musical and directed its performance before soldiers being deployed to Iraq; earned favorable publicity.

- **Leadership:** By word of mouth/reputation, increased class size 68% (35% above average). Managed 2 teachers' aides.

- **Teamwork:** Worked with Improvement Committee to develop recommendations and then with staff at all levels on project implementation.

- **Creativity:** Launched innovative year-long program to build students' knowledge base of musical theater.

Career Change: *From elementary school teacher to business project manager.*

Strategy: *Use functional headings to call attention to highly related skills used in her job as a teacher; downplay use of elementary education language.*

Donna Mazzei
donna_mazzei@hotmail.com

continued

Drama and English Teacher – Columbia High School, Columbia, SC, 1999

- **Teamwork:** Worked closely with team of teachers to implement the drama program across all grade levels.

Drama Director, Instructor, and Actor – South Carolina Youth Detention Facility; Dixieland Theater Academy; U.S. DoD School, Columbia, SC, 1998–2003

- **Performance:** Recruited for role in Dixieland Theater production of *Bridge to Terabithia*. Performed throughout region.

- **Creativity:** Conceived and executed original teaching methodology to improve language skills of at-risk youth. Success led to quick transition of volunteer role to part-time paid position.

Board Member/Member – Junior League of Columbia, Columbia, SC, 2000–2003

- **Leadership:** Elected by new class of members to head up major community project, a holiday toy drive that served 120 area children. Created project plan, delegated responsibilities, scheduled activities, and coordinated distribution.

- **Project Management:** Spearheaded annual scholarship drive that awarded 3 grants to outstanding local youth. Managed applications, coordinated judges' panel, and secured publicity.

- **Recognition:** Named *Provisional of the Year* for contribution to the organization, 2000–2001.

Board Member/Member – Downtown Club, Columbia, SC, 2000–2003

- **Project Management:** Chaired a key initiative to drive young adults to downtown enterprises. Secured 15 business sponsorships.

Board Member – South Carolina Youth Detention Center, Columbia, SC, 1999–2001

- **Strategy & Analysis:** Analyzed the organization's financial records, budget, and curriculum to develop long-term strategy for best use of facility and resources.

Campaign Volunteer – City Councilor Debra Clegg, Columbia, SC, 2002

- **Teamwork:** Participated in grass-roots campaign effort that resulted in 2-to-1 victory for new city councilor.

- **Project Management:** Coordinated volunteers and helped manage fund-raising events.

Education

University of South Carolina, Columbia, SC

- Master's in Early Childhood Education, 2001
- Certification in Theater Education, 1998
- Bachelor of Arts in Theater, 1997 – *Theater Student of the Year, 1997*

RESUME 16: BY GEORGE DUTCH, CMF, CCM, JCTC

J. Robert Martin

42 Covington Drive
Ottawa, Ontario K2L 4H9

Home: (613) 853-8146
Email: jrobm@internet.com

Business Process & Planning Specialist

Start-up Ventures / Information Systems & Technology / General Business

Specialist at planning and implementing processes to improve the effectiveness of business teams and business systems. Possess strong analytical and problem-solving skills and the ability to quickly determine how a process or system works, identify improvements, and envision any new procedures required. Excel at performing thorough research and synthesizing different ideas to create a complete process from the individual components.

Competent, dependable, self-reliant, and accurate professional, team player, and natural leader. Strengths include

- Strategic Planning & Growth
- Project Management
- General Management
- Business Development & Growth
- Revenue & Profit Maximization
- Client Relationship Management
- Team Building & Leadership
- Communications Skills
- Programming Life Cycle

Highlights of Achievements

- Prepared a report focusing on the future operations and structure of a start-up company. **Result:** Highlighted areas of improvement, reducing overlap and inefficiencies.
- Managed all aspects of a quarter-million-per-annum project. **Result:** Returned the project to profitability by managing contract scope and resources, as well as securing new revenue-generating opportunities.
- Initiated and led a discussion group for current and potential team leads. **Result:** Significantly shortened learning curve for new team leads and reduced training expenses.
- Initiated just-in-time training for team members lacking project-critical knowledge. **Result:** Significantly shortened learning curve for employees new to the technology without additional training expenses.

Professional Experience

Computer Support & Consulting, *Self-Employed*, Ottawa, Ontario   July 2003 to present

Environment: Small businesses and home offices requiring on-site and on-call assistance purchasing computer components, troubleshooting problems or software/hardware tutorials. Solutions often require learning new technologies quickly.

Sample Achievements

- Reduced or eliminated many program instabilities and errors from a computer system. **Result:** Significantly reduced computer downtime for small business owner.
- Evaluated and installed new software to access multiple file formats from different platforms. **Result:** System is compatible with all major file formats and platforms, greatly increasing efficiency of a core business function.
- Created procedures to streamline mass-mailing process. **Result:** Business now produces all mass mailings in-house, eliminating time and cost required to outsource the work.

Project Leader, *Local/Global Technologies*, Kingston, Ontario   July 2002 to July 2003

Environment: Start-up venture developing mobile electronic devices to automate logging, tracking, and reporting requirements for the trucking industry. Reported directly to the President on matters of marketing, company operations, internal structure, and policies.

Sample Achievements

- Designed customer-support policies in preparation for product launch. **Result:** Reduced training and issue resolution time while ensuring consistency when resolving customer-support issues.
- Managed team responsible for launching the company's marketing web site, as well as developed brochures and other marketing materials. **Result:** Increased awareness of the company in a professional manner, especially among potential clients and investors.
- Organized the company's first appearance at a national trade show. **Result:** Company and product were introduced to more than 12,000 attendees.

… /2

Career Change: *From computer programmer to business process specialist.*

Strategy: *Translate technical jobs to business language with documented results.*

J. Robert Martin page 2

IT Consultant, *CDI Management Systems Canada, Inc.*, Ottawa, Ontario   May 1999 to March 2002

Environment: IT systems integration company with the majority of clients in the government sector. Held different positions with a variety of projects, including programmer/analyst, project leader, advisor, and researcher. Also active in initiating or leading many internal projects, such as discussion groups, satisfaction surveys, and social events.

Sample Achievements

- Researched and created reusable document templates for current and future Internet Security projects. **Result:** Reduced time and training required to document Internet Security projects.
- Designed, analyzed, and reported to senior management findings of an internal survey focused on improving staff meetings. **Result:** Increased employee satisfaction and the effectiveness of staff meetings.
- Consulted on the development of an internal Lotus Notes database. **Result:** Shortened learning curve of development team and resolved errors so database could be launched as quickly as possible.

Application Designer/Builder, *National Pacific Railway*, Toronto, Ontario   June 1997 to May 1999

Environment: Maintenance and enhancement support for the company's mainframe payroll system. Responsible for designing, testing, and implementing program modifications as well as providing 24/7 on-call support for critical problems.

Sample Achievements

- Performed 24/7 on-call support for the highly visible payroll application. **Result:** Ensured time-sensitive systems completed successfully and as scheduled. Reduced future errors and support requirements through proactive system maintenance and detailed problem logs.
- Provided on-site support and training for a highly visible, time-critical payroll tax database. **Result:** Clients were able to produce and distribute required tax information to employees on time.
- Designed and produced all aspects of a promotional video for company relocation. **Result:** Employees could make an educated decision about relocating from Toronto to Calgary.

Technical Skills

Proficient in all aspects of the programming system life cycle, especially pertaining to mainframe platforms, as well as some knowledge of C, C++, PowerBuilder, and LotusScript. Always eager to learn new skills. Proven ability to deliver quality work when faced with a short learning curve.

Applications	Operating Systems	Languages	Internet
MS Office 2000,	Windows 9x/NT,	COBOL, JCL, C,	HTML, PKI architecture,
WS_FTP Pro,	MacOS, OS/390,	C++, PowerBuilder,	various browsers & mail
Lotus Notes, TSO	OS/2	LotusScript	applications

Education

Bachelor of Engineering and Management (1997), *McMaster University*, Hamilton, Ontario

Environment: Combined Engineering Physics degree with the core Commerce courses to gain a balanced appreciation of business and technology. Acquired management knowledge in courses such as marketing research, project management, finance and accounting, human resources management, and business law. Gained experience with technology studying solid-state electronics, laser and electro-optics, nuclear energy, hardware design, and statistical analysis. Extracurricular roles included President of the Engineering and Management Club (1993–1995) and member of the Residence Council (1990–1991).

REFERENCES AVAILABLE ON REQUEST

ANDRE MITCHELL

513-249-0090   9787 Covington Place, Apt. 7, Cincinnati, OH 45005   am@cinci.rr.com

Building Manager

Efficient and effective manager with experience in multiple facets of building construction, maintenance, and management and exceptional performance in critical areas of building safety, security, and tenant satisfaction. Maintenance/management experience includes multi-tenant commercial properties, food-service facilities, and entertainment venues as large as 25,000 square feet.

Skilled/licensed carpenter, HVAC technician, sheet metal fabricator, and auto mechanic with additional experience maintaining electrical and plumbing systems. Licensed real estate agent proficient at showing property and managing tenant relations.

General Manager: The Blue Note, Cincinnati, OH   1995–Present

Direct all business operations for 15,000-sq.-ft. nightclub with weekly revenues exceeding $100,000. On board since start-up; put in place the operating procedures, security standards, and revenue safeguards that have been pivotal to long-term success and profitable operation of the club.

Recruit, train, and manage 42 staff. Manage financial operations, including monthly budgets, payroll, assessments, and inventory. Ensure compliance with all building and safety codes; oversee building maintenance, including A/C, plumbing, and electrical.

- ☑ **Site selection & construction:** Assisted owners in locating and selecting site in up-and-coming downtown neighborhood. Oversaw building construction and club layout. Represented owners at community meetings and before licensing boards.

- ☑ **Revenue protection:** Established foolproof ticketing system that eliminates non-paying guests and guarantees revenue accountability. Set demanding standards for door staff and hold them accountable.

- ☑ **Safety & security:** Created effective security system that minimizes use of illegal substances and promotes a safe environment—since launched, zero incidents. In demand as consultant to introduce similar systems in other Tristate-area clubs.

- ☑ **Community relations:** Instituted street-side crowd control to minimize neighborhood disturbances. Personally visible and accessible to all neighbors.

- ☑ **City agency relations:** Personally secured and maintained up-to-date city licenses for fire safety and building security. Built excellent relationships with Cincinnati Police and Fire Departments.

- ☑ **Staff loyalty & reliability:** In high-turnover industry, retained staff long term—including 3 bar staff and 3 coat-check staff since opening of club. Constantly improve staff skills through training. Create a positive, team-oriented culture.

Property Manager: Downtown Spaces Realty, Cincinnati, OH   1998–2002

Managed multi-unit commercial property with close attention to safety, building maintenance, and swift resolution of tenant issues.

- ☑ **Maintenance:** Created maintenance schedules and performed or supervised all aspects of maintenance, repairs, cleaning, and rules enforcement.

- ☑ **Management:** Showed property to prospective tenants; managed leasing and evictions; maintained excellent tenant relations through professional approach to building management.

Career Change: From nightclub general manager to building/facilities manager.

513-249-0090   **ANDRE MITCHELL**   am@cinci.rr.com

Construction / Supervisor: Buckeye Mechanical Systems, Toledo, OH   1990–1995

Performed wide range of activities related to installation and servicing of residential and commercial HVAC systems.

- ☑ **Special skills:** Fabricating and installing sheet metal; rebuilding, servicing, and installing steam turbines and absorption units; all areas of pipe fitting for refrigeration and hot water boilers.

- ☑ **Staff and project management:** Supervised work crews to ensure efficient and timely project completion. Trained workers in all aspects of the job.

Manager: Lakeside Inn, Port Clinton, OH   1993–1995

Turned around unprofitable, inefficient, poorly managed seasonal facility and created a profitable inn/restaurant/nightclub that was so successful, owners invested in Cincinnati club (The Blue Note) and brought me on as GM from day one.

- ☑ **Operational turnaround:** Revamped entire operation for better efficiency; replaced 90% of staff; introduced new computer system for cash registers and office functions; instilled strict operational policies and procedures. Transformed lax operation to consistently profitable "tight ship."

- ☑ **Safety and security:** Implemented and maintained new security practices for bar, nightclub, and hotel.

Manager: Alhambra Nightclub, Toledo, OH   1988–1993

Worked in all areas of nightclub operations, beginning as busboy and advancing to manager of 25,000-sq-.ft. establishment with 1,800-patron capacity.

Managed stock and ordered inventory. Handled all employee payroll accounts. Hired and trained staff at every level. Managed all special events as well as day-to-day functions of the nightclub.

Licenses / Certifications / Technical Skills

- ☑ Cincinnati Fire Department certifications: Fire Drill Conductor, Maintenance, Public Assembly.

- ☑ Cincinnati Health Department License for Food Service.

- ☑ Certified auto mechanic. Sheet metal worker, fabrication and installation.

- ☑ Former union carpenter (employed full-time with Local 129 from 1984–1986). Scaffolding and rigging experience on high-rises.

- ☑ Licensed refrigeration and air-conditioning technician. Electrical and plumbing experience.

- ☑ Ohio Real Estate License; related education through College of Mount St. Joseph:
  — Changing Dynamics of Real Estate (11/03)
  — Real Estate Law (11/01)
  — The Management of Residential Property (11/01)
  — The Management of Commercial Property (10/01)

Strategy: *Pull out just the relevant experience from the most recent position, which involved broader sales, marketing, and supervisory experience than is detailed in this resume. Include part-time property manager role as key experience.*

RESUME 18: BY CINDY KRAFT, CCMC, CCM, JCTC, CPRW

717-222-8988
MICHAEL FISHER, MBA, CPA
fisher@email.com
2283 Atlantic Avenue, York, PA 17404

SENIOR MANAGEMENT EXECUTIVE
Finance ... Change Management ... Procurement ... Purchasing

Visionary strategist with a demonstrated ability to deliver corporate objectives. Solid 13-year career creating market advantage, reducing and controlling expenses, and fostering a culture of teamwork, shared mission, and dedication to customer satisfaction. Key strengths ...

> *"You quickly jumped in with both feet and made an immediate contribution to our team. Specifically, your analysis and projections of our financials and operational metrics within our group have been right on track."*
>
> John Jones
> General Manager

> Michael *"improved his revenue standing as the manager from the #6 position to the #2 position in about 60 days."*
>
> Loren Hughes
> Director
> Consumer Ops

Leadership ... Pioneered a service program to improve customer service ratings that exceeded quarterly targets and captured the #1 position among 7 teams. The program was adopted by corporate and rolled out in 21 offices.

Cost Reductions ... Collaborated with intradepartmental managers and senior executives to implement a cost-reduction plan companywide. Negotiated a telecommunications contract that generated $1.8 million in savings annually.

Change Management ... Drove the organization's ranking from #6 out of seven to #2 in sales performance within 60 days by introducing an empowering, team-based management style.

Vendor Sourcing ... Consolidated temporary services sourcing from 50 providers to one national contract, generating $200,000 in annual expense savings.

Team Building ... Championed employee development, recognition, and open communication that positioned the call center as #1 in product retention within a 9-state region in 5 months.

New Product Launch ... Introduced incentives and measurement tools that positioned the territory as #1 in telephone sales within a 5-territory region.

Participative Management ... Partnered with the Communications Workers of America (CWA) union to create a performance-based work environment, establishing best-in-class benchmarks for management practices.

Training & Development ... Key member of a 6-person team tasked with developing sales effectiveness training and implementing a certification process. Drove 15% annual sales increases post-implementation, garnering the VP/GM "Shining Star" Award.

PROFESSIONAL EXPERIENCE

BANK OF AMERICA, York, Pennsylvania

Director of Customer Service Operations—2002 to Present
Recruited to take over leadership of a department with a history of ineffective leadership, lack of performance, escalating expenses, and excessively high budgets. Manage a 15-person staff and $100 million expense budget; report directly to the Controller.

- Reduced expenses by $2.5 million through detailed reports and analysis of travel, telecom, express mail, copier leases, office supplies, document management, and cell phone policies.
- Partnered with the Human Resources Director to negotiate a 10% contract reduction on a national temporary services contract, yielding an annual expense savings of $200,000.
- Pioneered the department's first-ever incentive performance plans.

Career Change: *From call-center manager to finance executive.*

Strategy: *Create a skills-based resume to pull out financial accomplishments; add quotes from supervisors to provide even more emphasis on his qualifications in his target area.*

MICHAEL FISHER Page 2 717-222-8988

VERIZON, Tampa, Florida

Hired as a Financial Analyst, launching a successful ten-year career holding increasingly responsible management positions with this Fortune 100 communications services company. Recruited for a special assignment as Finance Manager with P&L responsibility for a $200 million expense budget.

Manager of Sales/Service/Retention, Consumer Services — 2001 to 2002
Selected to drive sales and ensure customer service and retention. Managed 12 direct reports and 100 union-represented employees.

- Personally selected by senior management from among 1,000 candidates to participate in the Gateway Leadership Program.

- Completely turned around sales performance, taking the team from #6 to #2 in 60 days. Maintained the second position for the balance of 2001.

- Initiated the customer service and satisfaction program that took ratings from #3 to #1 in 60 days.

- Built team unity and empowered employees to achieve corporate goals, establishing the team as #1 in product retention and beating the company's regional retention rate by 8%.

Manager of Sales Excellence, Consumer Services — 2000 to 2001
Personally chosen for leadership, product knowledge, vision, and financial expertise for this newly created position.

- Developed the Sales Effectiveness Training program that standardized training, strengthened the overall regional sales organization, and led to annual revenue increases of 15%.

Finance & Call Center Manager, Consumer Services — 1997 to 2000
Promoted to Finance Manager and within 12 months assumed additional responsibilities directing a 13-person team in the special-needs call center.

- Resolved a $20 million shortfall in sales goals to finish #1 in booked revenues by benchmarking internal performance, reallocating revenue goals between sales and service departments, and employing performance metrics for sales representatives.

Financial Analyst, Consumer Services Finance — 1992 to 1997
Conducted post-promotion marketing reviews for profitability; recommended marketing and operations funding prioritizations; reviewed income statement categories to evaluate financial trade-offs; and analyzed activity-based costing system results.

PRIOR RELEVANT EXPERIENCE

Financial & Compliance Auditor, FLORIDA AUDIT DEPT., Tallahassee, Florida — 1990 to 1992
Staff Accountant, Audit Staff, ERNST AND YOUNG, Nashville, TN — 1989 to 1990

EDUCATION

Master of Business Administration, University of Florida, Gainesville, Florida — 2001
Bachelor of Science in Accounting, Purdue University, West Lafayette, Indiana — 1989

CERTIFICATIONS

Certified Public Accountant (CPA) • Certified Internal Auditor (CIA)
Certified Information Systems Auditor (CISA)

DEREK STEPHENS

215 Churchill Street, Pittsburgh, PA 15212
412.322.1258
dstephens@msn.com

---

* MANAGEMENT CONSULTING *
Certified Six Sigma Black Belt

Consummate Research Scientist with a **synergistic proficiency between technical disciplines and Six Sigma strategies** to successfully integrate analytical insight and business knowledge. **Highly motivated** with a responsible work ethic and a **solutions-oriented** focus within a demanding environment to impact long-term process improvements. A **professional communicator** with the ability to build relationships based on mutual respect, trust, and benefit.

Business Analysis and Team Development

- Apply cross-functional communications to interface with high-profile business clients, consultants, teams, agencies, professors, and students.
- Integrate strong quantitative and analytical skills to re-engineer business processes using the **Six Sigma methodology** leading to optimum business efficiency.
- Present scientific data and information to non-scientific communities while leading and participating on project teams.
- Play instrumental role in bringing new products to market. Improve processes to make products more robust.

Technical Expertise

- Design experiments for product analysis and formulate strategies to reduce process variation.
- Recognized internally as **technical expert** in optical thin films. **Submitted three intellectual property applications.**
- Apply highly developed technical discipline to create process improvements through data-driven decision making.
- Astute understanding of air-sensitive and solid-state chemical manipulations.
- Extensive hands-on experience utilizing chemical vapor deposition, solvo/hydro-thermal, high-pressure synthetic, glass-blowing, glove-box, and vacuum-line techniques.
- Computer Skills—Statistical analysis software: JMP
  Silicon graphics crystallographic software: SHELXTL and Cerius2

WORK EXPERIENCE

SR. RESEARCH SCIENTIST, **RRT Industries,** Pittsburgh, PA	2001–PRESENT
RESEARCH ASSISTANT, **University of Michigan,** Ann Arbor, MI	1999–2001
RESEARCH ASSISTANT, **Arizona State University,** Tempe, AZ	1997–1999
TEACHING ASSISTANT, **Arizona State University,** Tempe, AZ	1997–1999
SYNTHETIC POLYMER CHEMIST, **RRT Industries,** Oak Creek, WI	1996–1997
RESEARCH ASSISTANT, **Carroll College,** Waukesha, WI	1996–1997

EDUCATION

PH.D., University of Michigan, Ann Arbor, MI   *Emphasis:* Materials Chemistry
   Project: Synthesis, design, characterization, and study of highly porous metal-organic materials for
   use in heterogeneous catalysis, gas and liquid separation, and storage applications.

M.S., Arizona State University, Tempe, AZ   *Emphasis:* Inorganic Chemistry
   Project: Synthesis and design of single-source molecular precursors for chemical vapor deposition of
   group III nitrides for use in light-emitting diodes.

B.S., Carroll College, Waukesha, WI   *Major:* Chemistry   *Minor:* Business Administration

---

Career Change: *From research scientist to management consultant.*

Strategy: *Create a layered resume with the option to use either two or three pages depending on the specific opportunity. Page 1 contains qualifications gleaned from past experiences; page 2 shows*

DEREK STEPHENS

215 Churchill Street, Pittsburgh, PA 15212
412.322.1258
dstephens@msn.com

Page 2

KEY PROJECT MANAGEMENT & LEADERSHIP

Challenge: **New Product Development**—To generate ideas and applications for new products that define value-added opportunities.

Actions: (1) Design and develop novel materials for next-generation products.
(2) Assess novel materials for unique product opportunities.
(3) Lead technical activities within team environments.

Results: Inventor of **Solarshade** self-cleaning glass product.
Launch Date: February 2003
Build intellectual property position—Application #US 5,215,348

Challenge: **Market Development**—To analyze problems and creatively generate solutions to overcome production issues.

Actions: (1) Develop process strategies and possible capabilities for producing materials.
(2) Perform online design of experiments at production facility.
(3) Establish trends using **Six Sigma methodology.**
(4) Design pathways to eliminate problematic issues.
(5) Provide technical input to assist and influence customer.

Results: Employ novel approach to overcome process issues.
Inventor of **Visiongate** statistical software to track and eliminate problematic technical issues.
Launch Date: December 2004
Build intellectual property position—Application #US 6,451,730

Challenge: **Academia Collaborations**—To leverage expertise within academia to bring new technology to RRT Industries.

Actions: (1) Collaborate with Materials Science and Environmental Engineering departments to initiate ideas to leverage expertise.
(2) Provide appropriate materials and assist with analysis to finalize project goals.
(3) Assess results using **Sigma Logic methodology** to define products and opportunities.
(4) Translate university work to RRT process technology.
(5) Recommend ways to improve RRT process.

Results: Define products and opportunities.
Build intellectual property position—Application #US 9,296,197

RECOGNITION AWARDS

Two awards for **technical project update presentations** to the CEO and Executive Committee of RRT—awarded by R&D Director of RRT.

Idea Generation Committee Award for **contribution and leadership** in uncovering new ideas for product opportunities—awarded by R&D Associate Director of RRT.

Successful online design of experiments that revealed process limitations to overcome product qualification hurdles—awarded by Manager of Glass Coatings Process Control Group of RRT.

Rackham Dissertation Fellowship (University of Michigan)—departmental fellowship awarded to most promising dissertation.

in-depth project leadership using the CAR approach; and page 3 documents publications and scientific instrumentation knowledge.

DEREK STEPHENS

215 Churchill Street, Pittsburgh, PA 15212
412.322.1258
dstephens@msn.com

Page 3

PRESENTATIONS / PUBLICATIONS

Presentations: "Precursors for Strongly Bonded Three-Dimensional Frameworks," D. Stephens, *Abstr Pap Am Chem Soc.* 220: 354-Inorg. Chem. Part 1, August 20, 2000.

"Synthesis of Cl_2InN_3, Br_2InN_3, and Related Adducts," D. Stephens, Departmental Seminar, Arizona State University, April 3, 1999.

"Combustion of Liquid Organic Compounds in a Bomb Calorimeter," D. Stephens, *Abstr Pap Am Chem Soc.* 213: 511-Chem. Ed. Part 1, April 13, 1997.

Publications: "Synthesis, Characterization, and Sorbtion Comparisons of $Tb_2(B_{10})_3$, $Tb_2(AnDC)_3$, and $Tb_2(DHDC)_3$." *Submitted.*

"Mixed Metal-Organic Frameworks Constructed from Benzene Tricarboxylic Acid." *Submitted.*

"Highly Porous Three-Dimensional Metal Formates." *Submitted.*

"Design of Secondary Building Units Using Functionalized Terephthalates." *Submitted.*

"Synthesis of New Azidoalanes with Heterocyclic Molecular Structures," J. Williamson, J. Miller, D. Stephens, Main Group Met. Chem., 24 (2): 77–84 Apr. 16, 2001.

"Synthesis and Structures of Heterocycle Azidogallanes $[(CH_3)ClGaN_3]_4$ and $[(CH_3)BrGaN_3]_3$ en route to $[(CH_3)HGaN_3]_4$: An inorganic precursor to GaN," J. Williamson, J. Miller, D. Stephens, T. Reiter, J. Huber, Inorg. Chem., 39 (17): 3805–3809 Aug. 21, 2000.

"Synthesis of Cl_2InN_3, Br_2InN_3, and Related Adducts," D. Stephens, J. Miller, J. Williamson, Inorg. Chem., 39 (7): 1615 Apr. 3, 2000.

"H_2GaN_3: A Facile Approach to GaN," J. Miller, K. Burnside, D. Stephens, J. Williamson, Inorg. Chem., 37 (26): 6638–6644 Dec. 28, 1998.

Complete publication and abstract bibliography available on request.

INSTRUMENTATION

Extensive experience
- FTIR spectroscopy
- High/low temperature x-ray powder diffraction
- Thermogravimetric analysis
- Mass spectroscopy
  Electron impact ionization
  Fast atom bombardment
- Gas chromatography
- Ultraviolet spectroscopy

Fluent background
- Single crystal x-ray diffraction
- Scanning electron microscopy
  BSE/ SEI/ EDS
- Solid state and solution NMR
  $^{13}C/^{31}P/^{15}N/^1H$
- Rutherford backscattering spectrometry
- Ultra high-vacuum chemical vapor deposition film growth processes

CHAPTER 5

Resumes for Career Changers Seeking Technology Positions

Despite outsource and offshore initiatives, the demand for qualified technologists continues to grow. It is important to have the right qualifications to be considered for these opportunities. Note how many of the resumes in this chapter emphasize recent training and list specific technologies and skill sets. These resumes represent the following specific career and industry changes:

- Carpenter to network administrator

- Graphic designer and musician to video game audio engineer

- Library science to information technology

- Certified surgical technologist to network administrator

- Education to publishing information technology

- Manufacturing engineering to IT

- Customer service to computer graphics

- Retail to network management

- Telecommunications account executive to video game producer

- Sales manager to Chief Information Officer

WILL GATEM

wgatem@construct.net

105 Outlook Drive   Nashville, Tennessee 37239   615.792.1412

NETWORK ADMINISTRATOR

➢ Versatile, hardworking individual; driven to meet or exceed expectations.

➢ Passion and exceptional aptitude for working with computers. Skilled in troubleshooting and identifying procedures needed to maintain a reliable and efficient network to keep the organization running smoothly and profitably.

➢ Knowledgeable in designing gates in hardware and software to allow free exchange of data, custom applications, and the computer power to process this information for authorized users; also skilled in setting up firewalls to protect proprietary information from outsiders.

➢ Effective interpersonal skills; work well as a team member with people at all levels of an organization and of various cultures. Equally capable working independently.

➢ Computer proficiency includes Microsoft Office (Word, Excel, Access, Outlook, PowerPoint), QuickBooks Pro, backup protocol, and scanning documents/graphics.

EDUCATION / TRAINING

Coursework in **Computer Technology,** 2003   4.0 GPA
Vanderbilt University—Nashville, TN

Coursework in **Microcomputer Familiarization,** 1984
Coursework in **Mechanical Engineering,** 1982
The Ohio State University—Columbus, Ohio

CERTIFICATION

Microsoft Certified Systems Engineer, 2004
Microsoft Certified Professional, 2003

- Networking Essentials
- Proxy Server
- NT Workstation
- NT Server in the Enterprise
- Internetworking with Microsoft TCP/IP on Microsoft NT 4.0

EMPLOYMENT

Brant Construction Co., Inc.—Nashville, TN   1982–Present
CARPENTER FOREMAN—1990–present
CARPENTER—1976–1990
LABORER—1972–1976

Earned respect of co-workers and supervisors in family-owned business through diligent observation and application of skills learned. Demonstrate remarkable work ethic.

- Supervise 3–10 carpenters and laborers in construction/renovation/maintenance of residential/ commercial buildings. Schedule subcontractors. Ensure accuracy of work.

- Calculate space estimates regarding material costs, labor costs, and time from start of project to completion. Organize job site and ensure tasks are completed in a timely and cost-effective manner.

Career Change: *From carpenter to network administrator.*

Strategy: *Emphasize recent education and use the introduction to detail transferable skills gained from multiple experiences.*

RESUME 21: BY LOUISE FLETCHER, CPRW

SAM ELLIOT
148 W 219TH ST., TORRANCE CA 90502
(310) 555-1212. SAMUEL@SAMUELELLIOT.COM

KEYBOARDIST/PROGRAMMER/ENGINEER FOR THE MEMORY CHAIN
– TRANSITIONING TO VIDEO GAME AUDIO ENGINEERING –

PROFILE

Built extensive original F/X library. Wrote, performed, engineered, and produced four albums. Advanced skills in session dialing for basic tracking, overdubs and voice-overs, Foley, mixing and mastering, and live mixing for clubs and national tour venues. Strengths include

**Sound Effect Creation ... Sampling/Looping ... Music Composition ...
Audio Engineering/Production ... Orchestral Scoring ... MIDI ...
Digital Audio Studio ... Musician: Guitar, Keyboards, Drums ... Audio Editing**

Skilled in a variety of studio applications including: **Pro Tools, Cubase SX, Sound Forge, DirectMusic Producer, Acid, Reason, Logic, SoundDiver, ReBirth, and Studio Vision Pro.**

SELECTED REVIEWS

"The Memory Chain takes sampling to a new level.... Sam Elliot has done it again."
LA Times, May 2002

"The Memory Chain's latest album is the one where Sam Elliot finally takes center stage ... and if this album is any indication, he should have been there long ago."
Q magazine, October 2001

"Sublime keyboards ... Sam Elliot is a musician's musician."
Musician magazine, June 2000

MUSICAL CAREER

Keyboardist/Programmer/Engineer, The Memory Chain, 1996–2001
Released four CDs as sound designer and performer with this critically acclaimed band. Toured U.S., Asia, and Europe extensively. Played keyboards on four CDs and 600+ live performances.

Clear Sounds Audio, 2nd Engineer, Paid Internship, 1998
Recorded, edited, mixed, and produced multi-track audio productions for major label artists and advertising agencies. Assisted outside engineers.

OTHER EXPERIENCE

Freelance Designer, Graphics and Web Design, 2001–Present

EDUCATION

BA in Music. Emphasis in Electronic Music and Recording

– Member ASCAP –

Career Change: *From graphic designer and musician to video game audio engineer.*

Strategy: *Use name recognition of well-known band to capture interest; combine this with emphasis on technical abilities and deemphasize design experience even though it is recent.*

MELANIE MARTINSON

34 Straight Path Avenue
Brentwood, New York 11717
(631) 887-0990
MMIT@techway.net

Transitioning from Library Science to Information Technology, bringing the following transferable strengths:

- Advanced Research Strategies
- End-User Support
- Staff Training & Supervision
- Information Systems Management
- Systems Infrastructure
- Customer Service Excellence
- Vendor Sourcing & Relations
- Purchasing/Inventory Control
- Expenses/Budget Control

CREDENTIALS

Info-Tech Training Center, Huntington, New York
A+ Certified Technician, 2004

Adelphi University, Garden City, New York
Master of Science, Library Science, 1990

C.W. Post at Long Island University, Brentwood, New York
Bachelor of Arts, Sociology, 1986

PROFESSIONAL EXPERIENCE

Career track in librarian science and business management, bringing the following transferable experience:

Information Systems/Database Management
- Developed reference tools for collecting, organizing, interpreting, and classifying information.
- Successfully trained users on Internet navigation techniques for use in complex reference searches.
- Accessed proprietary vendor databases with demonstrated expertise of complex infrastructure navigation.
- Applied advanced media, including the Internet, virtual libraries, and remote resources.
- Developed a strategic database-driven system that proved effective for generating Internet results.

Business Management/Customer Support
- Established brick-and-mortar and Internet-based bookstores with total responsibility for business operations.
- Cost-effectively purchased and resold books from publishers and wholesalers for global distribution.
- Maintained a strong vendor base to ensure a broad selection and availability of used and hard-to-find books.
- Recruited, trained, and supervised personnel in areas of product knowledge, research, and customer service.
- Delivered quality customer service tailored to individual customer needs, ensured open lines of communication between all concerned, and handled all aspects of financial management and reporting.

WORK HISTORY

Reference Librarian, Kennedy University, Coram, New York	2001–Present
Reference Librarian, Sheridan Community Library, Islip, New York	1996–2001
Reference Librarian, Lincoln Public Library, Brentwood, New York	1990–1996
Managing Owner, Skies The Limit Books, Deer Park, New York	1985–1990

Career Change: *From library science to information technology.*

Strategy: *Emphasize profile and keywords using a functional format that really highlights transferable experience.*

RENÉE ROVAN

4405 Georgia Avenue, NW, #412, Silver Spring, MD 20901, (301) 291-8512, rrovan@email.com

NETWORK ADMINISTRATION PROFESSIONAL

Pursuing **Cisco Certified Network Associate (CCNA)** and **Network+** credentials.

Proficient in Microsoft Office applications in a Windows XP/NT environment.

EDUCATION

Information Systems (IS), *IS Management Specialization* (Honors Graduate), Avery College, Arlington, VA
....2003

Northern Virginia College, Alexandria, VA 1999–2000

Medical Specialist/Surgical Technology, U.S. Armed Forces Health & Sciences College, Irving, TX 1997

APPLIED RESEARCH PROJECTS

Completed **Applied Research Projects (ARPs),** in conjunction with IS degree requirements, covering all aspects of design and management of organizational technical resources, as follows:

➢ **Organizational Culture and Leadership** (2003): Evaluated the organizational culture of Briarwood Surgery Center's endoscopy unit and operating room (OR) in order to ensure that the mission and vision statements were being appropriately applied at the staff level.

➢ **Human Resources (HR) Management** (2003): Established a comprehensive orientation package for the Briarwood Surgery Center's clinical staff.

➢ **Strategic Management and Planning** (2002): Conducted internal/external environmental assessments in order to identify an approach for Briarwood Surgery Center to expand its OR facilities.

➢ **Financial Accounting** (2002): Created a quarterly operating budget for the Briarwood Surgery Center and implemented an expenditure tracking system.

➢ **Database Management Systems** (2002): Created an inventory-control system that optimizes inventory maintenance in a cost-effective manner.

➢ **Networking and Telecommunications** (2002): Identified solutions to integrate Briarwood Surgery Center's two local area networks (LANs) into a single LAN.

➢ **Systems Analysis and Design** (2002): Created a project plan to automate and streamline Briarwood Surgery Center's cataloging of surgical supplies.

➢ **Management Support Systems** (2002): Identified solutions to resolve inventory-control vulnerabilities at minimal cost for Briarwood Surgery Center.

➢ **Statistics and Research Analysis** (2001): Generated graphics to illustrate the Merrifield Hospital Center's assisted-reproduction success rate statistics.

PROFESSIONAL EXPERIENCE

CERTIFIED SURGICAL TECHNOLOGIST

Briarwood Surgery Center, Silver Spring, MD 2002–Present
Merrifield Hospital Center, Vienna, VA 2000–2002
U.S. Army Reserves, Allen Reece Medical Center, Washington, DC 1998–2000
Kelway Ambulatory Surgery Center, Irving, TX 1997–1998

MILITARY EXPERIENCE

U.S. Army Reserves 1997–Present

Career Change: *From certified surgical technologist to network administrator.*

Strategy: *To paint the picture of an accomplished professional, focus on the numerous applied research projects she completed in conjunction with her IT/IS degree requirements.*

RESUME 24: BY TRACY BUMPUS, CPRW, JCTC

ROBERTA HENSLEY

Staten Island, New York 10306
H: 931-296-6949 ● C: 931-622-2511 ● rhensley@aol.com

SUMMARY OF EXPERTISE

INFORMATION TECHNOLOGY ● PUBLISHING

Publication Timeline Management	Editing and Preparation for Publication	System Management and Integration	Multimedia Presentation and E-Publication

Exacting, accurate professional with unusual combination of skills in language manipulation and technology application. Experience in publishing, education, and information technology with ability to synthesize knowledge across industries. Strengths in writing, research, information analysis, and intuitive system design.

TECHNICAL SKILLS

Operating Systems

Windows 2000	Windows NT/XP	Windows NT AS	MacOS

Database Technologies

Oracle	SQL Plus	Oracle Groupware
SQL	MS Access	

Network Management and Protocols

LAN Server	TCP/IP	LAN/3000/9000

Software Applications and Languages

HTML	CorelDRAW	Adobe Acrobat 6.0
PeopleSoft	Visio	MS Office Suite
Lotus Notes	MS Graph	
MS Exchange	MS FrontPage	

EXPERIENCE

CONSULTANT   2000 to 2004
Provided consulting services in areas of technology, publishing, and training.

McGraw-Hill
Served as **Project Leader** managing production schedule for highly complex, extensive educational publication encompassing traditional print media plus multimedia components including CD-ROM, cassettes, and digital artwork. Managed project schedule to ensure deadlines were met by more than 10 copy editors and three production areas. Maintained folios and content tracking.
IMPACT: Kept entire project on track and organized with high accountability to project editors. Provided top-notch hand-off of entire project *in situ* for future continuation or salability.

Bernstein, White, Nudelman & Gable
Executed high-level desktop publishing for financial and legal clients. Prepared dispositions, briefs, reports, contracts, and financial documents for presentation. Passed rigorous testing standards regarding software knowledge, proofreading abilities, and writing.
IMPACT: Eased workload/deadline pressure on executive staff and streamlined entire word-processing workflow.

Deutsche Bank
*Consulted in multiple roles, including **Project Leader, Trainer,** and **Desktop Publisher,** on various projects.*
Data Merge—Led team of two as Project Leader in data cleanup and merge in PeopleSoft for acquired company. Analyzed most effective methods of integrating divergent data sets and ran reports/queries to determine effectiveness of strategies.
IMPACT: Shouldered additional work where possible to free up permanent team members for deadline-critical, high-level system integration tasks. Streamlined entire data-merge process through intuitive identification of data integration techniques.

Roberta Hensley ● 1

Career Change: *From education to publishing information technology.*

Strategy: *Emphasize as much IT work as possible and enhance that information with highlights of her background in education, training, and writing.*

Concur Rollout—Served as Software Trainer on rollout of new expense reporting tool. Acquired software training and provided knowledge transfer to new users. Teamed on anomaly identification and escalation to development team during early stages of implementation.
IMPACT: Instrumental in rapid ramp-up of employees on key reporting tool, providing one-on-one instruction to senior executives and executive assistants.

<u>TManage, Inc.</u>
Supported IT department as Assistant Network Administrator during migration from AS400 mainframe to Windows NT environment. Assisted users in login procedures, set up new accounts, and managed account access.
IMPACT: Provided excellent customer assistance during highly volatile period of reduction in force and changeover in technology.

<u>Bornham Global Consultants</u>
Served as Internet Researcher uncovering employment opportunities and internships for Japanese professionals. Successfully placed more than 16 candidates via Internet research alone and trained others on effective placement methods.
IMPACT: Actualized numerous employment opportunities for overseas professionals and fine-tuned Internet tactics that benefited entire team.

SPECIAL PROJECTS EDITOR   1999 to 2000
Scriptor Publishing ● New York, New York

Served as editor and author for special projects for Dr. William Levy, world-renowned dermatologist. Maintained direct contact with senior editors of publications including *The Lancet* and *Dermatology World* for op-ed pieces. Authored first website content for Scriptor Publishing and the "Dermatopathology: Practical and Conceptual" publication. Worked to highly exacting standards of language and publication.

LITERACY EDUCATOR   1996 to 1999
Cason College ● New York, New York

Authored curriculum for English as a Second Language (ESL) to meet Cason program guidelines. Developed learning objectives, standards, and methods of evaluation. Designed all supporting materials, including consumables, evaluation vehicles, activities, and multimedia support materials. Published two editions.

Served as Instructor for ESL and GED classes serving heterogeneous student population with wide-ranging educational goals. Transitioned program from sequential learning to more freeform outline to accommodate non-traditional student lifestyles and enrollment.

LITERACY EDUCATOR   1992 to 1996
Kehring Bilingual ● New York Institute of Business Education ● Hope Institute ● New York, New York

Instructor in foundation classes—including Business Law, Business English, and Computer Literacy—for both adult and secondary students.

EDUCATION AND TRAINING

Microsoft Certified Systems Engineer ● CompTIA A+ and Network+ Certified
Cisco Certified Networking Associate ● Oracle Database Administrator
(In progress)—Futures in IT

Business Intelligence and RDBMS Technologies Certified: *Relational Database Management Systems incorporating Oracle 9i RDBMS, ERStudio, DBArtisan, MS Excel (PTS)/MS Access, Data Warehousing, MS SQL Server, MS Analysis Services, DTS, Business Objects 5i Reports, Business Objects 5i Universe Design*

Bachelor of Arts—English and Music
New York University and Hunter College ● Graduated with Honors

Hold Series 6, Series 63, and Series 26 securities licenses; New York State teaching certification

Roberta Hensley ● 2

RESUME 25: BY SUSAN GUARNERI, NCC, NCCC, CPRW, CCMC, CEIP, MCC

John Joseph Derry
176 Woodhaven Drive, Eatontown, NJ 07724
(732) 927-5555 • JJDer@bol.com

Web Applications Management
E-Commerce • B2B • Project Management

KEY QUALIFICATIONS

✓ **Technical Strengths:** Up-to-date, diverse training in e-Business Management coupled with years of experience in analytical, technical process engineering profession.

✓ **Project Coordination and Teamwork:** Highly productive in team environments as both team member and team leader. Efficient in handling multiple project priorities.

✓ **Communication:** Able to communicate technical information in an easily understandable way. Recognized for relationship building with team members and clients. An effective listener.

✓ **Personal Attributes:** Innovative problem solver. Committed to goal achievement. Dependable.

EDUCATION

✓ Cybersoft Internet Professional—CIP 1, Cybersoft, Inc., Woodbridge, NJ
December 2003, **Certified e-Business Architect, e-Business for Managers**
December 2002, **Certified Cybersoft Communications 1000** including Fundamentals of Networking, Database, Web Development, Web Design, Multimedia, and Internet Business

✓ Bachelor of Science, Industrial Engineering, Connecticut Institute of Technology

TECHNICAL SKILLS

e-Commerce: e-Business and B2B Infrastructures and Consumer Payment Protocols
Applications: ERP, e-Procurement, Selling Chain Management, Customer Relationship Management
Software Tools: MS Word, MS Excel, MS Access, HTML, MS FrontPage 2000, JavaScript
Operating Systems: Windows NT, Windows 2000, Windows 98

PROFESSIONAL EXPERIENCE

1988–2003 ENGINEERING SYSTEMS, INC., Astro Space Division, Eatontown, NJ
Manufacturing Engineer, Production Engineering Department

Provided assembly documentation and engineering floor support throughout all phases of production flow, including fabrication, assembly, and test operations, for manufacture of diverse satellite products contracted by major government clients (USSA and U.S. Air Force).

ACCOMPLISHMENTS

- Promoted to Team Leader for new equipment installation and upgrades. Performed research and analysis, and tested in production mode. Full authority to sign off on fully tested equipment.

- Reduced cycle time by 30% through development of assembly and test tolling. Improved recycle characteristics and cut hazardous emissions into atmosphere by 40%.

- Collaborated with 60-person design engineering team to ensure that designs were producible in manufacturing environment. Provided cost-effective manufacturing recommendations.

- Trained 8 entry-level engineers in 4-month period to prepare efficient, labor-effective work plans for multi-line production floor in 80,000-square-foot facility.

Career Change: From manufacturing engineering to IT.

Strategy: Showcase recent education and technical skills while also highlighting abilities in team collaboration, project coordination, communications, and problem-solving gained from prior experience.

 **Christine Steile**

2 Denver Court
Brentwood, NY 11717
(631) 766-1003
webdesigner@grafx.net

Seeking a position in Computer Graphics with an emphasis in Web Design

Education

Adelphi University, Garden City, NY
Certificate of Completion, Web Design, 2004

Preston School of Art and Design, New York, NY
Bachelor of Fine Arts, 2000
Concentration, Computer Graphics

Accomplishment
As one of Preston's web project leaders, guided a team of student webmasters recruited to design the school's 125-page website. Successfully optimized the site, achieving top 10 placements in all major search engines.

Computer Proficiencies

Platforms
Macintosh; Windows NT/2000

Web/Graphic Design
Adobe Photoshop, Illustrator, Premiere; QuarkXPress; Macromedia Flash, Dreamweaver, Director; Microsoft FrontPage; JavaScript; HTML

General Software
Microsoft Word, Excel, PowerPoint, FoxPro, Outlook; Easy Mail SMTP Express

Experience Overview

➤ Managing customer service and office support functions within banking and retail sales environments.

➤ Efficiently processing orders, invoices, and job orders.

➤ Streamlining workflow efficiencies and training others.

➤ Interfacing between customers and vendors, exercising strong follow-through and problem-solving skills.

➤ Maintaining account information on data-tracking systems.

➤ Contacting merchants and financial institutions to investigate and resolve transaction disputes.

➤ Monitoring and reconciling account discrepancies.

➤ Received numerous employee recognition awards.

Graphics / Web Design

➤ **Internship Experience**
Produced designs that captured the essence of marketing identities. Demonstrated an eye for color, shape, size, texture, and layout in the creation of promotional materials.

- MAGAZINE LAYOUTS
- CORPORATE LOGOS
- BUSINESS CARDS
- BOOK/CD COVERS
- BROCHURES
- COMMERCIAL WEBSITES
- E-PORTFOLIOS
- ELECTRONIC GREETING CARDS
- BANNER ADVERTISING
- ONLINE NEWSLETTERS

➤ **Academic Experience**
Completed extensive mock projects that incorporated the use of HTML, dynamic databases, templates, images, audio clips, and animation to create online and print materials.

Work History

Account Analyst, Montgomery Bank, Hauppauge, NY, 10/98—Present
Intern Graphic Designer, Dream Designs, Commack, NY, 4/99—10/99
Customer Service Representative, Fashion Frenzy, Huntington, NY, 9/97—4/98
Customer Care Associate, Precision Watches, Hauppauge, NY, 6/94—9/96

Career Change: From customer service to computer graphics.

Strategy: Express creativity while clearly categorizing relevant education, internship experience, and software proficiencies.

RESUME 27: BY PAUL WILLIS, CECC

Brannon P. Donovan

465 Blossom Lane
Cary, North Carolina 27511
brannontech@techline.net

(919) 756-4097 Home
(919) 688-3000 Work
(888) 610-7098 e-Fax
(919) 899-9898 Mobile

OBJECTIVE

IT network management or related network support position that will utilize current qualified training and management skills. Focused on obtaining a technical career with strong management responsibilities in a growth-oriented company.

MCSE and MCP+I Certified

SUMMARY OF QUALIFICATIONS

- *Outstanding analyst and project analyst/team member; a proven high performer able to deliver projects/programs—including help-desk operations, sales support, retail operations/sales, and technical support—and innovative ideas to increase sales, improve productivity, and reduce costs.*
- *Strong background in maintenance with associated mechanical skills/aptitude for technical networking opportunities in any industry.*
- *Extensive experience analyzing methods to improve technical operations environments, including extensive network hardware and software troubleshooting skills.*
- *Solid verbal and written communication skills from management, engineer/IT team, and end-user perspectives. Able to teach and explain highly technical skills in simplified terms so that new technologies can be quickly incorporated into the business development strategy.*
- *A highly dedicated professional with a track record for longevity and organizational loyalty in meeting daily and annual operational and sales objectives.*
- *Known as a valuable team player incorporating fairness, honesty, and a willingness to help others. Able to effectively resolve conflicts at appropriate times and assist new managers and other staff in becoming familiar with policies and operational standards.*

MCSE Focus
Implementing and Supporting Microsoft Windows NT Server 4.0; Windows NT Server 4.0 in the Enterprise; Windows NT Workstation 4; Internetworking with Microsoft TCP/IP on Microsoft Windows NT 4.0; Implementing and Supporting Microsoft Internet Information Server 4.0; Networking Essentials for XP

Networks/Operating Systems/Applications
Windows NT 4.0	*Windows 95/98/XP Home & XP Professional*
Windows NT Server	*Internet Information Server 4.0*
MS Word 2000/XP	*MS Excel*
MS PowerPoint	*MS Internet Explorer 4.0/5.0/6.0*

Hardware
Hands-on experience in assembly and installation of PCs. Understand all aspects of building PCs and installing operating systems, peripherals, and software packages. Configure operating systems (WIN 95, WIN 98, WIN NT, WIN NT Server, WIN XP) for optimum performance.

Network
Experience in installation of peer-to-peer and small client/server networks, including installation of interface cards, cabling, and configuration for file and printer sharing.

Protocols/Setups
TCP/IP, NetBEUI, IPX/SPX, DLC, DHCP, WINS, DNS, RAS

Career Change: *From retail to network management.*

Strategy: *Reflect recent technical certifications while also emphasizing skills and achievements from career experience.*

BRANNON P. DONOVAN   *Page 2*

PROFESSIONAL EXPERIENCE

PEP BOYS, Charlotte, NC, and Raleigh, NC
Store Manager, 1994 to 2002

Selected Achievements:
- *Named to President's Club two consecutive years as recognition for proven performance and leadership.*
- *Trained in an interviewing skills workshop to make hiring decisions for the company.*
- *Reached and exceeded previously unattainable goals at a location with a reputation for a difficult environment.*
- *Increased sales volume 48% during a single fiscal year (1996); this stands as a regional record.*
- *Increased net profit by 72% during two-year track (1998 and 1999).*
- *Reduced shrinkage by 26% average in both 1997 and 1998.*
- *Analyzed and improved departmental operations, resulting in increased productivity. Met and exceeded company goals for all six years, including averaging more than 34% in CSI four years running.*
- *Significantly increased production through departmental changes.*

- Recently selected to assist in a $12 million automation program for all North Carolina stores. Analyzed and identified the best equipment and training for more than 343 employees through written employee reviews, analysis of national plan for network automation, and related Microsoft-sponsored training.

- Totally responsible for team leadership in the generation of new-customer leads from various market opportunities. Developed quality relationship with new customers, offering them a sense of confidence in the business and the new service incentives; this led to five new contracts and two renewals for key commercial accounts.

- Recruited, hired, and trained all management personnel for main store and other stores since 1999.

- Supervised full- and part-time sales associates and managers; scheduled associates to cover the complete work week; controlled store from a managerial standpoint, including recruiting, interviewing, intensive training, supervision, evaluations, and delegation of responsibilities to the rotating shift of employees.

- Motivated and enhanced employee morale, resulting in low turnover and progressive staff development.

- Other special projects included serving as a trainer and representative during an acquisition of a smaller company in Greensboro, North Carolina. This included travel, setup, and automation of new store.

- Supervised setup, remodel, inventory, and sales staff for six new stores over the past five years.

- Directed new-product-development initiatives, including production and marketing strategies, budgeting, cost control, and advertising campaigns. Responsible for purchasing and vendor relations.

- Conducted sales training courses and orientation seminars for new employees since 1996. Provided ongoing assistance in that training process, which included computer training and proprietary Pep Boys software training.

EDUCATION

NORTH CAROLINA STATE UNIVERSITY, Raleigh, NC
- *Certification through NCSU Technical Training Institute*
- *5 semesters of Engineering Studies*
- *3 semesters of Business Management with courses in Accounting, Economics, HRM, and Business Law*

References Available upon Request

GREG DAVIES

189 Delaware Street
Columbus, OH 43206
(614) 204-9912
gregdavies@net.net

ASSOCIATE PRODUCER
– Video Game Industry –

*Combine a passion for video games with exceptional project
management skills and an absolute determination to succeed in the game industry.*

Results-oriented individual committed to building a successful career in the video game industry. Offer a strong background in technical project management, problem-solving expertise, and a proven ability to coordinate the work of teams. Dynamic and entrepreneurial with a track record of meeting deadlines in extremely stressful, fast-paced environments. Strengths include

- ✓ Highly organized with a hands-on approach to project management
- ✓ Extremely knowledgeable about games and the game industry
- ✓ Experienced managing contract and in-house staff
- ✓ Exceptional creative problem-solving skills
- ✓ Frequently recognized for outstanding work performance
- ✓ Strong background in staff development and training

SUMMARY OF QUALIFICATIONS

*Consistently excel when faced with new challenges, especially
when working under pressure or to tight deadlines.*

- ✓ **Organization:** Organized previously chaotic technical consultancy into highly efficient operation. Changes reduced turnaround time from three weeks to seven days and generated a 14% return on sales.

- ✓ **Self-Development:** Obtained four technical certifications, without company sponsorship, by studying after work and on weekends while paying all associated costs.

- ✓ **Performance Excellence:** Received several awards for performance excellence and consistently ranked among the top 10% of regional account executives.

- ✓ **Staff Development:** Developed training for new hires in two different companies in order to increase productivity and reduce errors.

- ✓ **Problem Solving:** Frequently selected to solve challenging technical-support issues despite the presence of more-experienced technicians on staff. Used reverse engineering to resolve many longstanding customer issues that no one else had been able to solve.

- ✓ **Relationship Building:** Turned around problematic relationships with major computer hardware manufacturers such as HP and IBM, with the result that SemTech received valuable assistance and technical support at no cost.

Industry Change: From telecommunications account executive to video game producer.

Strategy: Present accomplishments in areas that will be relevant to senior managers in this industry that is notoriously difficult to enter; include personal qualities to help him stand out as an individual.

GREG DAVIES   PAGE 2

PROFESSIONAL HISTORY

Commitment and exceptional work ethic have brought success in diverse positions and industries.

PACIFIC COMMUNICATIONS, INC., COLUMBUS, OH   2000–PRESENT
Commercial Account Executive

Generate new sales and manage existing accounts in the small to mid-market corporate IT/telecommunications environment.

- Generated $1.3 million in top-line revenue, an increase of 22% over region's prior performance, while consistently ranking among the top 10% of regional account executives over a two-year period.
- Designed training on proprietary CRM software to ensure that new sales reps could produce quickly. This training program was subsequently adopted by Human Resources for use with all new hires.

LEVEL10 COMMUNICATIONS, COLUMBUS, OH   1998–2000
Network Operations Technician

Recognized and resolved problems within legacy network, IP infrastructure, and worldwide frame-relay architecture, which represented 45% of Fortune 500 WAN connectivity.

- Consistently selected to solve challenging technical-support issues. Used reverse engineering to resolve complex customer issues that had been open for more than three days.
- Coordinated and developed new-hire training agenda to teach required technical skills to new associates. Program reduced orientation time from 6 weeks to 14 days.

SEMTECH, COLUMBUS, OH   1997–1998
Consulting Engineer/ Practice Manager

Managed PC hardware troubleshooting and repair for seven major corporations. Maintained database of service calls, product returns, and parts inventory. Diagnosed and fixed technical issues.

- Reduced turnaround time from three weeks to seven days and generated a 14% return on sales by implementing new systems that transformed this previously chaotic technical consultancy.
- Received Compaq five-star ratings for "outstanding service and customer support" for two consecutive quarters. Awarded SemTech Consultant of the Month twice in ten months.

EDUCATION

Demonstrated a continued commitment to personal development since leaving university.

CompaqTIA A+ Software Certification (2000)
CompaqTIA A+ Hardware Certification (1999)
CompaqTIA Network Plus Certification (1999)
Cisco Certified Network Associate (1998)

BS Management Information Systems and Finance, The Ohio State University, Columbus, OH (1997)

PROFESSIONAL ASSOCIATIONS

Member, International Game Developers Association (IGDA), 2000–Present

RESUME 29: BY DIANE BURNS, CPRW, CCMC, CCM, CEIP, JCTC

Jane M. Goodson

2398 Melancholy Lane * Columbia, MD 21045 * 410-555-3490 * jmgood@hotmail.com

CAREER FOCUS

Chief Information Officer ~ IT Director

PERSONAL & PROFESSIONAL VALUE OFFERED

Optimize your business investments with realistic IT solutions, build high levels of customer satisfaction, and bridge the gap between management and techies with a skilled business manager and IT professional proficient in the following:

· Policy Development	· Strategic Planning	· Leadership & Team Management
· Organizational Skills	· System Administration	· Computer Espionage & Security
· Financial Management	· Operational Procedures	· IT Implementation & Operations
· EDI Management	· Training/Staff Development	· Problem Solving & Analysis
· Web Design & Hosting	· High-Level Briefings	· Quality Customer Service
· Interpersonal Skills	· Federal & Corporate Contracts	· Oral & Written Communications

Technical Proficiencies & Tools

Coldfusion · HTML · MS FrontPage · JavaScript · SAP · Clarify · MS Office Suite · MS Project 2000 · Lotus 1-2-3 · MS-DOS · Ventura · Expert System · Expert Choice · WordPerfect 4.0 and 5.0 · Macintosh desktop publishing software and hardware applications · PageMaker · Mac Draw · Peachtree · Harbinger · SQL · Oracle · Sun System · WANG · Macintosh · IBM PC

Career Highlights

- More than 15 years of experience as a proven leader in technology management with working knowledge of computer platforms, applications, measurement systems, and performance standards. Able to teach/train others in such technology. Consistently worked in high-technology industries.

- **Certified CIO through the Office of Personnel Management and the University of Virginia.** Only three universities offer this new CIO Certification program, which is supported and backed by the U.S. federal government to bridge the digital divide within government agencies. Familiar with researching, analyzing, identifying, and developing strategic plans and objectives for the implementation and use of IT.

- Accomplished professional lauded for refined interpersonal and public communications abilities. Poised and polished public speaker. Articulate writer.

PROFESSIONAL EXPERIENCE

Motorola, U.S. Federal Government Market Division (USFGMD), MD   1994–Present
* *Motorola is a major manufacturer and seller of two-way communication equipment.*

Sales Account Manager, 2000–Present
- Manage 300 Department of Labor, Army Corps of Engineers, U.S. Navy, and Naval Ship accounts. Consistently generate new accounts. Started 2001 with a $3M quota and exceeded the quota by 30% by summer 2001, growing accounts by more than 26%.
- Determine strategies for the development of two-way communication systems, including wireless LANS, Voiceover IP, and VPNs. Assess technologies and the IT direction of each client. Formulate plans, determine upgrades or migrations for systems, and implement solutions to facilitate and strengthen the cost effectiveness and efficiency of IT and wireless solutions.
- Provide clients with superior customer service. Develop quotes, manage customer service problems/issues, and follow up on delivery. Conduct user training, on site or via telephone.
- Suggest appropriate systems, operations, and integration of new systems. Guide customers in understanding where new technology can add value while supporting or transforming program operations. Provide immediate technical support for information systems or telecommunications systems.

Career Change: *From sales manager to Chief Information Officer.*

Strategy: *Focus on IT and management skills, with technology expertise and recent certification as added value.*

Jane M. Goodson, Page 2

Web Master & EDI Manager (Concurrent Assignment), 1999–Present
- Independently researched, built, and maintained Electronic Data Interface transactions with various federal government agencies with more than 500 accounts and web-based technology for two of Motorola's divisions.
- Spearheaded the division's EDI objectives and maintained the department's web page. Worked with a web development team to determine content, placement, and accomplishment timelines. The company desired to be presented as superior in a web display to the world.
- Created the idea for a web page and brought the division in line with current-day technology with a web-based presence. Led a team to create, develop, upload, and maintain the department's web page.

Collection Manager & Web Master, 1995–2000
- Provided a superior level of customer satisfaction related to the maintenance and collection of accounts receivable generated by the sale of Motorola Parts and Equipment to the federal government. Supervised, trained, and evaluated a staff of four. Interfaced with division and field finance personnel.
- Instrumental in the creation and implementation of strategies and action plans. Co-wrote the collection and credit policy, and revised and updated outdated regulations. Managed international business and updated/implemented international collections policy, a subset of departmental policy. Handled European transactions and led a team responsible for Asia, South America, and Africa.
- Wrote a user-friendly collections guidance manual for junior employees, reducing the confusion in the department. Streamlined procedures to one plan and eliminated employees asking repeated questions.
- Member of the Critical Differences Total Customer Satisfaction (TCS) Team and Legacy. Discussed and recommended working solutions to complex customer problems and difficult customer issues.

Desktop Publishing Specialist, 1994–1995
- Assigned to Motorola, Inc., as a Macintosh subject-matter expert and Temporary Credit Analyst. Troubleshot programs and ensured computers were up and running. Designed a policy manual.

United States Marines, Active Duty, The Pentagon   **1990–1994**
Reserves (Called to active duty during Operation Iraqi Freedom)   **1994–present**

Intelligence Specialist (TS/SBI Clearance), Active Duty **Soldier** of the Year, 1993 *(Distinguished Professional)*
- Supervised and trained a team of six personnel that produced and distributed a daily, 18-page classified newsletter for the White House and Joint Chiefs of Staff.
- Presented high-level briefings and prepared briefing products and reports. Enforced cyber-security measures. Implemented communications security protocols.
- Instrumental in the integration of a new state-of-the-art desktop publishing system.
- Developed and published a comprehensive series of Standard Operating Procedures that served as a valuable tool for the conduct of the office during manpower turnovers and shortages.
- Participated in setting up the initial operating procedures for the secure video teleconferencing link that supported the daily morning brief to the Director of Marine Intelligence and his staff.
- Quickly mastered the procedures maintaining the office ADP system. Trained all incoming personnel.

EDUCATION

- **MS in Information Technology,** University of Virginia, Richmond, VA, May 2003
- *Certified CIO*, Office of Personnel Management and the University of Virginia (21 continuing-education credits), July 2002
- **BS** in Business Administration, University of Virginia, Richmond, VA, May 1995

CHAPTER 6

Resumes for Career Changers Seeking Sales, Marketing, Advertising, Public Relations, Writing, and Events Management Positions

To facilitate a successful transition to a sales or marketing career, resumes in this chapter highlight relevant knowledge and—wherever possible—proven abilities in the important functions of communica-tion, persuasion, and presentation.

- Network engineer to sales representative
- Software developer to sales/customer service professional
- Police officer to sales representative
- Flight attendant to pharmaceutical sales representative.
- Respiratory therapist to pharmaceutical sales representative
- Teacher to sales representative
- Nurse to sales professional
- Counselor to pharmaceutical sales representative
- Medical researcher to medical device sales professional
- Small business owner to pharmaceutical sales rep
- Paint-store manager to sales representative or sales manager
- Auto technician to marketing professional
- Pharmacist to marketing professional
- Fashion designer and medical office manager to marketing/PR
- Human resources to marketing/PR
- Retail manager to marketing professional
- Massage therapist to writer/editor
- Academic advisor to writer
- Underwriter to event manager
- Entrepreneur to marketing and events management

RESUME 30: BY MICHAEL LEVY, CPRW, CEIP, MCDP, PHR, GCDFI

JOHN E. COOPER

822 Clayton Street
N. Las Vegas, Nevada 89032

Residence: (702) 938-5802
Cell: (702) 573-8137

Email: JohnEcooper@cox.net

TECHNICAL SALES REPRESENTATIVE
TECHNOLOGY / COMMUNICATIONS / MANUFACTURING
First-class customer service—increased company revenue $3 million

AS400, Cisco, WAN, Routers, Hubs, Switches, Network Servers, Lotus Notes, Visio, ATM

- Account Development
- Customer Needs Assessment
- Global Marketing Strategies
- Client Relationship Management
- Team Building and Leadership
- Vendor Negotiations
- Consulting
- Revenue Growth
- Technical Knowledge

Organized and self-directed manager with 15+ years of experience in the technology industry. Excellent communicator and sound decision maker with proven people skills. Consistently delivered multimillion-dollar projects on time and within budget. Trained new technicians and developed processes.

PROFESSIONAL EXPERIENCE

Network Design Engineer   1999–Present
Sprint, Las Vegas, NV

Developed and maintain up to 225 business-to-business sales accounts both nationally and internationally. Supervise a team of 14. Coordinate with departments to prepare cost-effective solutions, provide buyer satisfaction, and create profits for the company.

- Achieved 25% reduction in customer turnaround and product delivery time—set a benchmark standard.
- Teamed with department heads to create an automated PC tool that enhanced tracking, coordination, and process flow.
- Brought customer service back online within 72 hours after 9/11 disaster.

Network Design Engineer   1987–1999
Qwest Corporation, Denver, CO

Managed multi-network accounts throughout the United States, Europe, and South America. Prepared design and managed delivery to customers; assisted the sales teams in product review for cost-effective solutions for customers; monitored customer networks to ensure 100% usage of circuits.

- Enhanced the profit picture by ensuring 100% accountability for 200+ client accounts.
- Created a test system to identify potential configuration problems—saved time and expense.
- Reduced wasted duplication, met deadlines, and improved efficiency of information by maintaining close communication with other department managers.

Network Technician   1986–1987
Level 3 Communications, Denver, CO

Lead technician overseeing the technical training, keeping informed of latest technology, managing customer accounts, and solving high-level problems.

- Developed a technician hands-on training process that reduced learning curve of new technicians.
- Initiated a high-speed upgrade project to support 800+ branch offices—the project was self-funded, was completed six weeks ahead of schedule, and returned $3 million to the company.

OTHER EXPERIENCE

Line Chief, Jet Maintenance, United States Air Force

EDUCATION AND CERTIFICATIONS

Louisiana State University, Baton Rouge, LA
Studies in Business (2 years completed)

Pace University, New York, NY
Certified in Network Skills (12-week course)

Career Change: *From network engineer to sales representative.*

Strategy: *Emphasize relevant technical knowledge, along with proven ability to work with people as demonstrated by delivering training and developing vendor and business relationships.*

RESUME 31: BY BARBARA POOLE, CPRW, CRW, CCMC

MARK J. DIXON

891 Arbor Lakes Parkway ▪ Maple Grove, MN 55311 ▪ (763) 555-8291 ▪ marjkdixon@qwestmsn.com

SALES / CUSTOMER SERVICE / OPERATIONS

A results-oriented professional with extensive experience in client relations. Excellent sales skills include thorough product knowledge and the ability to convey all pertinent facts to customers, staff, and management. Demonstrated ability in assessing problem areas and offering recommendations that profitably impact the bottom line.

AREAS OF EXPERTISE

Client Services ▪ Sales ▪ Marketing ▪ Prospecting ▪ Vendor Relations
▪ Complex Project Planning & Management ▪ Cross-Functional Training & Leadership ▪ Technology

SUCCESSES

SALES & MARKETING

- Closed sales and doubled business for an e-commerce leader and Top-10 revenue-based e-tailer.
- Featured multiple times in the *Minneapolis Star & Tribune* for building community-focused revenues.
- Generated new business in broad consumer markets ranging from health care to nail polish.
- Employed cold-call, referral, and other prospecting methods. Assessed client needs and made effective sales presentations, often involving technical product details. Commended by executives for "smooth" presentations.
- Performed research, promotions, and forecasting techniques to penetrate markets with an 80% success rate.

CUSTOMER CARE & COMMUNICATIONS

- Built and nurtured relationships with clients and member customers in reduced-pricing, partner-store purchasing, and redemption-center transactions with a blend of consumer products. Grew client base 70% in one year.
- Interacted with customers both in person and in a call-center environment.
- Commended by customers for positive attitude and willingness to go beyond the requirements of the job.
- Conducted customer needs assessments and illustrated cost-effective benefits and solutions.
- Coordinated a matrix of technical support services for small to large organizations, both for- and nonprofit.
- Officiated adaptive sports for a Minnesota statewide nonprofit association of public and private schools.

OPERATIONS & TECHNOLOGY

- Trained numerous individuals at all levels to effectively use state-of-the-art information technology.
- Led all phases of operations and project management; recognized for team-building skills and the ability to motivate others on all levels in the achievement of individual and organizational goals.
- Developed project specifications and communicated project goals to cross-functional technology teams.
- Considered technology "go-to" person for many organizations: MS Office software, web technology, programming languages, operating systems, and database technologies in systems design and implementation.

WORK HISTORY

SOFTWARE DEVELOPER, Milton Corporation (subsidiary of Darnet Enterprises, Inc.)—Minneapolis, MN   1989–present

PRIOR TECHNOLOGY POSITIONS   Pre–1989
- Supported the University of Minnesota's student recruitment technology; led Honeywell's technology support for HealthLine, Inc.'s online wellness education; and provided contracted systems development and support for the Minnesota Timberwolves, Aerospace, Children's Hospital, Grand Casino, and other organizations.

EDUCATION

Sales, Customer Service, Communications & Operations, METROPOLITAN UNIVERSITY—Minneapolis, MN
Graduate: Programming Technology, ST. PAUL TECHNICAL COLLEGE—Minneapolis, MN

Career Change: *From software developer to sales/customer service professional.*

Strategy: *Create a skills-based, functional resume that emphasizes relevant experience under an attention-getting "Successes" headline.*

TERENCE KEENAN

344-02 Parsons Blvd., Flushing, NY 11355 • 718-660-9033 • TKeenan@netway.net

ROUTE DISTRIBUTION

Five years of experience in route distribution preceding a 20-year career in law enforcement. Offer an impeccable New York State driving record and a proficiency in 18-wheeler operations. Work well with diverse populations and expertly handle potentially threatening situations throughout urban communities. Maintain a high energy level and strong stamina required for lifting heavy loads and working long hours in inclement conditions.

Select Areas of Qualification:

- Beverage Route Distribution
- Product Sales & Marketing
- Customer Service Excellence

- Promotional Display Merchandising
- Customer Needs Assessment
- Security Enforcement/Theft Control

- Purchasing/Inventory Control
- Receivables/Collections
- Vehicle Maintenance/Repair

Relevant Experience — *Route Distribution*

ROUTE DRIVER / SALES REPRESENTATIVE
Long Island Beverage Distributors, Bay Shore, NY, 1979–1984

- Recipient of 15 quarterly recognition awards for *Top Sales Production* and *Performance Excellence.*
- Managed a route distribution of Barley's Brew throughout competitive Suffolk County sales territories.
- Serviced an account base of 25–40 daily stops that included bars, restaurants, supermarkets, and delicatessens.
- Monitored and replenished daily/weekly inventory levels, and consistently met delivery schedules on time.
- Expertly managed tailgate deliveries and forklift operations for volume product loading and unloading.
- Effectively negotiated sales agreements and terms with potential and existing clients.
- Maintained ongoing expenses for inventory and vehicle maintenance; collected accounts receivable.
- Supported customers' merchandising needs with window displays and relevant promotional materials.
- Responded to customer requests, resolving problems directly and through appropriate channels.

Career History — *Law Enforcement*

POLICE OFFICER
109th Precinct, Flushing, NY, 1984–Present

- Currently work with the New York State Police Department/New York State Parole Department as part of a Joint Task Force to track and apprehend parole violators throughout all areas of the five boroughs.
- As part of the Department's specialized training, recently completed extensive criminal investigative studies in Forensic Science, Automotive Crime, and Organized Crime through the New York City Police Academy.
- Throughout career, worked collaboratively with all Bronx County precincts (nine) and numerous Brooklyn North precincts on diverse cases and assignments in high-crime vicinities throughout all five boroughs.
- Trained Academy recruits in all aspects of foot, car, and scooter patrol of high-crime areas.
- Extensively experienced in undercover surveillance work in connection with robberies and drug trafficking.

Education

John Jay College of Criminal Justice, New York, NY
Associate in Applied Science, Criminal Justice, 1984

Career Change: *From police officer to sales representative.*

Strategy: *Bring to the forefront similar experience, even though it occurred more than 20 years ago.*

DIANE M. SEYFERTH

122 N. Telegraph ▪ Southfield, MI 48024
(248) 555-3456 ▪ seyferth@aol.com

Highly motivated and results-driven professional seeking **Pharmaceutical Sales Representative** position to accelerate sales growth through effective product education and extensive relationship building.

SUMMARY OF QUALIFICATIONS

- ✓ Persistent in pursuit to build sales and provide solutions according to identified customer needs.
- ✓ Strong customer-service orientation as demonstrated by commendations earned while working for high-profile corporations, including Southwest Airlines—recognized for unparalleled service.
- ✓ Familiar with medical terminology and able to convey complex concepts in simpler terms.
- ✓ Frequently chosen for prime assignments based on performance and job dedication.
- ✓ Professional, confident demeanor; excellent public-speaking skills; willing to work extended hours.

Strengths: Goal Attainment ▪ Persuasion Skills ▪ Needs Assessment ▪ Time Management

RELATED EXPERIENCE

SALES
- One of selected few chosen to participate in sales campaign designed to promote new services within new-growth market. Utilized consultative-sales approach to educate customers on service packages and incentive programs, emphasizing advantages and features. Employed suggestive-selling strategy to maximize individual sales while selling travel packages to customers.

CUSTOMER SERVICE
- Recruited to serve needs of international dignitaries of presidential stature based on outstanding customer-service skills. Supported diverse needs of up to 137 customers daily through attentive, responsive service. Responded effectively to inquiries of up to 150 phone customers daily. Remained current on service packages and options to ensure accuracy of rapidly changing service information.

MEDICAL
- Assisted with medical situations of passengers suffering from cardiac arrest, strokes, hypoxia, diabetic comas, and Alzheimer's. Interfaced with doctors and medical professionals during medical situations. Volunteered for Airline Crisis Team to assist in emergency-recovery efforts. Participated in annual training seminars to remain current on medical procedures.

COMMUNICATIONS / PRESENTATIONS
- Educated groups of 100+ individuals on policies and practices. Communicated clearly and effectively with dignitaries, executives, colleagues, and customers. Wrote copy to generate interest in current events and stories presented by anchors of news station (during internship).

WORK HISTORY

Flight Attendant, Southwest Airlines, Detroit, MI, 1995–Present
Customer Service Representative / Flight Attendant, America West Airlines, Detroit, MI, 1987–1995
Corporate Flight Attendant, Execujet / Aramco Associated Company, Detroit, MI, 1992–1994

EDUCATION / TRAINING

Bachelor of Arts in Communications, University of Michigan, Ann Arbor, MI

Career Change: *From flight attendant to pharmaceutical sales representative.*

Strategy: *Bring relevant experience to the top and enhance its value by emphasizing other related areas that contribute to her capabilities. The bold subheadings call attention to the necessary skills.*

Colleen Quinn

Home: (937) 332-5390 | Cell: (937) 289-9875
1621 Southgate Circle, Troy, OH 45373

PHARMACEUTICAL SALES CANDIDATE with a track record in the Medical Field

Respiratory Therapist who has demonstrated and instructed on medical equipment and holds intimate knowledge of select medications covering patients with chronic lung problems such as asthma, bronchitis, and emphysema. Experienced in using a variety of inhaled bronchodilators and steroids to help treat and control patients with breathing problems. Capable of securing new business through aggressive sales and lead cultivation with physicians, medical facilities, and hospitals, while overseeing the complete sales lifecycle—from initial contact to sales closure. Possess a rapport with physicians, physician assistants, nurses, and medical interns.

Foundation in the medical arena will assist with:

Market Reach & Expansion • Sales Presentations • Territory Growth
Client Base Development • Sales & Marketing Strategies • Relationship Maintenance
B2B Customer Case • Lead Generation & Cold Calling • Sales-cycle Management
Business Development • Customer Need Assessments • Emerging Markets

---

EDUCATION / CERTIFICATION / TRAINING

B.S., Respiratory Care, 1996
Wright State University, Dayton, OH

Certificate, Registered Respiratory Therapist, Ohio Dept. of Health for Respiratory Therapy

Training: Pediatric Advanced Life Support, Advanced Cardiac Life Support, Neonatal Advanced Life Support; Pulmicort and Racemic Epi medications; ventilators and BIPAP equipment

---

PROFESSIONAL EXPERIENCE

RESPIRATORY THERAPIST, 2000–present   Kettering Memorial Hospital, Dayton, OH

Provide respiratory care, such as administering medications and assisting with treatments and equipment, for adult and geriatric patients. Deliver and set up mechanical ventilation, connect cardiac monitors, and work with physicians pertaining to patient treatments: inhaled aerosol and MDIs, pulmonary function and stress tests, and EKGs/ABGs. Instruct patients and family members in the use of home respiratory equipment and medications. Discuss with physicians the current and future use of respiratory medications and treatments for patients with respiratory ailments. Assist the emergency room and ICU with intubations and cardiopulmonary resuscitation efforts in critical care situations. Explain medications and therapy to patients, including side effects and benefits.

RESPIRATORY THERAPIST, 1997–2000   Franciscan Medical Center, Dayton, OH

Oversaw respiratory care to Pediatric and Neonatal units, tracked patient progress, and trained and advised patients and staff on equipment and medications.

HOME HEALTH EQUIPMENT DELIVERY, 1993–1997   US Health Equipment, Montgomery, OH

Trained and educated patients and family members on the features and proper use of home health equipment. Answered questions pertaining to usability or maintenance of equipment. Conducted patient follow-up every 3 months to inform physicians of status and to voice concerns regarding patient progress or other complications that deterred patient recovery. Networked with physicians and medical staff; attended meetings to discuss the use and delivery of home health equipment. Demonstrated respiratory care equipment to hospital staff and outlined the process for patient evaluation and instruction.

Career Change: *From respiratory therapist to pharmaceutical sales representative.*

Strategy: *Write a strong introduction that relates health care experience, knowledge, and skills to the demands of a career in pharmaceutical sales.*

Edward King

5 Falling Ledge Lane • The Woodlands, Texas 77381 • (936) 273-6785

QUALIFICATIONS PROFILE
Sales & Business Development

Well-educated professional offering a unique combination of professional skills. Successful educator and sales manager with core competencies in sales development, sales presentations, competitive market positioning, customer relationship management, teaching, training, and coaching. Excellent communication, organizational, and planning skills.

SALES EXPERIENCE

DIAMOND INTERNATIONAL, INC., Ontario, Canada   2002–Present
Area Manager & Distributor, Plink-o
Recruited by this Canadian-based vending machine manufacturer as an exclusive distributor to sell/lease a new product, "Plink-o Money Machine," to restaurants, convenience stores, and other retail establishments in Houston area. Assumed full responsibility for cold-calling and canvassing, sales presentations, contract negotiations, product delivery, and follow up. **Exceeded sales goal by 15%.**

TEACHING EXPERIENCE

Fifteen years of experience as a **Special Education Teacher** employed on educational grants within Texas, Massachusetts, New York, and New Hampshire. Taught all academic subjects and social and life skills to learning-handicapped, cognitively disabled, and emotionally disturbed youths in grades 5–12.

Houston School District, Houston, Texas	(2000–2001)
Nashua Children's Home, Nashua, New Hampshire	(1999–2000)
Worcester Public Schools, Worcester, Massachusetts	(1997–1999)
Seacoast Learning Collaborative, Kingston, New Hampshire	(1993–1996)
Crockett Intermediate School, Conroe, Texas	(1990–1992)
FM Black Middle School, Houston, Texas	(1989–1990)
Erasmus Hall High School, Brooklyn, New York	(1987–1988)

ACCOLADES FROM SENIOR MANAGERS

"Ed was extremely conscientious and worked hard to develop support programs for students…a dedicated professional."
Krista Osborn, Principal, Houston School District

"Ed shows a general desire to serve the children in his care…always presents himself in a professional manner."
Joanne Burdett Dion, Educational Director, Nashua Children's Home

"Ed's lesson plans were some of the best from my school, and he implemented them with success…his teaching style is firm yet flexible, caring and professional."
Jo Ann Beken, Principal, Worcester Public Schools

"You were our anchor in the BAC program…you did a great job in a tough situation."
Bourke Meagher, Principal, FM Black Middle School

EDUCATION

St. John's University, New York, New York, **MS, Special Education**
St. John's University, New York, New York, **BS, Management**
State of Texas General Special Education Certification • **Certified Special Olympics Coach**

Career Change: *From teacher to sales representative.*

Strategy: *Concentrate on recent part-time sales experience and downplay teaching career. Use quotes as strong endorsements.*

RESUME 36: BY JANICE M. SHEPHERD, CPRW, JCTC, CEIP

SUSAN JUSTIN

7777 Freesia Lane, Seattle, WA 98136
phone: 206-777-8767 — pager: 206-348-9021
susanjustin@email.com

Result-oriented self-starter seeking a position in SALES. Present a positive, professional attitude; thrive on challenge; work hard and passionately—always in the spirit of customer service. Demonstrate acute business insight with conceptual talent for seeing "the big picture" along with expertise in strategic planning, organizational development, team building, and staff enhancement. Willing to relocate.

QUALIFICATIONS

- Outstanding communication and presentation skills, articulate and expressive—able to tailor information to audience from laymen to experts, and diplomatically and persuasively relate new concepts and ideas—enhanced by medical training and experience.
- Talent for generating enthusiasm—use timely sense of humor to illustrate a point.
- Strong analytical, problem-solving, decision-making, and time-management skills.
- Strategic thinker, able to synthesize information quickly.

CAREER HISTORY

Staff RN, Critical Care Unit/Cardiovascular/Emergency/Special Procedures
St. Sophia Hospital, Benning, WA   3/2000–present
Travel Contract, Post-Anesthesia Unit
Petula Nielson Medical Center, Nielson, CA   11/99–2/2000
Travel Contract, Emergency Services
Nielson Medical Clinic, Nielson, CA   7/99–11/99
Travel Contract, Post-Anesthesia Care Unit
St. Agnes Medical Center, Liberty, CA   4/99–7/99
Travel Contract, Post-Anesthesia Care Unit
Liberty Community Medical Center, Liberty, CA   1/99–4/99
Agency Nurse, ICU, PACU, and ER for 5 metro-area hospitals
Health Care Staffing, Dover, CO   1/98–12/98
Staff RN, Intensive Care Unit
Columbia Medical Care Center of Denver, Denver, CO   1/97–12/98
Staff RN, Float Pool
St. Sophia Hospital, Benning, WA   7/95–10/96
Staff RN, Medical/Surgical Unit
Presbyterian–St. Luke's Hospital, Denver, CO   10/94–7/95

EDUCATION

B.S., Nursing, Creighton University, 1993
B.A., Humanities, Colorado State University, 1989

ACCREDITATIONS

Nursing Licenses—Washington, California, Colorado

Member—American Nurses Association; Washington State Nurses Association

Certifications—Advanced Cardiac Life Support, Pediatric Advanced Life Support, Trauma Nurse

Member—Air and Surface Transport Nurses Association

"...work ethic is outstanding...a pleasant person...willing and rapid learner...." JT, M.D.

"...good communication style and deals with problems directly... strong leadership and management qualities...." TCR, St. Sophia Hospital

"...a winning personality...very calm, level-headed...performs well under pressure... well respected among her peers...strong leadership abilities... able to communicate clearly and concisely...." MW, Lieutenant, U.S. Army Reserve

"...independent and knowledgeable and enjoys educating colleagues and patients alike...maturity and experience necessary to be a success...." SLK, Captain, U.S. Naval Reserve

---

Career Change: *From nurse to sales professional.*

Strategy: *Emphasize qualifications and spice up the resume with powerful and relevant quotes.*

John J. Cochran

16533 Sky Ranch Road
San Diego, CA 92138

Office: 619-555-6257   jjcochran@aol.com   Mobile: 619-555-5740

TERRITORY SALES—CUSTOMER SERVICE—BUSINESS DEVELOPMENT
PHARMACEUTICAL, MEDICAL EQUIPMENT, HEALTHCARE MANAGEMENT ORGANZATIONS

PROFILE

Results-driven professional with a career distinguished by consistent performance within both small and large organizations—focus on service organizations—operating in diverse business cultures, industries, and markets. Offer high-caliber cross-functional management qualifications and proven leadership talents. Strong orientations in business development, relationship management, and performance improvement. Highly motivated, innovative, and creative, with a big-picture perspective. Analytical, logical, and resourceful in approach to prospecting, relationship building, problem solving, and decision-making. Honest, ethical, and effective.

— Licensed Professional Counselor —

CORE QUALIFICATIONS

Strategic Business Planning	Team Building & Leadership
Organization & Follow-through	Purposeful Listening & Needs Assessment
New Business & Account Development	Solutions & Relationship Sales
Customer Relations & Negotiations	Persuasive Communication Skills
Account Revitalization	Large Group / Small Group Presentations

PROFESSIONAL EXPERIENCE

JOHN J. COCHRAN, MA, LPC COUNSELING, INC.—San Diego, CA   1992–Present

Owner, Licensed Professional Counselor serving largely physician and executive client base using cognitive-behavioral psychotherapeutic approaches and methodologies.

- Increased client base 300% in first two years of practice using aggressive, six-step solution-selling technique: approach, interview, demonstrate, validate, negotiate, close.

HUMANA HOSPITAL ACADEMY OF MENTAL HEALTH—San Leandro, CA   1980–1992

Executive Director, reporting to the Board of Directors, responsible for its 260-outpatient base, providing individual and group counseling on addictive behaviors.

EDUCATION & PROFESSIONAL ACTIVITIES / AFFILIATIONS

MA, Counseling—CALIFORNIA SCHOOL OF PROFESSIONAL PSYCHOLOGY, Los Angeles, CA
BS, Industrial Engineering—UNIVERSITY OF ILLINOIS, Chicago, IL

Keynote speaker—January 2000, New York Life Insurance Co.—*"Tying Self-Motivation to Performance"*
Ethics Committee Chair, California Counseling Association (CCA)

PROFESSIONAL REFERRALS

"Through his private practice, John has worked together closely with physicians and medical offices. He is well apprised of the intricacies of the medical services environment as well as familiar with the pharmacological therapies used for disorders of the nervous system. He is an excellent candidate for a medical-type services sales representative position ... I am sure that he will meet and exceed all expectations."
—Clarissa Schick Howisson, Ph.D., DABR, Chief, Division of Radiotherapy Medical Physics, University of California Medical Sciences Medical Center

"I have been in the practice of medicine for thirty-four years and have dealt with pharmaceutical representatives for all of them. I have known John for twelve years and have always been impressed with his communication skills and his ability to build and sustain an outstanding rapport with a wide range of professionals. I believe he will be much superior to the 'typical' sales representative that I see on a daily basis. I can guarantee that he will be an asset to any company."
—Richard G. Sullivan, MD

Career Change: *From counselor to pharmaceutical sales representative.*

Strategy: *Relate professional experience in the health care field to the challenge of a sales career. Enhance the resume with strong professional referrals from individuals in the medical field.*

J. PETER KESTER

421 Everwood Drive
Nashville, Tennessee 37220

Cellular 615.414.2374
jpeterkester@hotmail.com

Career Focus → MEDICAL DEVICE SALES

RESULTS-DRIVEN HEALTHCARE PROFESSIONAL proven to be a key contributor to business growth, team productivity, and operating efficiency. Background includes more than five years of experience in clinical-trial services, marketing, and physician recruitment for a leading clinical research organization. Additional experience in sales, promotions, small business management, and veterinary lab procedures. Thorough understanding of medical and pharmaceutical terminology, physician- and hospital-contract pricing, clinical-trials monitoring, Good Clinical Practices (GCPs), FDA regulations, and statistical reporting. Bachelor of Science degree.

KEY STRENGTHS

- **Communication**—Articulate and persuasive communicator with well-developed presentation and negotiation skills. Deliver high-impact presentations that communicate value and benefit to physicians and other key decision-makers. Effectively convey complex, technical information in meaningful terms. Strong statistical report-writing and documentation skills.

- **Relationship Management**—Cultivate and nurture profitable relationships with physicians, healthcare providers, senior management, and team members. Experienced in managing, training, supporting, and motivating team members. Effective business liaison and group facilitator.

- **Business Development**—Implement physician- and patient-recruitment strategies to ensure successful clinical-study enrollment. Proven history of achieving business-development and sales-performance goals in small-business environments. Proactive in cold calling and pursuing referrals to generate qualified leads.

Professional Experience

INFO CLINICAL RESEARCH, INC.—Nashville, Tennessee.. 1998–Present

A full-service Clinical Research Organization that manages Phases I to IV clinical-research studies ranging in size from small, local trials to large, global programs. Services include clinical research, biometrics, interactive technologies, laboratory, clinical pharmacology, and consulting services.

Advanced rapidly through a series of increasingly responsible clinical-research monitoring positions, earning five promotions in five years.

Therapeutic areas of experience include gastrointestinal system (IBS), skin and soft tissue (antibiotic), urinary system (antibiotic), and central-nervous system (migraine, post-operative pain management, and cognitive disorder).

Lead Clinical Research Associate (2002–Present)
Promoted to manage 10- to 15-member study team assigned to investigational-study sites and coordinate all study activities. Conduct weekly meetings with sponsor and CRAs, delegate team responsibilities, conduct site visits, and perform on-site quality reviews. Monitor study progress and serve as primary resource for team members regarding study-related issues.
- Identify and recruit physicians for study participation—generate physician leads through cold-calling techniques, evaluate their interest in study participation, motivate them to achieve recruitment targets, and train them on FDA regulations and protocol compliance.
- Deliver cost-proposal presentations to physicians that outline the full scope of ICR's service capabilities, highlight clinical team-management approach, and effectively justify cost proposals.
- Implement patient recruitment/outreach campaigns to maximize clinical-study enrollment. Marketing strategies include creative advertising; motivational site visits; newsletter, phone, and fax communiqués; and bonus incentives.

Career Change: From medical researcher to medical device sales professional.

Strategy: Emphasize persuasive skills used in his prior career, and pull out sales-related activities and skills from his earlier, less relevant experience.

Cellular 615.414.2374	**J. PETER KESTER**	Page Two

Professional Experience—Continued

Senior Clinical Research Associate (2001–2002)
Managed investigational (physician) study sites, including on-site monitoring, study-team management, new CRA training and assistance, and physician recruitment.
- Generated Study Specific Procedures (SSPs) for approval by sponsor companies.
- Created clinical-tracking system at beginning of each study to evaluate site performance.

Clinical Research Associate II (2000–2001)   **Clinical Monitor** (1998–1999)
Clinical Research Associate (1999–2000)   **Clinical Research Assistant** (1998)
Managed 10 to 15 investigational-study sites across the U.S., conducting routine on-site monitoring visits and acting as secondary resource for CRAs regarding study-related issues.
- Maintained query rate of <0.05% with research data submitted to sponsor.
- Completed in-house presentation training required by INFO Standard Operating Procedures (SOPs).

Additional Experience

LANDSCAPE & PROPERTY MAINTENANCE SERVICES—Nashville, Tennessee 1995–1998

General Manager
Provided landscaping and property-maintenance services to client base in the Belmont University community. Determined pricing, handled billing and bookkeeping activities, and hired and supervised contract workers during peak seasons.
- Developed business from initial concept and startup. Grew business from zero to 20 clients and expanded client base primarily through networking and referrals.
- Coordinated property maintenance for rental duplex with frequent tenant turnover. Prepared property for new tenants, including overseeing electrical and painting subcontractors and completion of project punchlist.

FIRECRACKER FIREWORKS—Nashville, Tennessee 1996–1997

Sales Representative
Managed all aspects of fireworks sales projects—site selection, tent set-up, inventory selection, merchandise displays, advertising and promotions, and sales performance.
- Achieved notable sales success in concentrated, seasonal sales cycle. Challenged during second season to manage and coordinate sales activities in larger market with greater sales potential.

BELMONT ANIMAL HOSPITAL—Nashville, Tennessee... 1993–1994

Laboratory Technician
Performed routine laboratory and clinical procedures—obtained blood samples, assisted with surgical procedures, prepared prescriptions, and advised pet owners on medication administration.
- Acquired hands-on experience with veterinary-medical equipment, including centrifuge, autoclave, and various surgical instruments.

Education and Technical Skills

Degree: **BACHELOR OF SCIENCE**—1997
                     Belmont University—Nashville, Tennessee
                     Pre-Med Curriculum—Major: Biology—Minor: Chemistry

Technical Skills: Proficient with Microsoft Office (Word, Excel, PowerPoint, Access, Publisher, Outlook), Adobe Photoshop, Citrix Clinical Trial Management software, and Internet protocols. Confident in learning and using new business applications.

JENNA B. WHITE

5900 Witte Road ▸ Turney, Missouri 64493
Residence: 816-632-5555 ▸ Cell: 816-632-5556 ▸ jennawhite@centurytel.net

SALES/MARKETING PROFESSIONAL

AGGRESSIVE/RESULT-DRIVEN SALES PROFESSIONAL with a consultative approach to customer service and a genuine commitment to customer satisfaction. Proven leader with an eye to the bottom line and record of double-digit-percentage revenue growth. Combine confident communication skills with a contagious enthusiasm and demonstrated ease in conversing across diverse audiences. Strong influencing skills exhibited among entry-level, professional, and senior-level executives and within the medical community (physicians/nurses). Possess an unshakable determination when challenged with strong personalities, demanding deadlines, and the rigorous assimilation of information.

▸ **Client-Driven Sales Consultations**	▸ **High-Impact Presentations**
▸ **Staff Training/Development**	▸ **New Market Development**
▸ **Competitive Market Intelligence**	▸ **Organizational/Planning Skills**
▸ **New Business Development/Retention**	▸ **Solutions-Building/Problem-Solving**
▸ **Time Management/Project Management**	▸ **Dedication to High-Quality Standards**

SALES/MARKETING HIGHLIGHTS

▸ Cinched **year-over-year profits** after launching fitness center from start-up planning—market research, identification of location and introductory advertising—to full operation. (Jazzercise)

▸ Captured positive media attention, cold-canvassing local reporters and leveraging cost-effective cable advertising to spur better-than-average business-launch results. (Jazzercise)

▸ Achieved **30% to 40% revenue increase** month over month. (Jazzercise) *Keys to performance:*
  - Identified/responded to customer needs by performing a consultative needs assessment survey.
  - Pinpointed, recruited, and trained customer-focused talent, ensuring staff's passions and abilities.
  - Excelled at customer retention: Cultivated personal relationships and facilitated a reaffirming, companionship-oriented, fun, and nonthreatening environment; performed a consistent written and spoken customer-appreciation program; and orchestrated special client events.
  - Developed client advocates who touted Jazzercise's value to potential customers.

▸ Key initiatives included promoting Chamber through media and attendance/promotions at other business meetings and helping members in concept-to-delivery project planning. (Junior Chamber)

▸ Concentrated on **high-profile projects/fund raising**—Halloween festival, homeless-shelter event, MS150 rest stop coverage—to increase Chamber's visibility. (Junior Chamber)

▸ Spearheaded highly successful Channel 9 Health Fair Site, in association with County Commissioner, three consecutive years. (Junior Chamber)
  - **Recruited physicians** (oncologists, podiatrists, opthalmologists, dermatologists, dentists, and general practitioners) and other medical staff to perform more than 60 medical screenings, evaluations, and referrals. Directed staff comprising approximately 80 volunteers.
  - Achieved **75% increase** in number of patients in program's second year, while maintaining leadership responsibility for one of Colorado's largest Health Fair sites.
  - Successfully **retained a majority of physicians** each year as a result of relationship building.

▸ **Boosted membership 120%** during tenure. (Junior Chamber)

▸ Won state Public Speaking Award and spoke at National Convention. (Junior Chamber)

▸ Delivered presentation at international convention in Kansas City, MO. (Christian Women's Club)

▸ Settled medical claims, communicating with physicians, nurses, and claimants. (Shelter Insurance)

Career Change: *From small business owner to medical or pharmaceutical sales representative.*

Strategy: *Use a functional format to spotlight sales- and marketing-related results as well as success influencing physicians.*

JENNA B. WHITE, page two Residence: 816-632-5555 Cell: 816-632-5556 ▸ jennawhite@centurytel.net

CAREER SUMMARY

Jazzercise, Streamwood, Illinois 1997 to Present
$62M in system-wide sales generated for Jazzercise franchisees in 2001/2002. (www.jazzercise.com)
OWNER/FRANCHISEE

▸ Built start-up franchise from the ground up, successfully promoting a dance-fitness program in a marketplace already supporting YMCA, Gold's Gym, and a recreational center.

▸ Developed a new market, investigating customer needs and delivering creative, effective fitness solutions that supported a healthy lifestyle.

▸ Instituted regular advertising and promotional programs, including customer newsletters, thank-you cards, and media press releases that boosted customer retention.

▸ Grew revenue 30% to 40% month over month.

Christian Women's Club, St. Charles, Illinois 1998 to 2000
TREASURER

▸ Reported funds to local/national offices; distributed A/P funds and performed audits.

▸ Delivered presentation at the club's international convention in Kansas City, MO.

Junior Chamber of Commerce (Jaycees), Highlands Ranch, Colorado 1991 to 1994
Provides tools to people to build bridges of success in business development and philanthropy. (www.usjaycees.org)
PRESIDENT/VICE PRESIDENT

▸ As vice president, achieved 120% membership increase via high-profile program orchestration.

▸ Boasted positive results three years running for healthcare screening event, successfully recruiting and retaining physicians and medical personnel.

▸ As president, managed staff; directed initiatives in membership, finances, fund raising, and projects; performed officer training; and acted as liaison between state and local chapters.

Shelter Insurance, Tulsa, Oklahoma 1986 to 1989
Industry leader in insurance and financial products and services. (www.shelterins.com)
CLAIMS ADJUSTER

▸ Challenged with negotiating claims settlements in a fair/equitable manner for insured and Shelter.

▸ Constructed settlements for medical claims, interfacing with physicians, nurses, and claimaints.

▸ Ranked 5th of 500 people company-wide in subrogation, applying persistence in collections.

United States Army, Kansas City, Missouri 1986 to 1991
CAPTAIN (RESERVIST)

EDUCATION/HONORS

BA in Communications/Minor: Business Administration, 1986
Missouri University/Internship – **Missouri State Legislature**

Honors: Debate Team ... National Forensics League High Honors in Speech/Debate ... Leadership Council (College), Company Executive (ROTC)/Leadership Training (Army) ... Homecoming Royalty

MICHAEL BLACK

33 Fairbairn Drive
Rocklin, CA 94677

Email: mickblack@verizon.net

Mobile: 415-205-3940
Residence: 415-939-2004

SALES & MARKETING MANAGEMENT

A resolute desire to sell and achieve, a passion for influencing consumer buying habits, and proven strengths in building sustainable market share have been the foundation of career successes over an impressive, achievement-filled career. Rare talent for simplifying and executing strategic ideas has generated widespread support, delivered strong revenue growth, and complied with budget constraints. Confidence, integrity, discipline, and vision have been key drivers in expertly nurturing relationships with team members, clients, senior management, and vendors.

Professional strengths:

- Market & Segment Expansion
- Strategic Marketing Plans
- Staff Recruitment
- Key Account Management
- Financial Management
- Market Intelligence
- Customer Retention

- Change Management
- Branding Concepts/Rollouts
- Team Development
- Multi-Channel Distribution
- Sales Force Motivation
- Customer Needs Assessment
- High-Impact Presentations

- Profit & Loss Accountability
- Campaign Management
- Contract Negotiations
- Supplier Relations
- Competitive Product Positioning
- Margin Improvement

EDUCATION

Bachelor of Science, Business Administration (Marketing)
University of California at Los Angeles

EMPLOYMENT NARRATIVE

PAINTGLOW PAINTS, Rocklin, CA
State Retail Manager

2002–Present

Appointed to steer statewide operations during a period where lack of strategic planning, pricing restrictions, and an absence of cohesive teamwork were limiting market expansion. Skeleton staffs of traveling sales representatives restricted campaigns to trade accounts, and multi-branded independent distributors were failing to make desired headway against aggressive competition in a static market. A total revitalization strategy was critical.

Immediately established a tactical rollout plan, spearheaded intense market research into competitor placements, and managed performance expectations by devising a series of KPIs to act as benchmarks for staff achievement.

Results were impressive:

- State revenues **up 20% over previous year.**
- Market share increased from **6.8% to 7.5% statewide.**
- **Capital expenditure and setup costs** delivered **25% under budget.**
- Rental **expenses 30% below budget.**

Key Contributions—In-depth

- **Reinforced team focus** towards core fundamentals of customer service, product quality, and competitive pricing. Despite a stationary market, clients remained receptive to opportunities for aggressive, value-added service with competitive advantages.
- Coordinated advertising and promotional campaigns to maximize impact and results.
- **Grew customer base by 20% per month** over 12 months by introducing cutting-edge sales prompts into the POS system and injecting new "customer-care" performance initiatives into shop-floor roles.

> **SNAPSHOT**
>
> **Report to:**
> CEO and National Sales and Marketing Manager
>
> **Direct reports:**
> 4 Decorator Center Managers and 5 Trade Sales Representatives
>
> **Operating Budget:**
> $2M per year
>
> **State Revenues:** $21.1M

Career Change: *From paint-store manager to sales representative or sales manager.*

Strategy: *Use a chronological format but minimize references to the specifics of his retail experience and focus on client accounts, marketing and promotional campaigns, and management skills.*

MICHAEL BLACK Mobile: 415-205-3940 Page 2
mickblack@verizon.net

EMPLOYMENT NARRATIVE
CONTINUED

PAINTGLOW PAINTS
State Retail Manager (continued)

- Launched greater market presence, establishing company-owned outlets with one "exclusive" brand.

- Spearheaded lucrative **relationship-marketing initiative** with RACV, Delfin Property Group, several health insurers, and Master Painters' Association.

- Recruited 20 new staff and rolled out a series of rewards and recognition programs that raised the bar for **sales performance excellence.** Incentive programs in conjunction with active succession career planning has set benchmarks for sales retention—**currently steady at 95%**.

- Reversed ad hoc approach to inventory control that had prompted overstocking, understocking, and widespread inefficiencies. Devised formula to optimize stock turns, and attained a **previously unprecedented rate of 86% OTIF** (on-time-in-full).

- Negotiated six leases, overseeing council planning permits for usage, parking, and signage.

Store Manager 2000–2002

Presided over a period of significant revenue growth that reflected a series of incremental yet substantial changes to key business processes, expense controls, and goal attainment.

Revamped marketing programs; instilled "Market Best" service standards; produced new branding strategies; devised an integrated approach to advertising, marketing, and promotions in retail and trade markets; and spearheaded a staff revitalization program that rewarded superior efforts for attaining newly conceived goals.

Results & Key Contributions

- Sustained operating expenses to 82% of budget, **steering savings in logistics** through improved warehousing and inventory controls.

- Propelled **sales revenues 34.6%** over previous year to $25.4 million.

- Boosted staff retention by more than one-third to achieve a 95% rating. Alleviated the "brain drain" of high-performance staff through training, incentives, and recognition for goal achievement.

- Orchestrated renewed focus on company-owned decorator centers that flourished under lower commissions and rebates. Decision proved significant, **increasing profitability by 38+%** to $3.2 million.

- **Increased market share** from 11% to 12.7% of the California market.

- Conducted group training sessions for up to 40 staff. Presentations **fostered a dynamic environment** where participants brainstormed new ideas—many of which were revenue-positive.

- Analyzed market and architected a doubling of the product range offered to customers, providing alternatives and value-added packages.

> **SNAPSHOT**
>
> **Reported to:**
> California State Manager,
> National Decorator
> Center Manager
>
> **Direct reports:**
> 12 California Decorator
> Center Managers across
> 12 locations and 7 Trade
> Sales Representatives
>
> **Operating Budget:**
> $3M per year
>
> **State Revenues:** $25.4M
>
> **Key Clients:**
> AV Jennings, Q-Build,
> Rocklin City Council,
> Main Roads Rocklin

Trade & Retail Sales Representative 1997–2000

Distinguished from colleagues for securing the lucrative Q-Build Industries account, contributing $1 million annually. The account spurred credibility in the California marketplace, being utilized for virtually all government maintenance projects.

Identified flaws in opposition strategy, focusing successfully on product performance and services in negotiations with major builders across Rocklin. Secured key accounts from major government contractors, project builders, and prominent hardware and paint groups.

Recognized for achieving maximum budget incentives 3 years consecutively, and doubling territory sales in 2 years.

Excellent References & Client Testimonials Available

James T. Manville

jimmyman@network.com

4609 Miller Street ♦ Mt. Clemens, MI 48043 ♦ 586.555.8730

Profile
- ♦ Committed to pursuing a career in marketing or public relations.
- ♦ Strong interpersonal skills and ability to build rapport with others.
- ♦ Creative and artistic.
- ♦ Computer skills include Word, PowerPoint, Excel, and other spreadsheets.

Education

Oakland University • Rochester, Michigan
Bachelor of Business Administration—Marketing   2003

Eastern Michigan University • Ypsilanti, Michigan
Course work in **Business** and **Afro-American Studies**   2000–2002

Specs Howard School of Broadcasting • Southfield, Michigan
Radio/TV program   2000

Relevant Experience

Pontiac School District—Owen Elementary • Pontiac, Michigan
Bridges to Success Instructor   2003–Present
- • Teach African-American Studies to 4th and 5th graders two days per week under auspices of grant-funded after-school program.
- • Adapt curriculum to students' levels; research and develop handouts to supplement lessons.

National Basketball Association • Atlanta, Georgia
Marketing Assistant (Volunteer)   Winter 2003
- • Assisted staff at NBA All-Star Weekend Jam Session.
- • Interacted with children and families; encouraged participation with the "Got Milk?" program.

Employment History

Ford Motor Co. Vehicle Operations Division • Allen Park, Michigan
Technician *and* **Team Recorder**   1997–Present
- • Conduct tests and inspect parts per QS9000 guidelines.
- • Elected by peers to record minutes during meetings on quality, throughput, safety, and communications. Generate weekly report based on meetings.

S&R Clothing • Detroit, Michigan
Assistant Manager   1995–1997
- • Assisted with daily operations of trendy retail store.
- • Performed merchandising; monitored inventory.

Community Affiliations
- ♦ P.A.L. (Police Athletic League)
- ♦ Zeta Phi Beta Fraternity (community service)

— References available on request —

Career Change: *From auto technician to marketing professional.*

Strategy: *Emphasize relevant education as a primary qualification and include a Relevant Experience section even though this is not his primary work experience.*

RESUME 42: BY DON ORLANDO, MBA, CPRW, JCTC, CCM, CCMC

JOHN MARTIN

2400 Greenville Place
Atlanta, Georgia 30040   jlm@earthlink.net   770.555.5555 (Home)
770.555.6666 (Office)

WHAT I CAN OFFER TopLine AS YOUR NEWEST **MARKETING PROFESSIONAL**

❑ Translate marketing analysis into sales ❑ Introduce the right product to the right market—faster than the competition ❑ Leverage market savvy into every aspect of corporate success ❑ Keep close enough to customers to anticipate their needs

---

RECENT WORK HISTORY WITH EXAMPLES OF PROBLEMS SOLVED

❑ **Pharmacy Manager,** Winn-Dixie, Conyers, Georgia   00–Present

My pharmacy operates 54 hours a week sharing a tough market with 8 competitors. We fill more than 54K prescriptions each year.

Supervise directly two full-time and one part-time pharmacy technicians.

Improved market data to realign expensive **inventory with customer demand.** *Outcomes:* Cut inventory costs by 29%—the lowest level in years—yet kept customer satisfaction very high.

Used informal demographic analysis to identify the benefit that captured most consumers in this very tough market: minimum waiting time. Redesigned our workflow and then retrained our workforce. *Outcomes:* We **gained market share**—and it **didn't cost us an extra dime.**

❑ Staff Pharmacist *promoted over ten competitors in just six months to be* **Pharmacy Department Manager,** REVCO (*later* CVS), Lilburn, Georgia   97–00

Brought this new store online. Entered a market already dominated by 20 competitors. We wrote more than 62K prescriptions annually.

Kept valuable customer relationships completely intact even as I changed corporate identity and location. *Outcomes:* **Exceeded corporate production standards by 240%** from the first quarter on.

❑ **Owner and Manager,** Winter Drug Company, Montgomery, Alabama   88–97

Operated two locations that employed a pharmacist and store manager, a bookkeeper, two pharmacy technicians, and six cashiers. Competed successfully against 20 competitors—some partially underwritten by nationwide corporations.

Compared national market trends with local demand to offer a new service. *Outcomes:* Market analysis was good enough to return my investment in just nine months. New service became **our highest marked-up** product line.

More indicators of performance TopLine can use …

Career Change: *From pharmacist to marketing professional.*

Strategy: *Focus on recent MBA and show how the business he ran benefited from his marketing skills.*

John Martin	**Marketing Professional**	770.555.5555

Stayed close enough to our customers to offer a new service faster than our competition could react. *Outcomes:* **Dominated** one new **segment for two years.** In another case, became a new organization's **sole provider for five years.**

❏ Staff Pharmacist *promoted over three very much more senior team members to be* **Director of Pharmacy,** General Hospital, Kronigsburg, Alabama 80–97

My operation supported a 157-bed, acute-care hospital.

Supervised a secretary, five pharmacy technicians, and an IV technician.

Applied market savvy to internal customers. Addressed the needs of "hold outs" and overcame all their objections. My plan for a closed formulary won corporate approval. *Outcomes:* Much **more cost effective—without compromising quality and service.**

EDUCATION

❏ MBA, Georgia State University, Atlanta, Georgia Expected Spring 05

Paying my own way to earn this advanced degree while working up to 45 hours a week. **GPA 4.0.**

❏ BS, Pharmacy, Samford University, Birmingham, Alabama 80

Carried a full academic load and worked 25 hours a week.

COMPUTER SKILLS

❏ Expert in **proprietary pharmaceutical software,** ProScrip and Rx200 (industry-standard, **comprehensive, LAN-based business software** suite optimized to pharmacies), Word for Windows, WordPerfect, and Outlook Express.

❏ Proficient in Adobe Acrobat, Excel, Internet search engines, PowerPoint, and Access.

PROFESSIONAL AFFILIATIONS

❏ Co-founder, Georgia Independent Drugstore Association 95–97

Found, marketed to, and captured an overlooked niche from scratch. *Outcomes:* **Grew** membership **rapidly from 3 members to 250 in just 2 years**—all with very little money and time to spend.

❏ Former Board Member, State of Georgia Medicaid Drug Utilization Review Board 92–96

❏ Former Committee Member, State Employees Insurance Board's Drug Program 92–96

CERTIFICATIONS AND LICENSURE

❏ Registered Pharmacist, State of Georgia Board of Pharmacy

Page two

Chantal Luz

24612 Railroad Lane
Fillmore, California 91333

Home: 805-263-8611   chantal@hotmail.com   Mobile: 661-263-1651

**MARKETING / BUSINESS DEVELOPMENT / ACCOUNT MANAGEMENT
ADVERTISING / MARKETING COMMUNICATIONS
PUBLIC RELATIONS / SPECIAL EVENTS**

Creative, dynamic, results-driven professional with expert qualifications in identifying and capturing market opportunities to accelerate expansion, increase revenues, and improve profit contributions across broad industries, markets, and accounts. Energetic, organized, self-motivated individual who is able to comprehend and manage multiple details while focusing on the overall picture. Natural communicator with strong motivational skills and the ability to build, produce, and succeed. Extensive travel.

- Proven ability to spot and analyze trends across product/services spectrum.
- Evolution of concepts into achievable business strategies.
- Product research, analysis, and justification for production.
- Negotiation and relationship-building skills; project planning and execution.
- Drive, visual creativity, and ability to reach objectives under demanding circumstances.
- Strong analytical and problem-solving skills with a focus on workable solutions.
- Creative and strategic planning abilities with solid implementation skills.
- Computer literate.

Career Highlights

SPECIAL PROJECTS COORDINATOR / PARTNER   1996–2001
Surgery Center—Granada Hills, CA

Authored the firm's strategic communications plan and orchestrated successful effort to establish corporate vision, mission, and values statement. Transitioned marketing focus to core customer types and segments. Architected new corporate advertising and client testimonial trade campaigns. Developed Human Resources materials such as employee handbook (researched laws with assistance of attorney) and confidentiality agreements; participated in hiring process of office manager.

- Built physician's name as **brand value.**
- Conceptualized ideas and worked with ad companies to develop ads and brochures.
- Developed marketing and advertising materials to attract new patients, educate the community, and build referral base among physicians.
- **Special events:** Set up educational seminars for the community and prospective patients, held both in office and at area hotels.
- Performed grassroots marketing to Chamber of Commerce, spas, gyms, salons, and other local businesses.

DESIGNER / OWNER   1999–2000
Claire de Lune by Chantal Luz—Montrose, CA   (concurrently)

- Started business from ground up. Designed a 30-piece line of fun, hip, contemporary sleepwear. Handled all creative, PR, and administrative functions. Retained and trained required staff to produce line.
- **Developed brand label** and showroom representation for market events.

Career Change: *From fashion designer and medical office manager to marketing/PR.*

Strategy: *Demonstrate her talent for delivering practical business solutions through her interpersonal skills and ability to manage complex projects, meet deadlines, and meet high quality standards.*

Chantal Luz   Page Two

Successful background developing, establishing, managing, and maximizing profitability based on loyal client, vendor, management, and staff relationships.

BUYER   1994–1995
Marie Springs—Houston, TX

> Oversaw advertising and organized store events. Bought better contemporary dresses for this women's designer specialty store.

DESIGNER   1992–1994
Cecilia—Los Angeles, CA

> Designed line of social-occasion dresses for better contemporary sportswear and dress manufacturer. Selected all fabrics and trims, developed styles from first sketch through production, managed sample room and extensive fittings.

FASHION COORDINATOR / MERCHANDISER   1990–1992
Nicole Delbain—New York, NY

> Developed color stories, fashion concepts, and presentation boards for each season. Shopped print market and developed original designs. Worked closely with managers and buyers to create a collection look for their stores.
>
> - Visited European and New York stores to provide constant flow of ideas and fashion trend information. Designed specific groups for direct vendors in Asia.
> - Directed domestic manufacturers to develop merchandise appropriate for Nicole Delbain.

                                                                     Prior to 1989

DESIGNER, Macy's Corporate Buying, New York, NY
ASSISTANT DESIGNER, Nicole Miller, New York, NY

Education

Bachelor of Science, Design
College of Design, Architecture, Art & Planning
University of Cincinnati, Cincinnati, OH

Courses in Microsoft Windows, Word, and Excel
Valley College, Valley Glen, CA

Devon Rodriguez

6598 Commonwealth Avenue
Brighton, MA 02135

drodriguez@email.com

Home: (617) 435-1598
Cell: (617) 505-5985

Targeting Positions in...

PUBLIC RELATIONS | MARKETING | EMPLOYEE COMMUNICATIONS

Customer-focused business professional eager to leverage more than six years of experience in corporate communications and community outreach gained from HR program/employee benefit management to achieve career transition into public relations. Repeatedly commended by senior management throughout career for superior written/verbal communication skills and strong combination of creative talents and analytical thinking. Adept in constructing "out-of-the-box" solutions and effective strategies/action plans to proactively address business problems and communication challenges. Demonstrated ability to interface effectively with diverse groups; build strong community ties; and win lasting buy-in from employees on new initiatives, programs, and policy changes. Successful in diverse-industry work environments (higher education, retail, hospitality).

EDUCATION & CREDENTIALS

EMERSON COLLEGE — Boston, MA
Graduate Certificate in Public Relations, 2003
(In-depth certificate program)

MEMA — Framingham, MA
(Massachusetts Emergency Management Agency)
Public Information Officer Training, 2003

BENTLEY COLLEGE — Waltham, MA
Bachelor of Arts (BA) — Major: Government, 1994

COMMONWEALTH OF MASSACHUSETTS
Notary Public

HIGHLIGHTS OF RELEVANT CAREER ACHIEVEMENTS

<u>Communications:</u>

- **Directed comprehensive, ongoing employee communications programs for workforces of up to 5,000** that clearly articulated corporate benefit options. *(Boston, Inc.; Domino Casino; College of Music)*
- **Wrote and distributed bulletins, brochures, reference guides, updates, newsletters, and manuals** translating often-complex insurance and 401(k) plans/procedures/policies into easily understood terms. Ensured desired key message points from executive team were incorporated into all communications. *(Boston, Inc.; Domino Casino; College of Music)*
- **Leveraged strengths in persuasive verbal/written communications to minimize negative fallout** from increases in employee-paid insurance premiums. *(Boston, Inc.)*
- **Researched and authored well-received articles** covering an array of human resources topics published in corporate newsletters. *(Boston, Inc.)*

<u>Employee & Community Relations:</u>

- **Commended by Operations SVP for ability to elevate morale of, build trust/strong rapport with, and instill a shared sense of corporate "family" among employees at all levels of the organization.** Recognized for maintaining a highly visible leadership presence; accurately conveying the value of corporate programs to employees; and listening attentively and responding appropriately to staff concerns, issues, and questions related to HR programs/ benefits/compensation. *(Boston, Inc.)*
- **Promoted community outreach programs to achieve record-high employee participation** in nonprofit fund raisers, local food pantry, community-based adult literacy task force, and local chamber of commerce. Efforts helped to broaden corporate visibility, support worthy causes, and encourage cross-functional teamwork. *(Boston, Inc.)*

<u>Market Research & Analysis:</u>

- **Investigated and compared the relative merits/shortcomings of** a full spectrum of insurance and benefit plans (e.g., HMOs, PPOs) offered by national and local carriers. Selected best-option solutions and negotiated favorable pricing and terms. *(Appleseed's, College of Music)*

continued...

Career Change: *From human resources to marketing and public relations professional.*

Strategy: *Create an extensive Highlights of Relevant Career Achievements section as the focal point of page 1 while relegating employment to page 2.*

Devon Rodriguez

Résumé ■ Page 2

RELEVANT ACHIEVEMENTS *(continued)*

<u>Corporate Profitability:</u>

- **Delivered $133K in annual savings** by converting health insurance plan from a self-insured to a fully insured plan. Simultaneously lowered employee-paid premiums by 13% for individuals and 8% for families. *(Boston, Inc.)*
- **Jointly led effort that lowered corporate costs** associated with disability coverage by 12%. *(Boston, Inc.)*
- **Facilitated rollout of ergonomic plan that slashed costly lost-time incident claims by nearly 70%** through work on corporate Safety Committee. *(Boston, Inc.)*

EMPLOYMENT HISTORY

BOSTON, INC. — Beverly, MA [Retailer of women's apparel employing 400]
Manager, Benefits & Compensation, January 2001–Present

Report to Operations SVP/Director of Human Resources — Direct all aspects of benefits and compensation programs, including the development/dissemination of an ongoing, comprehensive employee communication program detailing specifics, procedures, and value of various employer offerings. Completely redesigned benefit plan to achieve win/win outcomes for both employer and employees (expanded coverage, added benefit options, reduced premiums). Manage, administer, coordinate, and communicate insurance enrollments/billing; administer 401(k) plans; represent employers at unemployment hearings; and handle negotiations with vendors and brokers.

DOMINO CASINO — Uncasville, CT [Casino with 4,000 employees]
Benefits Manager, January 2000–January 2001

Reported to Director of Benefits & Compensation — Recruited, trained, and supervised an 11-member team of HR professionals, overseeing insurance enrollments, updates, and billing processes for 4,000 employees. Regularly communicated revised policies, procedures, and benefit changes to employees.

COLLEGE OF MUSIC — Boston, MA [Academic institution with 370 faculty/staff and 3,400 students]
Human Resources Programs Manager, April 1997–December 1999

Reported to Assistant VP of Administration/Director of Human Resources — Managed annual and quarterly insurance enrollments/updates, billing, and communication of these benefits and procedures to all college faculty, administrators, and staff. Redesigned benefit plans and coordinated/prepared/presented benefit orientations.

PROFESSIONAL AFFILIATIONS & COMMUNITY INVOLVEMENT

- **Public Relations Society of America (PRSA),** Member (2003–Present)
- **Society for Human Resource Management (SHRM),** Member (1999–Present)
- **Northeast Human Resources Association (NEHRA),** Member (1999–Present)
- **North Shore Chamber of Commerce,** Former Chairperson — HR Managers' Committee (2003)
- **American Political Items Collectors (APIC),** Member (2002–Present)
- **Peabody Institute Library,** Former Trustee (1998–2000)

Mark Adams

61 Havenhurst
Pasadena, CA 91101   madams@aol.com

Home: 818-138-0108
Cell: 818-572-9428

MARKETING MANAGEMENT / BUSINESS DEVELOPMENT

Creative, energetic, multifaceted professional with a BS degree in marketing and a career of successful accomplishments. Proven record of achieving significant sales and business-development goals. Ability to increase productivity and efficiency by building and effectively supervising strong teams. Knowledgeable leader and trainer with excellent communication and interpersonal skills. Experienced in all aspects of customer service. Work within budget requirements to meet or surpass company goals. Capable of substantially improving sales and operations by developing and implementing creative solutions.

AREAS OF EXPERTISE

Retail Sales	Product Promotions	Merchandising
Business Development	Operations Management	Strategic Planning
Policies & Procedures	Leadership / Team Development	Creative Display Building
Forecasts / Budgets	Training / Supervision / Motivation	Communication
Staff Scheduling / Coordination	Productivity / Quality Improvement	Customer Service
Inventory Control / Warehouse	Purchasing / Cost Containment	Problem Resolution
Contract / Union Negotiations	Process & Efficiency Improvement	Shipping / Receiving

PROFESSIONAL EXPERIENCE

ALPHA BETA, Pasadena, CA   1984–Present
GM/Drug Manager (2000–present)
GM Manager (1986–2000), Clerk (1985–1986), Courtesy Clerk (1984–1985)
Management/Operations:
- Hold leadership and strategic planning responsibility for total store operations.
- Implement company guidelines, policies, and procedures and set an example for others.
- Resolve problems and issues related to the store, employees, and customers.
- Monitor and evaluate staff productivity to ensure achievement of sales goals.
- Inspire co-workers with the organization's vision and culture.
- Initiate new ideas and solutions to meet the objectives of my position and the store.
- Prioritize daily activities and projects to maximize productivity.
- Anticipate problems and opportunities and make timely and appropriate decisions.
Customer Service:
- Ensure that all store personnel provide excellent-quality service to customers.
- Address problems quickly and furnish efficient solutions.
- Continuously promote our store by cultivating and developing customer relations.
Staff Training:
- Supervise, motivate, schedule, and train 12 staff members to increase their efficiency and productivity.
- Utilize team-building strategies, including coaching and constructive feedback, with an emphasis on training and development.
- Encourage a cooperative and cohesive work group by inspiring staff members to set and reach goals.
- Delegate authority and responsibility to others in an appropriate and effective manner.
- Exhibit a constructive team-spirit approach to attain individual and group goals.
Sales:
- Total profit-and-loss responsibility for Pasadena store with $3 million in annual sales.
- Continuously build the Pasadena Alpha Beta into a more profitable, higher-volume store.
Merchandising:
- Build and oversee the construction of displays for promotional and seasonal items.
- Plan, direct, and coordinate all special events and promotions in the store.
- Ensure visual standards of in-store merchandise and displays.

Career Change: From retail manager to marketing professional.

Strategy: Emphasize recent marketing degree and incorporate relevant skills into a strong profile. Use category headings in the experience section to help the reader focus on key points.

Mark Adams

Resume—Page 2

PREVIOUS EXPERIENCE

ALPHA BETA, Riverside, CA   1980–1984
GM Clerk (1984)
Courtesy Clerk (1980–1983)
- Responsibilities included ordering, stocking, customer service, and clerk duties.

2003 YEAR-END PERFORMANCE REVIEW SUMMARY

- Rated outstanding in meeting and exceeding sales projections 2 out of 4 quarters; sales were up more than 8% in all 4 quarters.

- Exceeded earnings and gross in all 4 quarters.

- Outperformed expectations in customer-service shop score 3 out of 4 quarters, with total score above company guidelines.

- Rated **Outstanding** in Customer Service, Change Management, Action and Speed Management, Continuous Improvement, Education, People Development, Leading by Example, Decision Making, Communications, Planning, Goal Reaching, and Overall Performance.

- Rated **Above Expectations** in Positive Leadership, Diversity, Recognition & Reward, and Partnerships.

EDUCATION

Master of Science: Marketing (2003)
California State University, Fullerton, CA

Supervisory Skills and **Management Training** (2003)
Sponsored by Alpha Beta

Bachelor of Science: Marketing (2002)
California State University, Fullerton, CA

INSTRUCTOR / TRAINER / MENTOR

Train and coach future Alpha Beta store managers (2003)

Conducted Management Training in Operations, Inventory, Ordering, Scheduling, Reporting (2001–2002)

KATHERINE D. SCHOLLINGER

51027 Deerview Drive • Cleves, OH 45002
Phone: (513) 792-6127 • Mobile: (513) 505-6180

OBJECTIVE

Full-time, part-time, or freelance work involving

> ➤ Writing and editing articles, business biographies, marketing materials, newsletters, brochures, articles, and short stories
> ➤ Research and interviewing services for writers, publishers, and journalists
> ➤ Reading and evaluating manuscripts

QUALIFICATIONS

Demonstrated ability to develop prose that is clear, concise, and inviting to read. Exceptional interpersonal skills; proven ability to put people at ease and interview effectively. Experienced in conducting research through printed materials, online resources, and interviews. Well organized; efficient in coordinating multiple simultaneous projects and meeting tight deadlines. Accurate, prompt, dependable, and attentive to detail. Proficient with Microsoft Word and WordPerfect.

RELATED EXPERIENCE

OHIO MANUFACTURING, Cheviot, OH   1988–1997
Newsletter Editor/Administrative Assistant—Performed research, conducted interviews, and wrote articles for company newsletter that was instrumental in keeping employees informed and motivated. Reviewed and edited articles submitted for publication. Composed letters, memos, and other correspondence. Prepared reports in formats that were well organized and eye-appealing. Organized and maintained files. Position required the ability to prioritize multiple simultaneous projects, meet deadlines, and work well independently (1994–1997). Previous position: Press Operator (1988–1994).

SOUTHWEST REGIONAL SCHOOL DISTRICT, Cleves, OH   1985–1988
Teacher's Aide—Assisted teachers with all facets of classroom management, including researching, preparing lessons, grading papers, recording grades, and preparing written materials. Tutored individual students and small groups in all subject areas. Gained the ability to simplify subject matter, adapt lessons to fit different learning styles and levels of ability, and make lessons interesting.

DAILY JOURNAL NEWS, Hamilton, OH   1979
Proofreader, Advertising Department—Proofread copy, delivered proofs, and worked with advertisers to ensure copy was accurate. Consistently met all deadlines.

SUBJECT INTERESTS & RESEARCH EXPERIENCE

Sociology, family, women's issues
Health: psychology, holistic approaches to wellness, addictions, massage therapy, nutrition
Nonfiction (biographies, American history, current events, self-help), literature, mysteries, historical novels

Continued...

Career Change: From massage therapist to writer/editor.

Strategy: Use a combination format that brings older, relevant experience to the fore.

KATHERINE D. SCHOLLINGER   Page 2

ADDITIONAL EXPERIENCE

TRI-STATE HEALTH NETWORKS, Cincinnati, OH—Massage Therapist	10/01–Present
DAYLIGHT SALON & DAY SPA, Lawrenceburg, IN—Massage Therapist	11/99–9/01
OHIO REGIONAL CLINIC, Blanchester, OH—Addictions Technician	12/98–6/99
UNIVERSITY GENERAL HOSPITAL, Cincinnati, OH—Addictions Technician	5/98–12/98
PERFECT DAY SALON, Cincinnati, OH—Massage Therapist	11/96–5/98

Massage Therapist—Provided massage therapy for clients in support of major national and regional health plans in Ohio and Indiana. Administered therapeutic Swedish and deep-muscle massage. Coordinated appointments with other professionals. Identified opportunities and cross-sold other salon services with a professional, customer-focused and low-key approach.

Addictions Technician—Provided administrative support for drug and alcohol counselors. Observed and charted patient behaviors, including notation of physical and emotional issues, new medications, and other pertinent facts. Position required the ability to handle confidential information with absolute discretion.

EDUCATION

UNIVERSITY OF CINCINNATI, Cincinnati, OH   Present
Bachelor of Arts in progress. Major: English Literature. Minor: American History.
Attending school part-time to allow full-time employment. Degree expected December 2004.

- **GPA: 3.7**
- **Dean's List**
- **Relevant Courses:** Writing from Research • English Composition I & II • Interpersonal Communication

Additional Training:

Additional studies: *Mastering Research Using the Internet,* computer training (Windows, Word, WordPerfect, and Excel), and several psychology seminars.

Center for Holistic Therapy Studies, Independence, IN   1996
Healing Massage Techniques: Completed 168-hour program.

Charlotte School of Massage Therapeutics, Charlotte, IN   1995
Completed comprehensive 427-hour program, approved by the American Massage Therapy Association and accredited by the State of Indiana. Curriculum provided classroom training and practical experience.

RESUME 47: BY GAIL TAYLOR, CPRW, CEIP

Rita Cantor

1250 Vista Diego Road   Santa Clarita, CA 91310   (661) 449-5255   ritawriter@ezmail.com

Business & Creative Writing

Foreword   *"To whom much is given, much is required."* —French proverb

For 14 years, I have enjoyed the privilege of helping others develop their writing abilities. In this time, I have conceived and developed learning tools, conducted classes and writing workshops, and helped students realize potential and achieve goals. Now, I look forward to pursuing full-time my first passion: Writing.

The Writer   *"Ease in writing comes from art, not chance."* —A. Pope

Well-versed in: Business Communications • Speeches • Marketing • Poetry • Nonfiction
Publications: *The Tribute* (Nonfiction, 2003) • *Women of the Decade* (Nonfiction, 2000)
Featured in: *Poetic Path* • *Ascension* • *Living Arts* • *Reader's Choice* • *MasterWorks*

The Teacher   *"Teaching is an instinctual art, mindful of potential."* —A.B. Giamatti

Writing Courses: Advanced Essay • Creative Writing • Business Writing • Writing About Literature
Writing Proficiency Exam Workshops • Science Fiction & Film
English Courses: Basic Grammar • English & ESL • English Rhetoric • Linguistics

---

The Change Agent   *"Things do not change; we change."* —H.D. Thoreau

✓ Developed Writing Proficiency Workshop to help students prepare for exam.
✓ Served on Education Planning & Advisory Committee (EPAC).
✓ Created lunchtime classes that helped employees meet degree requirements.
✓ Started well-received annual clothing drives for underprivileged high school students.

Education   *"Education is for improving the lives of others..."* —M.W. Edelman

M.A. and B.A. in English & Creative Writing, Ojai University, CA   1988—Dean's Honor List

---

Experiences   *"Creativity seems to merge from multiple experiences."* —C. Edwards

Pepperdine University, Malibu, CA
Academic Advisor   1999–2000 / Site Manager   2000–Present

Write all commencement speeches, marketing materials, outgoing correspondence, and recommendation letters for faculty and students. Counsel students and resolve grievances. Manage MBA & MA programs.

Haverhill University, Ojai, CA
English Instructor   1993–1998

Taught English Rhetoric, Writing About Literature, Creative Writing, Advanced Essay Writing, Linguistics, English/ESL, Drama, and Speech. Conducted Writing Proficiency Exam Workshops.

Palm Grove College, Huntington Pointe, CA
English Teacher / ESL Instructor   1990–1993

Initiated and administered for Japanese & Korean businessmen an English Language Proficiency program. Also taught English; tested & assessed language proficiency for military personnel at nearby air force base.

###

Career Change: *From academic advisor to writer.*

Strategy: *Play up literary mindset using an unconventional format, literary style conventions, and quotes. The result is an interesting and attention-getting resume that speaks the language of her target audience.*

RESUME 48: BY LOUISE GARVER, CPRW, CMP, JCTC, CEIP, MCDP

MARILYN NOLAN

22 Meadow Lane ▪ Chicago, IL 78966 ▪ (975) 433–5889 ▪ MNolan@media.net

■ PROFILE

Conferences ▪ *Fund Raising* ▪ *Trade Shows* ▪ *Meeting Planning* ▪ *Cultural Programs*

Creative professional with expertise in all aspects of successful event/program planning, development, and management. Excel in managing multiple projects concurrently using detail, problem-solving, and follow-through strengths. Demonstrated ability to recruit, motivate, and build cohesive teams. Sourced vendors, negotiated vendor contracts, and managed project budgets. Possess superb written communications, interpersonal, and presentation skills.

■ SELECTED ACCOMPLISHMENTS

Special Events Management:

Planned and coordinated conferences, meetings, and events for companies, professional associations, and arts/cultural and other organizations. Developed program content and administered budgets. Arranged all on-site logistics, including transportation, accommodations, meals, guest speakers and entertainers, and audiovisual support. Coordinated participation and represented companies at industry trade shows. Recognized for creating and planning some of the most successful events ever held statewide.

- **Created cultural events for an arts organization that boosted membership enrollment.**
- **Organized 5 conferences for 2 national professional associations, surpassing all prior attendance records.**
- **Designed successful community educational campaigns promoting safety awareness.**

Fund Raising & Public Relations:

Created, planned, and managed all aspects of several major fund-raising campaigns, resulting in a significant increase in contributions raised for each function over prior years. Recruited volunteers and developed corporate sponsorships. Generated extensive media coverage through effective promotional and public-relations strategies. Created newsletters distributed to employees, customers, and others.

- **Co-chaired capital-fund campaign that raised $3.5 million for new facility.**
- **Coordinated 3 auctions that generated more than $140,000 for an educational institution.**
- **Initiated successful publication, generating $25,000 to finance community programs.**

Sales & Marketing:

Selected by management to spearhead opening of regional office, including all logistics, staff relocation and business development efforts. Designed and implemented creative sales and marketing strategies to capitalize on consumer trends and penetrate new market. Coordinated and conducted sales training.

- **Developed and managed 17 key accounts, generating $10 million annually.**
- **Recognized for managing top revenue-generating program company wide.**
- **Consistently exceeded sales forecast and led region to rank #1 out of 6 in profitability nationwide.**

■ EXPERIENCE

Financial Underwriter—Marcon Financial Services Company, Chicago, IL (1990–2003).

Event/Program Coordinator—Arts Council, Botanical Gardens and Cultural Exchange, Chicago, IL (1998–2002).

■ EDUCATION

B.A. in Business Administration, Springfield College, Springfield, MA

Career Change: *From underwriter to event manager.*

Strategy: *Design a one-page functional resume that showcases experience related to event planning—even though this experience was unpaid. Background in underwriting is downplayed.*

KAREN M. MITCHELL

25 Adams Drive   H: (617) 345-1457
Braintree, MA   kmitchell@yahoo.com   C: (617) 505-4917

Business Marketing and Events Coordinator
Business Services / Hospitality / Business to Consumer / Special Events

PROJECT MANAGEMENT–FINANCIAL CONTROL–TRAINING & COACHING

Creative business manager and entrepreneurial professional with 15+ years of experience in a marketing management capacity. Team coordinator, leader in business development, and director of business operations. Consistently increased profitability and market expansion.

- Entrepreneurial Spirit
- Employee Management
- Staff Training
- Financial Control
- Critical Thinking
- Strategic Planning
- Business Startup
- Time Management
- Problem Identification
- Profit Improvement
- Idea Generation
- Relationship Building

PROFESSIONAL EXPERIENCE

T&T PARTNERSHIP, Boston, MA

Operations Manager, Partner
1985–2002

Directed all operations and marketing activities associated with multi-business partnership. Developed and initiated organization and operating plans; recruited staff; conducted demographic research; and initiated creative marketing strategies that grew second-year business **300%** over year one. Maintained client retention at **90%.** Focused on quality customer service, standards, and price strategies to keep a competitive edge. Controlled financial operations and budgets up to **$500K** for multi-business partnership. Implemented marketing strategies that created and retained new business.

MASSACHUSETTS SPECIAL OLYMPICS, Boston, MA

Co-Director and Coach of Figure Skating
1990–1999

Coached and organized figure-skating events at the Massachusetts Summer Games. Supervised participants and sporting events. Achieved maximum student participation. Organized and recorded all qualifying and winning scores of each athlete in all events.

EDUCATION AND PROFESSIONAL TRAINING

Boston University, BA Candidate (2 years completed)
American Academy of Dramatic Arts, Theatre

Career Change: *From entrepreneur to marketing and events management professional.*

Strategy: *Show strengths and skills related to her goal, highlighting relevant details from business ownership.*

KAREN M. MITCHELL   PAGE TWO

SELECTED ACHIEVEMENTS

MARKETING AND SALES

PRESERVED A COMPETITIVE ADVANTAGE WITH A CREATIVE MARKETING APPROACH. Developed an innovative marketing promotion focusing on each client. Increased new-client base by 45% and earned more positive feedback from clients than any other promotion.

ORGANIZED AND DEVELOPED PLAN TO INCREASE SALES IN THE OFF-SEASON BY 20%. Trained staff in areas of in-depth presentation, product specials, and expanded product line. Successfully achieved company goals and improved product awareness.

PLANNED AND COORDINATED REUNION EVENT FOR 600+ ATTENDEES. Researched history of organization 1950–1981. Maintained tight budget requirements. Prepared publicity for local newspapers and television news shows.

MANAGEMENT

SERVED AS COACH AND CO-DIRECTOR OF FIGURE SKATING for the Massachusetts Special Olympics for 9 years. Developed into one of the best-organized events each year at the summer games.

RELIEVED A STRESSFUL SITUATION AND POTENTIAL LOSS OF BUSINESS. Screened, recruited, and trained 3 new employees, quickly responding to unexpected employee turnover. Avoided loss of business and customer dissatisfaction.

APPLIED NEW STATE REGULATIONS. Trained staff to focus on customer needs and how they could help. Enhanced customer and employee awareness.

RECEIVED NUMEROUS REFERRALS AND MAINTAINED 90% CLIENT RETENTION RATE. Recognized by clients and colleagues as a consummate professional with the utmost creativity and personal integrity. Perceptive, patient, and persistent; nurture trust and confidence.

BUSINESS ANALYSIS AND FINANCIAL OPERATIONS

CONTINUOUSLY ACHIEVED 12-MONTH FINANCIAL BUDGET GOALS. High standards of service and products were instrumental in consistent increase of capital for reinvestment in business.

NEGOTIATED A WIN-WIN SITUATION WITH MANUFACTURER. Analyzed prices of manufacturer and its competitors. Resulted in $20,000 annual cost savings.

INITIATED AND EXECUTED PLAN TO PURCHASE SECOND BUSINESS. Designed a market strategy to analyze business finances and local demographics. Commitment to detail resulted in a lower purchase price of business.

EXPANDED STORE SPACE TO ACCOMMODATE RAPID BUSINESS GROWTH. Business exceeded first-year projections by 50%.

CHAPTER 7

Resumes for Career Changers Seeking Health Care, Social Services, and Personal Services Positions

Retraining is often necessary to earn the qualifications and credentials for a switch into the health care industry. Many of the resumes in this chapter make this current education the centerpiece, with prior experience playing a supporting role. These resumes represent the following career changes:

- Priest to human services administrator

- Health educator to surgical technologist

- Customer service representative to a position in social services

- IT recruiter to social worker

- Sales representative to speech/language therapist

- Controller to counselor

- Nurse to legal consultant

- Flight attendant to personal assistant

- Nurse to researcher

- IT analyst to health care administrator

ANTHONY FONTINI

28 Abbotsford Avenue
Springfield, Massachusetts 01118
413.205.5432
fontini2358@mindspring.com

HUMAN SERVICES ADMINISTRATOR

- Highly skilled not-for-profit management professional with outstanding multitasking ability.
- Visionary leadership style that encourages "out-of-the-box" solutions to unique problems and challenges.
- Articulate, accomplished communicator and motivator.
- Strong team-builder, comfortable working with diverse populations in terms of both cultures and ideas.
- Seasoned traveler, fluent in Italian, Spanish, and Polish.

MANAGEMENT

- Chosen to provide strong, decisive organizational leadership through period of change, transition, and revitalization.
- Established and maintained team atmosphere and high morale level.
- Developed successful grassroots fund-raising campaign for major building project; **pledges / donations surpassed goal by 60%.**
- Designed and coordinated reconstruction of three facilities to better suit needs of residents. First stage of construction underway.
- Composed and presented motivational articles and speeches.

TRAINING

- Developed high-performance leadership training for organization volunteers.
- Trained and supervised staff of seven plus 50 volunteers.
- Led public-speaking seminars.
- Introduced in-house language training to meet needs of diverse community.

COUNSELING/ADVISING

- Regularly sought by members for family and marriage counseling.
- Assisted members needing guidance for ethical and moral dilemmas.
- Motivated members to set and accomplish goals.

(continued next page)

Career Change: *From priest to human services administrator.*

Strategy: *Design the resume so that it is not apparent that he is a priest, using a functional format and "secularized" language (for example, "motivational speeches" rather than "homilies" or "sermons").*

ANTHONY FONTINI – PAGE 2

EXPERIENCE

Pastor   1998–Present
St. Cecelia Church, Springfield, MA

Parish Administrator   1997
Corpus Christi Church, Holyoke, MA

Associate Pastor   1991–1997
St. Anthony's Church, Chicopee, MA

EDUCATION

San Carlos Seminary, Rome, Italy
Master of Divinity / Pastoral Theology

University of Connecticut, Storrs, CT
Master of Arts, Counseling. GPA 3.85

Holy Cross College, Worcester, MA
Bachelor of Arts, Double Major: Philosophy and Theology.
Graduated Magna Cum Laude.

RESUME 51: BY VIVIAN VANLIER, CPRW, JCTC, CEIP, CCMC

BRIANA MARTIN

5555 Las Flores Canyon Rd.   (323) 555-5555
Los Angeles, CA 91406   brianamartin@email.com

Surgical Technology Student
—Qualified for Position Managing Pre- and Post-Operative Care—

- Well-qualified and dedicated professional with 10+ years of related experience in nonprofit healthcare field.
- Work well in a fast-paced environment… proven ability to respond to problems and emergencies in a calm, organized, and effective manner.
- Managed and supervised paid and volunteer teams.
- Performed educational in-services, community outreach, patient care, client relations, grant writing, and training.
- Coordinated wellness fairs, health classes, and prevention workshops, increasing community awareness of health issues and services available.
- Natural communicator with excellent interpersonal and customer-relations skills.
- Quick learner who enjoys challenges and works well both independently and collaboratively in a team setting.

—Working Knowledge of Health-Related Rehabilitation and Medical Management Process—

EDUCATION

Surgical Technologist; GPA 4.0
LOS ANGELES CAREER COLLEGE, Los Angeles, CA; Completion, May 2005

B.A. in Social Services / Minor in Communications
UNIVERSITY OF CALIFORNIA, Los Angeles, CA (UCLA)

Certifications

CPR Certified—American Red Cross
Certified HIV Educator—American Red Cross

PROFESSIONAL EXPERIENCE

Health Resource Educator   2000 to Present
LOS ANGELES COMMUNITY SERVICES, Los Angeles, CA

Child Welfare Specialist
CALIFORNIA DEPARTMENT OF CHILDREN AND FAMILY SERVICES   1997 to 2000

Health Educator
LOS ANGELES COUNTY HOSPITAL, Los Angeles, CA   1993 to 1997

COMMUNITY / VOLUNTEER ACTIVITIES

Red Cross Blood Drive—Blood Drive Volunteer   2001 to Present
Sunlight Foundation—Healthcare Volunteer   2000 to Present
Big Sisters of Los Angeles—Big Sister to Middle School-Aged Girl   1999 to Present

Career Change: From health educator to surgical technologist.

Strategy: Emphasize recent retraining and relevant health care experience.

RESUME 52: BY CAROL ROSSI, CPRW

JOAN KAMINSKY

4 Baywood Boulevard   jkaminsky@aol.com   Home: 732-477-5172
Brick, NJ 08723   Cell: 908-810-4139

Target: Youth & Family Services Positions
Juvenile Counselor / Home Studies / Foster Child Placements / Victim-Witness Counselor

Energetic, people-oriented professional with excellent listening and communication skills. Respond well to difficult situations and skilled at juggling multiple responsibilities. Earned bachelor's degree in criminal justice with dual minors in psychology and sociology, plus a concentration in juvenile delinquency. Experienced in:

- Government Agency Communications
- Problem Resolution / Informal Counseling
- Positive Relationship Development

- Home Studies / Positive Child Environments
- Community Outreach Program Participation
- Performance Reviews / Written Assessments

EDUCATION

B.S. in Criminal Justice, Dual Minors in Psychology and Sociology, Juvenile Delinquency Concentration
Georgian Court College, Lakewood, NJ, 1991

Selected Courses:
Deviance: Reviewed common juvenile delinquency problems, how to deal with them, and policy enforcement.
Intervention Methods: Discussed juvenile problems, available intervention programs, and counselor roles.
Juvenile Delinquency: Defined which crimes are termed delinquency and when a delinquent is considered an adult, reviewed treatment steps, and explored types of facilities.
Juvenile Justice Independent Study: Conducted in-depth research on impact of juvenile detention vs. jail, damage of trying youths as adults, and crime rates when intervention programs are or aren't available.

SOCIAL SERVICES BACKGROUND

International Adoption (Personal Experience) • Brick, NJ, and Beijing, China • Apr. 2003–Present

Cooperated in 2 home studies and 2 office visits with in-depth interviews to assess family members, lifestyles, and environment for potential adoptive child. Fingerprinted by the INS, the State of New Jersey, and the federal government. Completed multiple in-depth forms. Successfully passed criminal background and medical checks. Performed 2 extended visits to overseas orphanage. Appeared in American courts and embassies. Cooperated in post-placement visits to ensure positive welfare of child.

Volunteer Juvenile Counselor • Ocean County Juvenile Detention Center, Brick, NJ • Jan. 1991–Jan. 1992

Assisted in the supervision of 25 incarcerated juveniles. Enforced rules about attitudes, behavior, and safety. Planned and participated in sports activities to promote teamwork and physical fitness. Attended, observed, and contributed to small, informal group counseling sessions for juveniles. During counseling sessions, listened to problems, helped them to realize why they were incarcerated, talked one-on-one, and offered opinions or advice on changing behaviors or overcoming difficulties.

RECENT EMPLOYMENT HISTORY

Sovereign Bank (formerly Bank One and United Jersey Bank), Toms River, NJ • Sept. 1994–Sept. 2001
Customer Service Representative • 01/98–09/01
CSR Supervisor • 08/95–01/98 // **Customer Service Representative (CSR)** • 09/94–08/95

Supervised 4 customer service representatives. Assisted with applicant interviews. Served as intermediary to resolve problems between employees and between employees and customers. Assessed employees' performance and completed written reviews. Participated in community outreach programs including United Way, Habitat for Humanity, and Toys for Tots. Received excellent performance reviews from supervisor.

Career Change: *From customer service representative to a position in social services.*

Strategy: *Highlight relevant education and personal experiences that qualify her for the role she is seeking. Eliminate irrelevant information from her employment history.*

RESUME 53: BY DEBRA O'REILLY, CPRW, CEIP, JCTC, FRWC

Marie Samuels, MSW

203-555-5885   160 Terryville Road, Fairfield, CT 06430   samuelsm@email.com

EDUCATION

MSW, Sacred Heart University, Fairfield, CT   May 1998
    Concentration: *Clinical Practice;* Specialization: *Children and Families*   GPA: 3.9
BSW, University of New Haven, West Haven, CT   May 1996
    Graduated *magna cum laude*   GPA: 3.8

SOCIAL WORK EXPERIENCE

Social Work Intern, Claire M. Brousseau Elementary School, West Haven, CT (1997–1998)
    Provided individual and group therapy for children and adolescents with emotional and behavioral disorders, using cognitive behavioral techniques. Conducted biopsychosocial evaluations; implemented and reviewed clinical services; developed individual programs (IEPs) to maximize therapeutic potential. Coordinated assistance with other social service providers. Communicated with parents to improve family dynamics.

Social Work Intern, Learning for Life School, North Haven, CT (1995–1996)
    Provided behavioral, social, and emotional support for students; implemented behavior-modification curriculum. Participated on interdisciplinary team providing counseling and crisis intervention.

Social Work Intern / Resident Counselor, Desjardins Healthcare, West Haven, CT (1994–1995)
    Conducted psychosocial evaluations / assessments; developed goals and treatment plans. Established rapport with patients, colleagues, and families to support achievement of goals.

Volunteer Facilitator for recreational activities for youth in foster care, New Haven Youth Trust.

ADDITIONAL PROFESSIONAL EXPERIENCE

COMPUTER PERSONNEL, INC., New Haven, CT   1999–2002
Technical Recruiter
    Supported market reps in the recruitment, sourcing, and placement of IT professionals for contract and permanent positions. Conducted candidate evaluations to assess skills, interests, and availability. Maintained communication from initial contact through post-placement follow-up.

MEDICAL SERVICES, San Rafael, CA   *Leader in transtelephonic pacemaker monitoring*   1990–1998
Pacemaker Medical Technologist III
    Advanced through increasing responsibilities. Conducted high-tech EKG monitoring via telephone for patients with pacemakers and ICD devices. Assessed and instructed patients throughout testing process. Analyzed cardiac data; prepared physician reports. Responded to emergencies, notifying medical personnel as necessary. Assisted in technical staff training and quality assurance.

DANCE ABROAD, INC., Los Angeles, CA   1987–1989
Dance Captain / Lead Dancer
    In addition to domestic performances, performed / lived in Far East for two six-month contract terms. Liaison for business relations and show manager.

    Computer skills: MS Office, including Word, Excel, Outlook, and Access.

Career Change: *From IT recruiter to social worker.*

Strategy: *Spotlight relevant experience as an intern and only briefly summarize her additional employment experience. Lead off with strong education credentials.*

KATHERINE RICHARDS

8595 Apple Tree Lane
San Diego, California 92109

(619) 444-2131
krichards@hotmail.com

SPEECH-LANGUAGE PATHOLOGIST

Dedicated professional offering a Master of Arts in Speech and Language Pathology. Hands-on experience providing evaluation and treatment services for adults and children with communication disorders. Easily develop rapport with a variety of clients. Dependable, organized, and creative.

Proficient in PC and Macintosh environments, Excent IEP, Microsoft Word and Excel, and QuickBooks.

Member, National Student Speech Language Hearing Association

EDUCATION / TRAINING

M.A. in Speech and Language Pathology, University of California, San Diego, CA   2003
B.A. in Communication Disorders and Psychology, University of California, San Diego, CA   1983

Professional Development	**Current Certifications**
Excent Computerized IEP Training, 2003	Interactive Learning (INREAL), University of California
Feeding and Swallowing In-Service, 2003	Cardiopulmonary Resuscitation, American Red Cross
Lee Silverman Voice Training (LSVT), 2003	Personal Trainer, American Council on Exercise

RELEVANT EXPERIENCE

Substitute Teacher, San Diego School District, San Diego, CA   2001 to Present
Work in elementary schools covering long-term assignments and daily substitute teaching.

- Substituted full-time for literacy teacher. Taught decoding and reading strategies to K–3 students (long-term assignment, 2002).

Student Clinician, San Diego School District, San Diego, CA   2003
Assumed duties of school speech pathologist. Provided evaluations and developed treatment plans for students ages 5 to 18 with learning disabilities, apraxia, stuttering, articulation disorders, autism, and hearing loss. Prepared progress reports and communicated results at staff meetings.

- Implemented therapy plans for 60 students.
- Established creative treatments that met IEP goals of each student.

Student Clinician, University of California, San Diego, CA   2002 to 2003
Evaluated and diagnosed clients for the Speech, Language, and Hearing Center. Planned weekly therapy for clients with aphasia, dysarthria, apraxia, stuttering, learning disabilities, and organic voice disorders.

- Served on child diagnostic, adult motor disorder, learning disability, and child screening teams.

OTHER EXPERIENCE

Partner/Owner, Richards & Smith Promotions, San Diego, CA	1996 to Present
Assistant Manager/Sales Associate, Hatfield & Company, San Diego, CA	1998 to 2002
Buyer/Sales Associate, Robin's Boutique, San Diego, CA	1994 to 1998

Career Change: *From sales representative to speech/language therapist.*

Strategy: *De-emphasize sales experience by listing it under Other Experience at the end of the resume. Focus instead on education, training, and relevant activities.*

Barbara Edwards

413 Half Mile Run • Hermitage, PA 16148
(724) 555-1212 • barbedwards@verizon.net

COMMUNITY COUNSELING / THERAPEUTIC SUPPORT / WRAP-AROUND

▶ Utilize listening and analytical skills to provide psychological or behavioral counseling to children, adolescents, and adults (and teachers and families of clients as appropriate).

▶ Identify resources and follow up to ensure services are helpful to client. Assist in creating treatment plans and monitor treatment progress.

▶ Intervene, support, and educate children and families to promote healthy, safe environments. Establish goals, interventions, and progress reports; consult with treatment team.

▶ Demonstrate high standard of integrity, exemplary attention to detail; and precise record keeping. Capable team member or team leader; equally effective working independently with no supervision.

▶ Possess exemplary communications skills. Streamline operations to expedite the flow of information. Clearly communicate results of work orally and in writing.

▶ Computer software proficiency includes MS Word, Access, Publisher, PowerPoint, and Excel; accounting software.

EDUCATION

Master in Community Counseling, anticipated 2005
Macom University—Macom, Pennsylvania

- Psychopathology of Child and Adolescent
- Models of Adaptive Behavior
- Human Development
- Foundations of Counseling

- Family Therapy
- Psychology of Adult
- Introduction to Community Counseling
- Counseling Theory and Research & Development

B.S., 1993, **Accounting.** *Consistently placed on Dean's List/Honor Roll*
Montara College—Montara, Pennsylvania

EMPLOYMENT

Doberman, Inc./Pinscher Industries—Wontom, Pennsylvania   *1997–2003*
CONTROLLER *(1998–2003)*
ASSISTANT CONTROLLER *(1997–1998)*

- Selected as member of management team, reporting to parent company. Improved employee morale; created more relaxed work atmosphere. Made recommendations to alter established procedures to create a more smoothly functioning office with increased efficiency, accuracy, and productivity. Analyzed reports and asked questions, initiating cost-savings changes.

  ▶ Developed form for tracking vendor criteria for ease in comparing items and pricing.
  ▶ Influenced reduction in cost of sales by 11% and operating expenses by 2.5% within 4 years.
  ▶ Created Excel spreadsheets for all daily, weekly, monthly, and annual reconciliations of general ledger accounts, four bank statements, financials, balance sheet, income statement, inventory reports, A/R, and A/P.

- Served as liaison to Virginia-based parent company, reporting to CFO. Managed accounting staff of five. Hired and trained employees on procedures and company policy.

- Subsequent to merger of Doberman and Pinscher in December 1998, spearheaded drive to bring harmony between the companies' employees, creating a more comfortable working environment.

- Negotiated annual health, disability, and life insurance. Formulated annual budget in coordination with corporate, working within their cost-savings strategies. Prepared documentation for corporate tax filings.

STAFF ACCOUNTANT, Progresso and Peabody, CPAs—Brownsville, Pennsylvania   *1995–1997*
BOOKKEEPING / CUSTOMER SERVICE, Modern TV and Appliance—Brownsville, Pennsylvania   *1994–1995*
REGIONAL ACCOUNTING ASSOCIATE, Crystal Cellular—Plankton, Ohio   *1993–1994*

Career Change: *From controller to counselor.*

Strategy: *Use middle-of-the-page placement to draw attention to recent education; start off with a comprehensive introduction that describes personal and professional attributes.*

DONNA DUGAN, RN

E-mail: Donnadugan@hotmail.com
663 Shadow Court, Las Vegas, Nevada 89015
Phone: (702) 654-8015 / Cell: (702) 873-4804 / Fax: (702) 564-4605

LEGAL NURSE CONSULTANT

MEDICAL / PARALEGAL / INSURANCES

Knowledge:

Risk Management — Quality Assurance — Regulatory Compliance
Workers' Compensation Torts — Personal Injury — Medical Malpractice

Qualifications:

- Eighteen years in the medical profession.
- Knowledgeable in state and federal regulations.
- Trained in trial law—depositions, discovery, legal research, motions, and client interviews.
- Thorough understanding of medical terms, client/patient assessments, and life planning needs.

Skills:

• Staff Management	• Medical Terminology	• Compliance Manager
• Communication	• Medical Administration	• Case Management
• Clinical Experience	• Disease Etiology	• Community Outreach

PROFESSIONAL EXPERIENCE

Staff Nurse, Sierra Health Services, Las Vegas, NV   1998–Present
Oversee a 14-bed psychiatric unit for acute mentally ill patients. Directly supervise 4 employees. Perform monthly, bi-yearly, and peer review of unit-based audits ensuring 100% compliance with standards of care requirements. Recognized a decrease in standards of care and implemented a staff training program that is showing increases toward 100%.

Veterans Health Administration, Knoxville, IA, 1985–1998

Primary Nurse, MHC	1996–1998
Nurse Manager, Psychiatric Unit	1992–1996
Acting Nurse Manager, Extended Care Unit	1991–1992
Lead RN, Alzheimer's and Related Dementia Unit	1989–1991

EDUCATION
Diplomas and Professional Training

Legal Nurse Consultant, Kaplan College of Professional Studies, Boca Raton, FL
Registered Nurse, Iowa State University, Ames, IA

Advanced Health Assessment Course, Parkland Community College, Champagne, IL
Health Assessment Course, Vennard College, University Park, IA

PROFESSIONAL PRESENTATIONS

Keynote Speaker on "Care of a Patient and Caregiver Support for Alzheimer's"
Crescent City, Community Center
Vermilion County Nursing Home
Iowa City Alzheimer's Support Group

AFFILIATIONS

(Active) Secretary, South Valley Ranch Homeowners Association

Career Change: *From nurse to legal consultant.*

Strategy: *Emphasize related experience and industry expertise to position her as an expert in the emerging field of health care legal consulting.*

RESUME 57: BY GAYLE HOWARD, CERW, CCM, CPRW, CRW

CLAUDIA WHITE

1001 Homestead Circuit
Victoria, 3803

Email: cwhite@earthlink.com

Mobile: (61) 5566 7898
Residence: (61) 6600 0323

"FIRST IMPRESSIONS"
S P E C I A L I S T

PERSONAL ASSISTANT • BUTLER • CABIN SERVICES MANAGER

First-class customer service, impeccable personal presentation, superior problem- and conflict-resolution talents, and meticulous attention to detail have been the hallmarks of an eight-year career spanning front-line client service and challenging nursing-care assignments. People-focused and logical; intuitive, empathetic, and proactive in responding to emergencies. A spirited leader and team participant; enjoy devising solutions and enhancing business reputation through the quality of personal communications and professional demeanor. Exposure to citizens of all nationalities via extensive global travel has further refined capacity for demonstrating patience, tolerance, and quick thinking.

Professional Strengths:

✓ "Red Carpet" Customer Service	✓ Safety & Security Processes	✓ Crisis Management
✓ Team Leadership & Direction	✓ Staff Training & Development	✓ Issues Resolution
✓ Conflict Resolution	✓ Medical/Nursing Intervention	✓ Catering/Food Delivery
✓ German/English Translations	✓ Cardiopulmonary Resuscitation	✓ Hygiene Protocols
✓ Quality Assurance	✓ Public Speaking	✓ Sales/Product Promotions
✓ Post Operative Nursing	✓ Risk Evaluations	✓ Counseling/Listening

Technology skill set includes Microsoft Office, WordPerfect, Windows XP, Internet, email.

EDUCATION | TRAINING

Certificate III in Airline Operations
Equivalent: Hospitality Certificate III
Australia Airlines

Advanced German Language
Institute of Languages

Nursing Diploma of Health Science
University of Sydney

Training also includes Security Awareness for Corrective Services.

EXPERIENCE SUMMARY

✓ "Top-scored" in all airline performance evaluations as a Long-Haul Flight Attendant since 1995—outpacing similarly experienced colleagues.

✓ Devised several initiatives for improving levels of safety, functionality, and efficiency across catering, medical, and occupational health and safety areas.

✓ Awarded several "Notices of Appreciation" from airline management recognizing the challenges faced during chartered distress flights that transferred "Bali Bombing" survivors from Bali to Australia.

✓ Conducted group training on safety, service procedures, and cardiopulmonary resuscitation.

✓ Recipient of numerous complimentary letters from passengers praising courtesy, empathy, and understanding displayed during all interactions.

✓ Volunteered to serve as part of the Risk Intervention Team dealing with prison inmates demonstrating suicidal tendencies.

✓ Managed medical ward and coordinated nursing team caring for up to 30 prisoners simultaneously at Short Bay Jail's Correctional Health Services unit.

Career Change: *From flight attendant to personal assistant.*

EMPLOYMENT CHRONICLE

AUSTRALIA AIRLINES   1995–Present
Long-Haul Flight Attendant

Service excellence, safety consciousness, superior grooming, and willingness to "rise to the occasion no matter what the challenge" are attributes cited on each performance evaluation since 1995 and further reinforced through positive feedback from the traveling public.

Regularly supervising up to 12 cabin crewmembers on international flights, provide leadership in areas such as in-flight conflicts, medical emergencies, staff education, and passenger communiqués—overseeing timely observation of departure schedules and the safety and security of all on board.

Contributions, Highlights, Accomplishments:

✓ Demonstrated superior knowledge of emergency aviation procedures during intensive airline operations training, including evacuations, "ditching," fire-fighting, administering oxygen, survival techniques, and hostage resolution.

✓ Selected to perform emergency medical treatments on doctor's verbal authority via air/land Medlink hook-up. Maintained communication stream by constantly briefing doctors on passengers' vital signs and visual observations.

✓ Devised several initiatives for improving levels of safety, functionality, and efficiency across catering, medical, and occupational health and safety areas.

✓ Volunteered services for Australian Airlines distress flights, evacuating "Bali Bombing" survivors back to Australia from Bali. Dispensed counseling and empathy to relatives traveling to seek missing friends and relatives or identify remains post-attack. Managed wounds previously concealed by survivors, administered first aid and comfort, and calmed distressed passengers. Awarded several "Notices of Appreciation" from management and passengers recognizing the challenges faced.

✓ Defused the violence level of an abusive passenger affected by alcohol and intimidating passengers and crew. Built rapport and eventually won agreement for the passenger to abstain from alcohol during the flight's final 2 hours. The calmed and cheerful passenger disembarked without further incident with thanks for a "lovely flight."

✓ Instigated emergency CPR upon a passenger's collapse during descent. Selected a crewmember to assist and, drawing upon qualifications as a registered nurse, continued to administer CPR procedures until landing and ambulance takeover.

✓ Recipient of numerous complimentary letters from passengers citing courtesy, empathy, and understanding displayed during all interactions.

CORRECTIONAL HEALTH SERVICES   1993–1995
Short Bay Correctional Center's health services division
Registered Nurse/Acting Nurse Unit Manager

Senior staff member and Acting Nurse Unit Manager of the challenging "B Ward"—a medical unit of Short Bay correctional facility caring for inmates with a variety of conditions from fractures and post-procedure care through degenerative and chronic conditions, drug dependencies, and mental illnesses. Personal safety and security of the nursing team and officers was a top priority requiring active awareness of surroundings and scrupulous attention to preventative measures such as storage of sharp objects and medications. Dealt professionally with up to 30 prisoners in the ward and a personal caseload of up to 4 patients daily.

✓ Won the respect of many prisoners by providing group training that prepared inmates for eventual release with a range of daily living skills.

✓ Co-produced reports to stringent guidelines when documenting assaults, suicides, or inmate injuries.

✓ Presented security awareness training to nursing staff, including such topics as hostage survival techniques in a correctional facility.

Claudia White   Page 2   Confidential

Strategy: *Avoid typical language for a flight attendant resume and focus instead on a series of examples that showcase her abilities to manage crises, solve problems, and deal effectively with diverse people.*

RESUME 58: BY JOHN O'CONNOR, MFA, CRW, CPRW, CCM, CECC

AMY J. SULETTO, R.N.

496 Talissan Road
Cary, North Carolina 27987
(919) 397-8300
ajsrnct@bellsouth.net

CLINICAL TRIALS ASSOCIATE & CLINICAL RESEARCH ASSOCIATE
Clinical Trials, Drug Safety, and Medical Focus

SUMMARY OF QUALIFICATIONS

- Knowledge of project leadership, clinical data management, clinical research, clinical trials, and related areas from experience with PPD Pharmaco in a drug safety internship role and outstanding patient-based medical background as a nurse, primarily with UNC Hospitals.
- Experience conducting clinical trial drug studies in difficult international environments.
- Understand the relationship with clinical trials and scientific research that has direct/indirect clinical applications.
- Research experience includes analyzing, gathering, writing, evaluating, and producing detailed reports on a variety of projects. Able to collect, review, and produce critical documents.
- Consult physicians for protocol continuation and principal investigator decisions.
- Excellent project management and overall organizational skills.
- Strong clinical background and orientation.
- Professional experience has provided training and exposure to drug development process, clinical monitoring processes, collaborative opportunities, compliance analysis, monitoring, training, data management, data collection, data analysis, source documentations, and validations.

SELECTED TECHNICAL TRAINING

Introduction to MedDRA, 2004
MedDRA Training of Coders, 2003
Database/Software: *Clintrace 2+, Argus; Microsoft Access, Word, PowerPoint, Excel.*

EDUCATION

Wake County Technical Community College, Raleigh, NC
Beginning ICD-9 CM and Advanced ICD-9 CM, May 2003

University of North Carolina at Chapel Hill, Chapel Hill, NC
Bachelor of Science in Nursing, May 1998

Planter County College, Planter, VA
Associate Degree in Nursing, June 1996

LICENSURE   Nursing—NC 0089589

SKILLS SUMMARY

- **Clinical Trials/Management**
- **Clinical Data Management**
- **Study Team Leader**
- **Clinical Trials Site Buildups**
- **Scientific Methods/Research**
- **Client Design-Build Solutions**

- **Drug Safety Monitoring**
- **Quality Assurance**
- **Event Follow Up/Case Closure**
- **FDA Audit Issues/Protocol**
- **Source Documentation Definition**
- **Source Documentation Verification**

Career Change: From nurse to researcher.

Strategy: Call attention to her recent training and use her prior experience as added value for her new career goal.

AMY J. SULETTO, R.N., page 2

PROFESSIONAL EXPERIENCE

PPD PHARMACO, Durham, NC
Intern—Drug Safety, 2001–Present
- Liaison to project manager and coordination work as the lead on five projects since 2001; helped start two of these projects, performing project review, Drug Safety–specific project protocol planning, scope of work and budget reviews, project change coordination/communication, site monitoring, and clinical trial site management assistance.
- Responsible for obtaining and processing adverse event data in accordance with Good Clinical Practice (GCP) and other regulatory guidelines.
- Analyze, plan, and ensure proper execution of clinical trials.
- Project budget work on studies includes budgeting setup and budget section review for Drug Safety Unit. Work closely with project manager during study to ensure time and finance remain under budget.
- Assist with ongoing client consultations regarding databases and database setups; validate systems after system setup by technical staff.

UNC HOSPITALS, Chapel Hill, NC
Staff Nurse, Electro-Physiology Patient Lab, 1999–2000
- Specialized duties included providing patient care during pacemaker insertion and radio-frequency ablation utilizing conscious sedation. Participated in A-fib/A-flutter protocol; maintained equipment, set up equipment, and recorded information during the study. Maintained QI by successfully implementing, collecting, and recording data on unit projects; revised unit base procedure and policies.
Staff Nurse, Post Anesthesia Care Unit, 1998–1999
- Conducted assessment and assisted in writing treatment plans; ensured that these plans were followed through all shifts; conducted assessment, intervention, and definitive care for post-anesthesia patients; performed in Relief Charge Nurse role. Served as Member of QA/QI Committee.
Staff Nurse, Level I Trauma, Emergency Department, 1997
- Performed administrative and clinical duties in the trauma/emergency area; provided multiple patient care work in triage to discharge planning.

BOWMAN-GREY HOSPITAL, Winston-Salem, NC
Staff Nurse, Critical Care Float, 1996
- Functioned in critical care area; coordinated patient and nursing activities, supervising healthcare technicians as well as handling other floor administrative responsibilities.

References and Further Information Available upon Request

PAUL DUNMAN

7 Moore Street
Sydney, Australia

Email: pdunman@iprimus.com

Cell: (360) 5441 3344
Business: (360) 5111 1221

Senior Executive	**HealthCare / Medical**

Profile	Results-focused senior executive offering 20 years of experience positioning hospitals and healthcare facilities for growth, increased shareholder value, and refined business infrastructure. Acknowledged for capacity to build consensus and drive solutions that meet short-, medium-, and long-term goals. Communicative, energetic style coupled with strategic vision has transformed multimillion-dollar losses to strong profit performances in months, while projects under personal direction have won national awards for innovation. Expert in restoring profitability, assessing potential acquisitions, devising case-management programs, and managing sensitive cultural-change integrations that challenge the status quo yet win the unqualified support of key stakeholders and staff.

Areas of Expertise

- Organizational/Cultural Change
- Business Analysis/Management
- Executive Presentations & Negotiations
- Mergers & Acquisitions
- Healthcare Management/Operations
- Strategic Planning & Market Expansion
- Revenue Growth Strategies
- Communications/Success Recognition
- Project Management
- Due Diligence Research & Recommendations

- Process Reengineering
- Business Development
- Not-for-Profit Organizations
- Clinical Process Revitalization
- Quality Healthcare Delivery
- Case Management Solutions
- Tendering Processes
- Team Building
- Succession Planning
- Hospital Business Administration
- Healthcare Industry Best Practice

Executive Performance

Change Management

Executed comprehensive change-management program for **Lutheran Church Community Care**—a not-for-profit organization that had experienced significant growth, yet remained stagnant in terms of processes and service delivery protocols. Incrementally introduced new philosophies and methods that automated routine tasks, cut inefficiencies, and slashed costs, winning the support of key stakeholders via step-by-step communication programs encouraging problem "ownership."

Cut administration errors by up to 15%, and elevated direct nursing care by 200% through reduced reliance on administrative follow-up.

Program delivered return on $255K investment within 15 months, outstripping all board expectations.

• • •

Case Management

Revolutionized **case-management practices** across New Zealand for the **Accident Compensation Corporation** as part of a $100M collaborative initiative to arrest escalating claims costs and introduce holistic infrastructure change. **Project-managed $880K bid** against aggressive competition, and presided over a team of eight to design, develop, and commission a multi-part organizational-change project integrating revitalized case-management protocols contributing **$37.5 million p.a. in savings.**

Against a backdrop of intense media and public scrutiny, **created transparent and accountable work practices** and regularly briefed the CEO to convey expected healthcare service improvements across New Zealand. Curtailed lead times; elevated customer service delivery; cut paperwork; employed dedicated caseworkers for each case; introduced recuperation plan negotiations; and reduced rehabilitation, compensation, and follow-up costs.

• • •

Due Diligence

Enhanced salability of business unit, conducting all due diligence work on behalf of **WorkCover S.A.** Examined products, internal processes, liquidity, debt position, markets, demand and supply capabilities, competitors, management, and skill retention post-sale. Board fully embraced all product and service recommendations.

Executive Performance

Efficiency Improvements

Inadequate systems, procedures, and controls were the key challenges faced by **Sullivan Nicholas Pathology.** Produced a complete suite of recommendations to refine

Career Change: From IT analyst to health care administrator.

Paul Dunman page 2

workflows and internal controls, and revamp business methods. Pruned costs and delivered 10% improvement in operational and customer-service efficiencies.

• • •

Cost Savings & Revenue Growth

Revealed numerous cost-saving and revenue-growth opportunities to principals of **The Wenton Hospital.** Worked in partnership to deliver a long-term business/growth strategy, formalize information and clinical management, and optimize financial operations. Recommended methods to enforce compliance to debt collections, assume a stronger commercial stance, restructure divisions to prune budget expenditures, introduce technology enhancements, and review clinical management processes.

Recommendations accepted and implemented across the board, resulting in **reduction in days accounts outstanding from 90+ days to 9.** "Payment on Discharge" recommendation **tripled cash flows** and **slashed cost of debt by $200K per annum.**

• • •

Tender Evaluation

Countered public concerns over the integrity of **California Health's** tender process in awarding the multimillion-dollar HAFT software project. Under "impossible" deadlines and a zero-tolerance error environment, meticulously reevaluated assessment processes; tenders; and the veracity of solutions offered for effectively managing medical records/reports, admissions/transfers/discharges, surgery/theatre/pharmacy management, billing, and more.

Produced comprehensive report of findings to the Crown, citing minor "human error" breaches; tender was given "green-light" and **system implemented with no political fallout.**

• • •

Hospital Metrics Analysis

Assessed financial health of the **South Eastern Private Hospital** to leverage improved performances across all divisions at the lowest practicable cost. Analyzed all key hospital metrics that reflected desired outcomes, and produced reports forecasting trends, winning management support.

Employment Chronology

BUSINESS/TECHNOLOGY CONSULTANT 6/2003–Present

Devised a formal value creation model for management to analyze the validity of proposed infrastructure expenditures over multiple timeframes of up to 10 years.

QUEENSLAND RAIL

Examined future business and technology infrastructures and identified a need to realign perceptions and practices to reflect technology as a business "investment."

United existing processes with industry best practice to create a methodology that integrated seamlessly with evolving activity-based costing initiatives and strategic goals. **Model forecasted productivity savings of up to 30%,** together with improved focus on technology investments and business value.

• • •

TRANSCOM, INC.

VICE PRESIDENT, BUSINESS DELIVERY 6/2000–6/2003

Reported to: Chairman & CEO (Monaco); Managing Director, Asia Pacific
Projects: AUD $600K–$4 million

Advanced business and technology solution provider servicing medical, healthcare, human resources, education, and executive management.

Instrumental in transforming a fledgling business unit to the most prominent and successful unit in the group—despite the challenges of global downturns in technology.

In 2001, the international intellectual property development group was relocated to Brisbane from the UK, with a renewed sense of purpose to transition to a long-term strategic focus from an operations-driven enterprise.

As the pivotal operations-based driver, steered complete solution-development phases—from creation to market launch and project implementation. Sustained momentum, scheduling, and delivery objectives, while simultaneously building client relationships through intense communication and scrutiny of individual business strategies, objectives, and infrastructure.

TRANSCOM, INC. (CONTINUED)

Turned around employee reluctance for merging intellectual property development and client development areas by exposing key international staff to the advantages of linking these complementary operations; devised well-received training programs conveying future vision. Relocation saved $2 million per annum, and in service delivery areas **delivered 70% productivity improvement.**

Strategy: *Create a powerful Executive Performance category to present his bottom-line business achievements that relate to today's hot health care issues, such as change management, case management, cost savings, and hospital metrics analysis.*

Paul Dunman

page 3

Devised and developed corporate and program-based activities spanning organizational management, corporate profile enhancement/creation, funding, capital-raising, budgeting and planning, strategy and financial planning and execution, and business and market development.

• • •

UNISYS AUSTRALIA LTD.

Business Solutions, Consulting, e-Business Divisions.

Key clients included: Lutheran Church Community Care, Accident Compensation Corporation NZ, Ergon Energy Corporation, The Public Trustee of Queensland, Brisbane City Council, Australian Stock Exchange, MIM Holdings, Coles-Myer Limited, ANZ Banking Group, Department of Primary Industries, Suncorp, and more.

PROGRAM (EXECUTIVE) DIRECTOR   7/1994–6/2000

Reported to: South Pacific Director, Sydney, Australia

Consulted to large corporate entities, healthcare/medical facilities, and government. Led team of 10 in project implementations, bids, and delivery of specialist healthcare engagements. Key catalyst in spearheading the innovative "Organizational Agility" practice that positioned the company for more responsive service delivery and allowed greater flexibility to meet market demand. Initiative prompted significant interest from the U.S.–based head office, inviting input on methods to drive cultural change.

Consultancies/Project Scope: Business strategy formulation, process reengineering, training and education, organizational and cultural change, operational analyses, executive guidance, productivity improvements, and cost-containment programs.

Project Highlights:

Winner, Silver National Government Productivity Award, for contributions in boosting employee productivity as part of a $15 million office management system for the Department of Primary Industries.

Reduced "tail" costs by $2 billion as part of a collaborative $100 million national business process reengineering initiative to contain spiraling litigation and accident insurance issues for the **Accident Compensation Corporation in New Zealand.**

Consolidated myriad disparate technology systems, designing a comprehensive knowledge base for the City of Brisbane that connected all systems for consolidated access from all areas. **Cut annual running costs by 96%.**

Advised ASX executive on planning, budgeting, change management, business communications, process reengineering review, and resolution of existing issues for the **Australian Stock Exchange.**

• • •

COOPERS & LYBRAND

Key clients included: WorkCover South Australia, Sullivan Nicholas Pathology, Queensland Health, Wesley Hospital, Department of Primary Industries, Department of Lands, Victorian Casino Control.

SENIOR MANAGER   7/1989–6/1994

Direct Reports: 12 (managers, senior consultants, consultants, support staff)
Operational budget: $12 million

Profit-and-loss accountability in this senior management role overseeing daily operations while driving tactical market plans to capture new business within premium markets. With high fees and high-quality deliverables, expectations were strong and necessitated continuous monitoring. Steered client relationship management strategies, delegated priorities, monitored project progress, identified trends, hired consultants, appraised staff performances, and positioned the business for continued prosperity.

Chaired *Quality Review Board* to review project progress and identify policy issues. **Winner, Gold National Government Productivity Award.**

Received **Silver National Government Productivity Award** for developing a government bid process to select quality tenders.

Education

Master of Business Administration, University of Southern Australia

Bachelor of Science (Business Administration), University of California, Berkeley

Graduate Certificate in Quality, National Association for Quality

CHAPTER 8

Resumes for Career Changers Seeking Training, Human Resources, Teaching, and Educational Administration Positions

Many jobs contain elements of teaching, training, and human resources functions even when this is not the primary role of the position. People seeking to transition to this role full time need to bring relevant experience to the forefront on their resumes. Quite often they can successfully position themselves as an experienced professional with relevant skills and achievements, rather than a career-transition candidate who needs to show transferable skills. It's all in how you present the material! This chapter contains examples for the following transitions:

- Teacher to corporate trainer
- Teacher to human resources/organizational development professional
- Client services manager to human resources generalist
- Prevention counselor to training and development professional
- Adoption specialist to employee relations and recruitment professional
- Office administrator to recruiter
- Marketing professional to teacher
- Boiler operator to teacher
- Farmer/rancher to teacher
- Dental office manager to teacher
- Retail salesperson and manager to teacher
- Police officer to teacher
- Computer programmer to college instructor
- Military officer to university administrator

RESUME 60: BY CINDY KRAFT, CCMC, CCM, JCTC, CPRW

Lorraine T. Wilson

919-223-8888
wilson@email.com

2813 Twilight Avenue
Raleigh, NC 27613

Training & Development

Expert in delivering training programs that drive productivity and performance improvements.

Dynamic training professional with an outstanding reputation for integrity and results. Effective interpersonal skills with an ability to meet and train people at their level. Skilled in facilitating groups through complex problem solving to action and improvement. Enthusiastic with a positive and motivating management style. Core competencies include …

- Strategic & Tactical Planning
- Performance Management
- Cross-Cultural Communications
- Train-the-Trainer Development
- Needs Assessment & Analysis
- Mentoring Programs

Lorraine "is a highly skilled professional with a wealth of experience in working effectively with individuals and groups across the district to effect change."

Coordinator
North Carolina Diagnostic &
Learning Resources System

"She is an extremely well-planned and structured individual. She models perseverance and encourages others to do the same…. Lorraine has an articulate ability to convey even complicated information in a very clear and concise manner."

Susan Smith
Guidance Counselor

Notable Highlights

- Repeatedly selected by the county to serve as a consultant to *develop training materials for alternative assessments and lead training workshops.*

- Following the requirement of federal- and state-mandated training procedures, *selected by the school district to develop the training modules and train 5,000 teachers to retain critical governmental funding.* Created the highly regarded and very effective PowerPoint presentation, "Solving the Puzzle," incorporating all learning modalities for ease of learning.

- *Created highly successful community-based training program to prepare disabled students for the workforce.* Established long-term, mutually beneficial relationships with major employers, including Sheraton, Marriott, St. Joseph's Hospital, Wal-Mart, Kash n' Karry, and Target. Served as the administration liaison monitoring student progress. *Enjoyed an unprecedented success rate in getting students hired into long-term employment.*

- *Chosen to author the curriculum and teach English to foreign-born nationals.*

- *Recruited to "train the trainer,"* authoring the program to successfully coach experienced teachers in the art of mentoring new teachers to reduce turnover.

- *Recruited by University of North Carolina to develop the "Classroom Manager," standardized web-based lesson plans.*

- *Invited by North Carolina State University* to participate as a key member of the Special Education Consortium conducting alternative assessment field testing for its Life Career Center *as a precursor to becoming a state-certified trainer.*

Career Change: *From teacher to corporate trainer.*

Strategy: *Focus on career accomplishments beyond the classroom and incorporate third-party comments as powerful endorsements of her training abilities.*

LORRAINE T. WILSON   Page 2   919-223-8888

Evaluation Form Excerpts:

"Excellent presenter. Lively presentation of DRY topic!"

"Lorraine has an awesome personality."

"Wonderful job, Lorraine. Very informative, yet fun!"

"Fantastic job."

"Very informative and helpful."

"Good workshop. Brought everything together. Fun activities."

"Excellent! Excellent! Excellent!"

"Great instruction and activities."

"Good information. Well presented."

Professional Experience

GREEN COUNTY SCHOOL DISTRICT, Raleigh, NC

Teacher—1999 to 2004
EMH Teacher, Central High School—1998 to 1999
VE/ESE Class Instructor, Springville Adult School—1992 to 1999
ESOL Instructor, Springville Adult School—1988 to 1992
ESE Department Head, Washington High School—1972 to 1998

Broad-based experience in training teachers and students within the 13th largest school district in the nation. As Department Head, supervised and mentored paraprofessionals; served as liaison with outside agencies; and developed effective training materials.

- Developed the coaching programs that resulted in new teacher orientation and professional day training policies.

- Chosen numerous times to serve on committees aimed at improving teacher training.

- Proven record of success in teaching and graduating the most dysfunctional students.

- Repeatedly selected by the District as a model classroom for visiting foreign educators.

Certification

North Carolina Certified Associate of Behavior Analysis (CABA)

Education

Master of Administration—Ohio University, Athens, OH
Bachelor of Arts—Pennsylvania State University, York, PA

RESUME 61: BY GAYLE HOWARD, CERW, CCM, CPRW, CRW

SHANE PAGE

200 Rathdown Street
San Francisco, CA 94109

Email: shaneyp@bigpool.com

Mobile: 415-205-9090
Residence: 415-392-8492

HUMAN RESOURCE MANAGER • CONSULTANT • PROJECT LEADER
Member, SHRM

Career background in education, leadership, and training is underpinned by advanced studies in human resource management, providing the backdrop to project, HR management, and consultancy engagements in the commercial sector. Acknowledged for capacity to inspire, achieve consensus, mediate, and deliver predefined goals despite a diversity of personal agendas, tight deadlines, and changing priorities. Adept at managing multiple tasks and isolating and resolving problems. A poised, entertaining, and influential speaker, presenter of ideas, and leader.

Professional strengths include

- Project Planning, Implementation & Delivery
- Team Leadership & Training
- Strategic Planning
- Employee Empowerment
- Public Relations
- HR Management

- Program Development
- Policy Development
- Resource Management
- Competency-based Performance Analysis
- Presentations/Training
- Organizational Change

- Goal Setting
- Training & Education
- Mediation/Consensus Communications
- Process Improvements
- Information Technology
- Cultural Change Management

Technology skill set: Word, Excel, PowerPoint, Windows, LAN/WAN, Internet, email

EDUCATION

Graduate Diploma in Human Resource Management
University of San Francisco, San Francisco, CA (2004)

M.Ed.
Fairfield University, Fairfield, CT (1996)

B.S., Elementary Education
Fairfield University, Fairfield, CT (1993)

Hundreds of hours devoted to ongoing professional development through on-the-job training, formal coursework, and information sessions. Includes Myers-Briggs Type Indicator, Behavior Management, Internet Development & Privacy, Workplace First Aid, and more.

BENCHMARKS & MILESTONES

- Served as project manager for the winning submission for the National Literacy Award 2003. Developed presentation, co-devised strategic goals, and produced finance documentation.

- Spearheaded new policy, establishing the strategic vision for future technology expansion and institution-wide access to Internet resources. Analyzed existing system, calculated future user demands, and devised processes and filtering for safe Internet research. Generated at-a-glance reporting systems for continuous statistical analysis. Administered budget.

- Elevated to first senior appointment (Coordinator) presiding over curriculum development, budgets, and departmental administration after only two years. Regularly selected for caretaker management roles driving the future direction and administration of two prominent training/development portfolios. Managed a staff of 12.

- Appointed by Catholic Education Office to launch intensive professional development program introducing fresh training initiative to senior educators across the region.

- Managed construction and start-up of $35K computer laboratory to service existing and future users.

- Personally selected to drive the introduction of an issue-sensitive training initiative—presenting information at workplace and community gatherings.

Career Change: *From teacher to human resources/organizational development professional.*

Strategy: *Focus less on daily classroom activities and instead emphasize abilities in leadership, training, people skills, and management, all supported by relevant "success stories."*

EMPLOYMENT CHRONICLE

SAINT JOSEPH'S SCHOOL, San Francisco, CA   2002–Present
270 students, 10 full-time and 20 part-time staff.
Teacher
Report to: Principal; Direct Reports: 8 Classroom Teachers and an Events Coordinator.

Key member of the teaching team, working with the principal, teachers, and parents to resolve educational issues and adjust curriculum to students' needs. Construct creative lessons to maintain interest yet thoroughly cover established curriculum.

Selected accomplishments:

- Presented to a diversity of groups both internally and externally; spearheaded information sessions for professional development days.
- Co-developed medical forms for Camp 2003, ensuring all potential litigious matters were highlighted for parental review.
- Produced significant content for inclusion in a three-year school-development plan reviewing student welfare, staff support, and goal orientation.
- Assumed a leadership role providing staff with empathetic, experienced, and insightful counsel in resolving a range of classroom and welfare issues.
- Led and coordinated winning submission for the prestigious National Literacy Award of 2003—the highest recognition possible for a school. Established and steered the submission committee throughout goal-setting, project-planning, and documentation-development phases.

OUR LADY OF VISION, San Mateo, CA   1996–2001
Educational institution offering diverse curriculum to 160 students, plus 8 full-time and 6 part-time staff.
Acting Principal, Educator, RE Coordinator, IT Coordinator
Budget: Operational $50,000; Special Projects $5,000. Staff: 12.

Track record of progressive career growth into leadership roles. Initially focused on hands-on classroom management for 27 children, progressed to developing curriculum and presenting information to make learning come alive. In 2001 was offered extended appointment as Acting Vice Principal during incumbent's personal leave. Devised timetables, chaired mediation meetings, and led professional development and parent events. Coordinated curriculum development, processed stationery acquisition needs for 2002 school year, co-produced class lists, and actively participated in five-year planning strategies for curriculum and school development.

Selected accomplishments:

- Actively promoted multi-skill development in all teaching staff; devoted considerable personal time toward mentoring, delivering, and evaluating professional development training to peers and subordinates in the prominent areas of information technology and religious education.
- Spearheaded personnel training initiatives, including lectures, presentations, and practical performance demonstrations that accomplished goals.
- Managed resources and operational and special project budgets; monitored and authorized expenditures.
- Built convincing argument outlining need for computer laboratory in 1997. Acquired necessary $35K budget to expand technology area to support unique classroom experiences and skills development in students and teachers.
- Developed school IT and Internet policy and formulated reporting system.

COMMUNITY ACTIVITIES

- Parish Committee, Our Lady of Vision, San Mateo, CA   2000–Present
- Volunteer, Cancer Council   2002–Present
- Fund Raiser, Kidney Foundation   2002–Present

LISA A. JOHNSON

23 Ocean Avenue ♦ Greenlawn, New York 11740 ♦ (631) 262-1817 ♦ Cell: (631) 466-5431
ljohnson@optonline.net

PROFILE

Talented Client Services Management professional with excellent qualifications in the development and management of HR functions eagerly seeking to **transition into HR Generalist** position. Demonstrated success with major projects in benefits and compensation, succession plans, quality orientation, and training. Skilled at developing business support functions, aligning organizational processes, and performing HR functions to deliver standards of productivity, efficiency, and quality. Extremely successful in facilitating cooperative relationships among employees, technology/operations, and senior management. Areas of support include

**HRIS • Compensation/Benefits Administration • HR Policy Communication
Retirement & 401(k) • Administration & Development • Regulatory Compliance & Eligibility
Open Enrollment/New Hire Orientation • Budgeting • Qualified Plans**

TRANSITIONAL STRENGTHS

Human Resources Administration & HRIS
~ Provide direct point-of-contact and liaison for HR call-center operations through division managers and staffs supporting a population of 12,500 employees.
~ Spearhead organizational development initiatives, leadership, employee empowerment, and process re-engineering.
~ Initiate innovative change-management programs focused on core efficiency and productivity improvements. Redefine staffing levels and service models to increase efficiencies.
~ Manage communication of HR policies and procedures and author comprehensive training materials; formulate analyses, prepare forecasting/projections, and review reports.
~ Initiate HRIS system enhancements; interface with technology management to accomplish upgrades and employee/client training.
~ Lead team-building efforts between company and clients.

Compensation / Benefits Management & Training
~ Provide support and field inquiries about employee benefits and insurance programs, including Executive Compensation, Indemnity Plans, HMOs, POSs, PPOs, Flexible Spending Accounts, Life Insurance, Dependent Life Insurance, Accidental Death and Dismemberment, Long/Short-Term Disability, 401(k), Profit-Sharing Plan, and COBRA.
~ Author high-level benefit training material and customer-service training material; train customer service representatives (CSRs) to support open enrollments for employees in petroleum companies, media communications, and financial institutions.
~ Provide client-site training on Cyborg 4.5 navigation and inquiry training for classes up to 25.
~ Assist in the development and scripting of a knowledge base utilized by customer service reps to support inquiries on benefits and HR policy and procedures for active, retiree, and terminated populations.

Public Relations & Presentations
~ Conduct open-enrollment road shows and presentations to large audiences, including union workers and corporate HR management personnel.
~ Write and present quarterly/monthly business reviews for clients, i.e., financial institutions and participating company senior management.
~ Assist sales department with demonstrations and presentations.

Career Change: *From client services manager to human resources generalist.*

Strategy: *Highlight "transitional strengths" in key areas related to her new job target.*

LISA JOHNSON
- Page Two -

PROFESSIONAL EXPERIENCE

<u>AUTOMATIC DATA PROCESSING</u> • Melville, NY　　　　　　　**1/90 to Present**
(Human Resources / Benefits & Payroll Outsourcing • 200 Divisional Employees)
Client Service Manager • 9/00 to Present
　Provide call-center implementation and support management of Human Resources, Payroll, and Compensation/Benefits for J.P. Morgan and Citibank. Write training material for open enrollment for Chevron Phillips, Cablevision, and HSBC. Hold departmental budget responsibility. Recruit, train, develop, schedule, evaluate, and supervise teams of up to 20 CSRs, verification clerks, and pre-processors.

- ~　*Collaborated with technology department to upgrade and enhance HRIS.*
- ~　*Currently participating in the implementation of a call center providing support on Limited Benefits Enrollments, New Hire Benefit Enrollments, Life Event/Status Changes; provide internal training for team of 25 to support enrollments. Direct liaison with JCPenney's human resources staff, insurance representatives, the underwriter, and third-party administrators (TPAs); perform call/process analyses.*
- ~　*Meet and exceed all contractual service levels; volumes exceed original projections.*
- ~　*Recipient of three "People Make the Difference" Awards.*

Supervisor • 3/96 to 9/00
Senior Customer Service Representative • 1/92 to 3/96
Customer Service Representative • 1/90 to 1/92

EDUCATION

Hofstra University, Garden City, NY
Bachelor of Arts in Business Administration

PROFESSIONAL DEVELOPMENT

Incoming Call Center Management Institute (ICMI)—
Essential Skills & Knowledge for Effective Incoming Call Center Management
How to Supervise People • Progressive Discipline Training • Service Excellence Training

COMPUTER SKILLS

Microsoft Office: Excel / Word / Outlook / PowerPoint
Tivoli Case Management System
Netscape Navigator
Tesseract HR & Payroll
Cyborg HR & Payroll 4.5 • Cobra Travis
Humanic HR
Erlang C
Business View Observer

MATTHEW BENSON

1234 5ᵗʰ Street   Indianapolis, Indiana 46240   (317) 555-6789   E-mail: MBenson@hotmail.com

CAREER PROFILE

ACCOMPLISHED HUMAN RELATIONS PROFESSIONAL with **6+ years** of experience in marketing, clinical counseling, investigation and case management, human services, curriculum development, program facilitation, and training. Proven track record of success in the education, medical, insurance, and human services fields. Comprehensive experience with a top-ranked research university, a Level 1 trauma medical center, a **Fortune 1000** insurance company, and two highly respected human services agencies. Passionate professional driven by a desire to see clients advance and develop personally and professionally. Consistently achieve excellent performance evaluations. Honors student with an extensive history of community involvement, public speaking, and volunteerism.

PROFESSIONAL OBJECTIVE

Seeking to contribute to a company's training & development function in the human services, human resources, and/or workforce development field.

COMPUTER SKILLS

Windows 95, NT, 98, ME & XP   Microsoft Office 95, 97 & 2000
Microsoft Outlook Express   Internet Research
Proprietary Human Services, Insurance & Medical Software

EDUCATION

M.S., ADULT EDUCATION, DEPARTMENT OF EDUCATION, INDIANA UNIVERSITY, BLOOMINGTON, IN
❖ Concentration in *Staff Training & Development.*
❖ Expected date of graduation: 2005.
❖ Work full-time while in school full-time.
❖ Financing **100%** of education.

CERTIFICATE, MANAGEMENT & SUPERVISION, SCHOOL OF CONTINUING EDUCATION, INDIANA UNIVERSITY, BLOOMINGTON, IN (2004)
❖ Worked full-time while in school full-time.
❖ Financed **100%** of education.

B.S.W., SOCIAL WORK, INDIANA UNIVERSITY, INDIANAPOLIS, IN (1999)
❖ G.P.A.: 3.4 / 4.0
❖ Worked part-time as an Indiana University Ambassador, giving tours to hundreds of prospective students.
❖ Successfully completed an intensive internship with Wishard Hospital in Indianapolis, IN (1999).
❖ Member, Golden Key National Honor Society.
❖ Member, Phi Alpha Honor Society, School of Social Work.

THE UNIVERSITY OF MIAMI, CORAL GABLES, FL
❖ Completed two years of coursework toward a Bachelor of Science degree in *International Relations.*
❖ Participated in the College Work-Study program by working as a Referee for the Basketball, Football, and Soccer Intramurals.
❖ Transferred to **IU** to target the respected **B.S.W.** degree program.

Career Change: *From prevention counselor to training and development professional.*

Strategy: *"Repackage" him as a soon-to-graduate student with recent and relevant education and position prior experience as added value rather than the primary qualification.*

MATTHEW BENSON   **Page Two**

PROFESSIONAL EXPERIENCE

CROSSROADS, INDIANAPOLIS, IN
Prevention Counselor, New Directions (2003–2004)
Crisis Hotline Counselor (2002–2003)
❖ Enthusiastically provide individual/group on-site clinical counseling services for teenagers at three local high schools.
❖ Address substance abuse prevention and treatment topics, including academic achievement, anger identification & management, family & peer relationships, problem-solving, and self-esteem.
❖ Implemented the ***Parenting Wisely*** program in the home for "families at risk" to strengthen family communication. Utilize cutting-edge computer laptop technology to present vignettes that depict commonplace situations.
❖ Facilitate family members role-playing and discussing possible solutions for the scenarios.
❖ Participate in ongoing staffing meetings to review the family's progress.
❖ Coordinate continuity of care case-management services with school personnel, Department of Children & Families caseworkers, and other professionals relevant to the client's achievement.
❖ Researched various topics and helped develop the curriculum for parenting and substance-abuse topics.
❖ Completed extensive documentation within tight deadlines.
❖ Speak to other interested community groups about substance abuse prevention in Marion County.
❖ Consistently earn praise for curriculum development, motivational speaking, and enthusiastic training style.
❖ Began working part-time as a Crisis Counselor; promoted to Prevention Counselor.

THE TEEN SCENE, INDIANAPOLIS, IN
Residential Counselor (2002–2003)
❖ Coordinated admissions, treatment plans, progress reports, and discharges for this highly respected children's home.
❖ Provided crisis intervention and individual, family, and group counseling to residents ages 5–17.
❖ Received consistently high performance evaluations for counseling and documentation skills.

FIRST PLACE INSURANCE, DANVERS, MA
Automobile Claims Adjustor (2000– 2001)
❖ Successfully case-managed hundreds of automobile claims totaling hundreds of thousands of dollars for this **Fortune 1000** insurance company.
❖ Contacted and established rapport with all appropriate personnel to determine coverage, exposure, and liability.
❖ Consistently earned praise for defusing difficult customer situations, expediting claims, and preparing thorough documentation.

WISHARD HOSPITAL, INDIANAPOLIS, IN
Social Work Intern (1999)
❖ Provided extensive social work education and intervention services for up to **120** patients and their families in a **700**-bed *Level 1 Trauma Center* hospital psychiatric unit.
❖ Reviewed clinical treatment plans for each patient and assisted the respective psychiatrists, physicians, and psychiatric treatment staff with individual, family, and group counseling for patients.
❖ Researched various clinical diagnoses and therapeutic interventions for immediate implementation on the unit.
❖ Thoroughly learned the in-depth patient assessment, admissions, financial options, and discharge-planning processes.
❖ Gained experience with culturally diverse patients and their various diagnoses, including dual-diagnosis patients.

COMMUNITY / VOLUNTEER ACTIVITIES

Completed the Toastmasters International Communication & Leadership Program, Indianapolis, IN (2003)
Volunteer, The Great American Teach-In, North Central High School, Indianapolis, IN (2003)
SERVE Volunteer, Delaware Trails Elementary School, Indianapolis, IN (2003)
Guest Lecturer, "Teambuilding," Butler University, Indianapolis, IN (2004)

RITA M. BAYLOR

2500 East Shea • Phoenix, AZ 85028 • baylorrita@cox.net • **602.222.4444**

TARGET POSITION: EMPLOYEE RELATIONS / RECRUITMENT

AREAS OF EFFECTIVENESS

<u>*COACHING*</u>*:* Developing individual plans and conveying feedback to facilitate behavioral change. Delivering orientation programs and articulating critical information to guide program participants. Negotiating difficult situations between conflicting parties. Training new hires to expedite transition to new environment.

<u>*LEGAL AWARENESS*</u>*:* Ensuring strict compliance with government regulations and remaining current on related information through continuous training. Collaborating effectively with attorneys / judges in preparation for and during court proceedings. Maintaining confidentiality of sensitive records.

<u>*LEADERSHIP*</u>*:* Hiring, training, mentoring, and evaluating performance of support staff. Leading retreats and monthly meetings to drive departmental planning and issue resolution while advancing team-building efforts. Maximizing productivity and performance within office. Interfacing effectively with management.

<u>*RECRUITMENT*</u>*:* Executing targeted and general-recruitment strategies, including dissemination of information and conducting large-group presentations at community events. Interviewing individuals to discern relevant information and matching parties according to guidelines. Representing agency on television and radio spots.

SKILLS / STRENGTHS

Mediation • Information Dissemination • Public Speaking • Conflict Resolution • Networking
Organized • Self-directed • Compassionate • Poised

PROFESSIONAL EXPERIENCE

Family Specialist / Recruiter, *Adoption Services*, Phoenix, AZ, 2001–Present

- ♦ License adoptions and manage up to 22 cases simultaneously, guiding families through all phases of process.
- ♦ Execute targeted and general-recruitment activities to build program awareness and increase referrals and prospects.
- ♦ Increase market presence for programs through television and radio appearances as well as newspaper articles and public-speaking engagements.
- ♦ Distribute materials to hundreds of individuals while working information booths to promote program.
- ♦ Design and maintain flowchart outlining adoption process to distribute to prospects during recruitment within community.
- ♦ Train new employees on policies and procedures.

Continued…

Career Change: *From adoption specialist to employee relations and recruitment professional.*

Strategy: *Highlight core capabilities within four skill sets that are relevant to her goal.*

– RITA M. BAYLOR –

Professional Experience continued…

Social Worker, *Mesa Health Systems*, Mesa, AZ, 2000–2001
- Maintained ongoing caseload of more than 45 clients with varied needs, including completing thorough needs assessment and collaborating with partner agencies.
- Functioned as client advocate to address grievances and determine viable solutions.
- Thoroughly investigated and maintained detailed records pertaining to case families.
- Consistently received positive feedback from clients and managers acknowledging outstanding dedication and performance.

Case Assistant, *The Carey Support Program*, Tucson, AZ, 1999–2000
- Hired, oriented, trained, scheduled, and conducted performance reviews for 12-person team.
- Charged with development, design, editing, and distribution of multi-page, visually appealing newsletter targeted to families.
- Played integral role in planning major conference to promote new adoption-support system.
- Quickly received increased responsibilities, including case management, after initially being hired to manage records of long-term cases.

Case Worker, *Department of Economic Security*, Tucson, AZ, 1997–1999
- Served as legal guardian and advocate for up to 52 children.
- Collaborated with Attorney General's office to strategize on cases.
- Gained broad-based understanding of individuals in need of rehabilitation programs.
- Orchestrated case meetings to bring together all parties to share cases and solutions.

EDUCATION / COMPUTER SKILLS

Bachelor of Arts in Sociology, University of Arizona, Tucson, AZ, 1996
Intermediate PowerPoint skills; Proficient in Word, Excel, Outlook, and Publisher

Kathleen Hunt

453 Roth Drive ◆ Souderton, PA 18964 ◆ 215-660-5498 ◆ khunt@dotresume.com

Goal

Recruiting position that will utilize my strengths in employee matching, sales, and customer relations to deliver top-notch service to candidates and customers.

Qualifications Summary

- ◆ Creative problem solver; proven ability to match people to jobs and products to customers utilizing active listening and persuasive presentation skills.
- ◆ Self-starter; demonstrated talent for building sales and providing high-quality service.
- ◆ Excellent interpersonal skills; easily develop rapport with people from diverse backgrounds; experience working with individuals in broad range of occupations.
- ◆ Highly organized; facility for multitasking and prioritizing in fast-paced environment.
- ◆ Computer literate and Internet savvy; knowledge of Microsoft Office.

Experience

Career Coaching

OPTIONS FOR WOMEN, Lansdale, PA, 1999–2001

Helped clients discover skills and personal strengths, match qualifications to occupations, and find employment.

Sales/Customer Service

FABRIC CITY, Quakertown, PA, 2000
SILK IMPORTS, INC., Doylestown, PA, 1999–2000
BUSINESS OWNER/OPERATOR (Faux Painting), Souderton, PA, 1991–1999
CEDARBROOK SCHOOL, Souderton, PA, 1989–2000

As business owner/operator, grew client base through networking and relationship building, direct calling, and flyer distribution. Sold products for Silk Imports and Fabric City to designers and consumers, evaluating customers' needs—spoken and unspoken—and matching with company products. In all positions, won customers' appreciation with respectful attitude and fast, friendly service. At Cedarbrook School, developed network as committee/event chairperson and informally championed school to increase enrollment.

Administration

A. JAMESON ASSOCIATES, CENTRAL MONTGOMERY HOSPITAL, Lansdale, PA, 2003–present
MONTGOMERY COUNTY TECHNOLOGY COUNCIL, Norristown, PA, 2000–2001

Researched member companies and industry trends for sales representatives, provided input for event planning, attended events, and managed office functions for organization serving 500 member companies doing business in high-tech arena. Currently serve as point of contact for busy medical practice serving 600+ cardiac patients per month. Screen, prioritize, and schedule patients, negotiating to obtain appointments with outside providers when necessary. Help maintain calm, professional atmosphere in high-stress environment.

Education

M.A., University of Pittsburgh, Pittsburgh, PA
B.A., Indiana University of Pennsylvania, Indiana, PA

Career Change: *From office administrator to recruiter.*

Strategy: *Group experience into categories in order of relevance to her target position, rather than chronologically. The most prominent experience (career coaching) was as a volunteer.*

Margaret Lemeshaw

414 Acorn Court, Lawrenceville, NJ 08648
(609) 771-5555 ▪ marlem@earthlink.net

Spanish Teacher at the Middle or High School Level

EDUCATION & CERTIFICATION

New Jersey Teacher's Certification, Spanish K–12

BA, Spanish Language & Civilization / Teaching (cum laude), Rutgers University, New Brunswick, NJ
Two semesters at University of Valencia, Spain. Summer study at University of Madrid.
MBA, International Business / Marketing, Columbia University, New York, NY

PROFILE

☑ Fluent Spanish. Basic conversational Portuguese and good reading ability. Familiar with French.
☑ Experienced Spanish teacher with demonstrated track record of obtaining outstanding results by utilizing highly effective interpersonal and communications skills.
☑ Detail-oriented, analytical professional with proven organizational and problem-solving abilities.
☑ Computer literate: MS Windows 2000, Word, Excel, Outlook, and Internet Explorer; Broderbund Print Shop.

PROFESSIONAL EXPERIENCE

TEACHING / COMMUNICATIONS

▪ Designed Spanish-language curriculum and taught one 2½-hour class weekly for The Princeton Community School. Used text, multimedia, and visual aids to make classroom learning relevant to adults. Resulted in high re-registration rate for following semesters.

▪ Trained small groups of end users on computerized banking services for Mercantile Banking and Trust Company. Conducted product presentations and consultative interviews with clients and prospects. Created and implemented marketing plans for corporate clients in Latin America.

▪ Consulted with clients of International Research Corporation to determine specifications for customized market / opinion research projects. Wrote proposals and translated textbook chapters and questionnaires from Spanish to English. Developed marketing collaterals and account relationship management techniques to ensure top-notch company image and service.

ORGANIZATION / PROJECT MANAGEMENT

▪ Coordinated complex, comprehensive multinational research projects for Research Analysis Corporation and International Research Corporation. Ensured timely completion of projects within budget.

▪ Coordinated translations from Spanish to English for scholarly magazine, obtaining and evaluating board-member input on editorial content, all while meeting strict publication deadlines. Streamlined procedures for foreign-language advertisement and order fulfillment (Medical Learning Systems).

EMPLOYMENT HISTORY

Director of International Marketing	International Research Corp., Somerset, NJ	1998–2004
Spanish I Teacher	Princeton Community School, Princeton, NJ	1998–2003
Field Administrator	Research Analysis Corp., Skillman, NJ	1997–1998
Coordinator—Latin American Services	Medical Learning Systems, Skillman, NJ	1995–1996
Community Volunteer Activities and Family Child Care	Lawrenceville, NJ	1989–1995
Senior Marketing & Sales Rep.	Mercantile Banking and Trust Co., New York, NY	previously

Career Change: From marketing professional to teacher.

Strategy: Margaret discovered her passion for teaching while conducting Spanish classes at a community school. Her resume relates her professional and volunteer experiences to her new target.

BRYCE CARLSON
265 Charlotte Street
Asheville, NC 28801

(828) 555-7893 *home*
(828) 254-7893 *cell*
gatehous@aol.com

HISTORY TEACHER
North Carolina License, Social Studies 9–12

PROFILE

Proactive, uncompromising advocate of improving critical reading, writing, and thinking skills. Use creativity, flexibility, resourcefulness, and organizational and interpersonal skills to facilitate learning through positive, encouraging environment.

Strengths

- Capable teacher thoroughly grounded in U.S., Middle Eastern, World, and European History.
- Rapport builder with parents (they think they're all alone out there), able to gain their positive involvement, trust, and respect in creating a participative environment.
- Adept, available, and adaptable classroom manager—combine discipline plan with effective procedures and varied lessons to attract the inattentive and enforce student accountability.
- Student motivator—can use cooperative learning, jigsaw, and other student-directed, process learning techniques to incorporate diverse students, foster a team spirit and inclusive group identity, and build teamwork and goal-setting skills.
- Develop useful daily lesson plans and instructional resources.
- Friendly, interactive, and dependable.
- Some fluency in Spanish (can read Spanish newspaper).

"A page of history is worth a volume of logic." —Oliver Wendell Holmes

EDUCATION

B.A., History, Magna Cum Laude, December 2002
University of North Carolina at Asheville

Coursework

- U.S. History, Medieval Europe, Politics of the Middle East, Political Science, Chinese History (Revolutionary China), Afro-American History, Human Rights & International Politics, Humanities. Dean's List every eligible semester.

Student Teaching

- Charl High School, Spring and Fall 2002—rotating 11th-grade college-prep classes in U.S. History. Selected to teach AP U.S. History class due to knowledge of material.

  · Contributions included judging senior projects, proctoring end-of-course tests, and sponsoring the fledgling debate club.

  · Because my co-op supervisor was on the school improvement team, was able to observe planning and goal-setting functions in the effort to meet constantly changing requirements. Participated positively in parent-teacher conferences.

"I teach skill in asking questions through my skill in asking the right question...."

Honors & Affiliations

- Selected for Phi Alpha Theta History National Honor Society (high GPA and faculty recommendation).

- Selected by History Department faculty for the Moses Lowe History Scholarship as most promising student in the field of history, despite being on an education track.

- Participant, UNCA History Association.

- Alpha Phi Omega National Service Fraternity—Chapter President. As Vice President of Service, initiated projects involving Boys and Girls Clubs; fund raising for Ride for Kids 2000 (pediatric brain tumors); highway beautification; hunger food bank (packing); and RiverLife (river clean-up).

Cited by department faculty for original, critical thinking....

Career Change: *From boiler operator to teacher.*

gatehous@aol.com • (828) 254-7893 *cell* • (828) 555-7893 *home*   **BRYCE CARLSON**

Prior Education	**Diploma, Welding** (one-year program), 1980 Carolina Technical Community College Coursework in Anthropology, Biology, and Spanish, 1973 University of Massachusetts—Boston
PRIOR EXPERIENCE	BOILER OPERATOR: Crawford Plant Works, Summerville, NC—1980–1997 Operated steam- and electric-generating utility for largest textile mill of its kind in the world, on 10 acres, with its own waste-treatment and water-filtration system. Member of 2-man team: managed electrical control room, maintenance, welding, machinery repair, and pipefitting. ENGINEER: 100-foot *Lad In Blue* fishing boat, Gloucester, MA—1971–1980 MACHINIST MATE: United States Navy—1967–1971 Served on the U.S.S. *Georgetown* (spy ship—traveled to Mozambique Civil War; the Indian Ocean; and Havana, Cuba) and U.S.S. *Severn* (oil tanker refueling ships at sea in the Mediterranean). Trained Navy personnel (including firemen and 3rd class petty officers) to work with tools and operate equipment.
COMMUNITY REINVESTMENT	<ul><li>Coached Roller Hockey for Boys and Girls Clubs, ages 13–18, in league competition.</li><li>Tutor, Afterschool Club, Salvation Army.</li><li>Big Brothers/Big Sisters, 1981–1983. Mentored 7-year-old boy (gardening, movies, sports, homework).</li><li>Member of Church Inquiry Committee—answer questions to assist one in deciding whether to join the church; prepare lesson plans and curriculum for those interested in doing so.</li></ul>

Strategy: *Emphasize teaching and academic skills, adding quotes and a graphic to make the resume stand out. Briefly summarize experience on page 2 and add a strong community involvement section to show a trend of working with youth.*

JOHN BRYAN ATKINS

345 Evergreen Terrace
Milton Mills, NH 03852   **jbatkins@aol.com**   Home: (603) 222-9871
Mobile: (603) 393-7610

PROGRAM SPECIALIST
Dedicated to the development and education of all students

Highly skilled professional dedicated to making a positive impact on students' lives by creating an atmosphere conducive to learning. Caters to diverse modalities of learning to promote and enhance individual student strengths, instilling in youth a love of knowledge and the desire to meet and exceed expectations. Skilled use of positive reinforcement, communication, and problem solving to establish outstanding rapport with students. Exceptional team-builder and leader, creating a strong sense of community for students and staff.

☑ Progress Monitoring   ☑ Budget Planning
☑ Classroom Management   ☑ Student Motivation
☑ Curriculum Design & Development   ☑ Parental Involvement
☑ Visual & Tactile Learning Methods   ☑ Vocational Development
☑ Individual Educational Plans (IEPs)   ☑ Team-Building Techniques

QUALIFICATIONS

Bachelor of Science, Special Education   2003
UNIVERSITY OF SOUTHERN MAINE

Bachelor of Science, Vocational/Occupational Education   2001
UNIVERSITY OF SOUTHERN MAINE

EDUCATIONAL EXPERIENCE

GABE FOUNDATION SCHOOL—*Maine*   1996 to PRESENT
Program Specialist (Volunteer)
Report to Director of Special Education for this private school developing educational programs. Research and develop curriculum, write IEPs, attend meetings in accordance with IDEA, teach integrated curriculum, interact with school districts, and manage classrooms.

Program/Curriculum Development
- Initiated and implemented three educational programs for at-risk youth, actively engaging students and creating programs to satisfy the school's growing referral base.
- Independently developed curriculum for elk farming program, enabling students to run the day-to-day operation of the elk herd, including TB testing, worming, and cutting velvet.
- Taught an integrated curriculum in all content areas by adapting curriculum to accommodate vastly diverse functioning levels, and accelerating achievement of educational objectives.
- Expanded programs to serve more students and promote active learning; started programs on new sites by adding new themes on current sites, including aquaculture, scuba diving, and boat building.
- Researched and developed curriculum requirements, ensuring programs were within curriculum frameworks and state content standards and benchmarks.

Student Learning/Interaction
- Encourage student involvement in their local community by having students complete community project each year. This year's project involved building offices in a community center. Past projects have included developing a park, building a bandstand, and roofing town buildings.
- Collaborated with students in resolving fish and wildlife concerns about contamination of local fish populations with the importation of tilapia. After persisting for two years to resolve issues, students received permits to import and raise tilapia.
- Provided a more structured and intense program that increased student interest and learning in reading.
- Directed the foundation's Fertile Farm Program, providing tutoring for up to 14 students diagnosed with AD/HD, ADD, and Bipolar disorder.

Career Change: *From farmer/rancher to teacher.*

Strategy: *Focus on educational experiences related to a volunteer position he has held for several years.*

RESUME 68, CONTINUED

JOHN BRYAN ATKINS   Page 2

Educational Experience, Continued

Communication/Relationship Building
- Develop and maintain professional business relationships with district administrators to ensure adherence to IDEA by attending meetings and interacting with directors and superintendents in seven school districts and two states.
- Collaborate with parents, fellow teachers, and school-based support team members to develop Individual Educational Plans (IEPs), enabling all students to progress toward individual goals.

RIVERTON SCHOOL—*Maine*   1991 to 1996
Substitute Teacher—Special Education Aide
Shop Teacher
- Substituted all grades K–8 in art, music, and gym, creating and implementing lessons in the absence of lesson plans or daily schedules to support student academic, social, and personal development.
- Provided tutoring to special-needs students to enhance student learning and understanding of subject matter. Ensured effective behavior management by incorporating motivational activities and positive reinforcement strategies.
- Instrumental in developing middle school woodworking shop program, creating educational activities to make learning enjoyable and exciting.

PROFESSIONAL EXPERIENCE

ATKINS ELK FARM—*Maine*   1976 to PRESENT
Business Owner/Manager
- Engage special-needs students in educational activities to make learning enjoyable and exciting; transport students to and from the elk farm, allowing them to interact with animals.
- Manage and execute all operational processes for 20-head elk farm, including managing aquaculture hatching and grow-out facility.
- Appointed as manager by the State of Maine to operate the abused farm animal facility, ensuring the proper care and well being of the animals.
- Astutely control all budget forecasting and management, performing statistical analysis relative to expense control, planning, and forecasting.

MAINE NAVAL SHIPYARD—*Maine*   1977 to 1987
Nuclear Crane Electrician/Chief Steward

CERTIFICATIONS

Vocational Special Needs
Vocational Electrical
Vocational Electrical/Electronics

PROFESSIONAL AFFILIATIONS

Member, North American Riding for the Handicapped Association (NARHA)
Member, Aircraft Owners & Pilots Association (AOPA)
Member, Civil Air Patrol (CAP)

REFERENCES AVAILABLE UPON REQUEST

NANCY ADAMS

473 Baywood Boulevard
Brick Township, NJ 08723

Residence: 732-477-5172
nancyadams@hotmail.com

TARGET: HIGH SCHOOL SCIENCE TEACHER

Biology • Physical Science • Environmental • Marine Biology • General Science

Solid science background with a bachelor's degree in biology, experience in a wildlife refuge, and instructional experience in a variety of settings. Possess a passion for science and children and for making a difference. Currently a certified scuba diver to enhance marine biology studies. Pending New Jersey Teaching Certificate. Creative, self-motivated, and enthusiastic. Developed strong abilities in the following areas:

- Needs Assessments and Progress Evaluations
- Laboratory Studies and Animal/Reptile Handling
- Advanced Planning and Group Presentations
- Microscope and Computer Instruction

Personal Teaching Philosophy

A friend with an education makes a better teacher than a dictator with a book. Children deserve patience and respect in an environment where the subject comes to life, producing children who attend class and want to learn.

CREDENTIALS

- New Jersey Teaching Certificate Eligible, Final Certification Anticipated June 2005
- Biology Content Knowledge Part 2 Praxis Series Certification, Completion Pending June 2005
- General Science Content Knowledge Part 2 Praxis Series Certification, Completed July 1997
- General Science Content Knowledge Part 1 Praxis Series Certification, Completed July 1997
- Brick Township Substitute Teacher for all grades during sophomore year of college, 1994–1995

EDUCATION

The Ultimate Supervisor's Workshop (time management, organization skills, budget management) • April 2003
Biology Course • Georgian Court College, Lakewood, New Jersey • Fall 2002
Dealing with Difficult People (verbal & written communication skills, handling toxic personalities) • Oct. 2002

Bachelor of Science in Biology • Georgian Court College, Lakewood, New Jersey • 1997

Invertebrate Zoology Lab—Microscopic examinations, detailed diagrams, and classifications of invertebrates.

Genetics Lab—Handling, anesthetizing, and classifying fruit flies.

Organisms & Evolution Lab—Dissections of multiple animals.

Marine Biology Lab—Collection of physical and biological samples during multiple hours on a boat in the Metedeconk River. Review of samples under microscopes in the lab and recording of data.

Additional Courses—Animal Behavior, Ecology, Cells & Molecules, Ichthyology, Marine Plants, Biology of Marine Mammals, Conservation Biology, and Environmental Crime.

SCIENCE INSTRUCTION EXPERIENCE

Volunteer, Snake & Small Animal Education Center, Ocean County Wildlife Refuge, Brick, NJ • Spring 2003
Regional wildlife and nature education, rehabilitation, and refuge center open to the public.

Educated children and adults in the importance of wildlife to the community and the characteristics of various wild animals. Handled and cared for screech owls, opossums, turtles, python snakes, rat snakes, corn snakes, and garter snakes.

Accomplishment
- Transitioned children terrified of snakes into children willing to touch them through demonstrations; through explaining why snakes look, feel, and move the way they do; and through clarifying the importance of snakes in our environment.

Page 1 of 2

Career Change: *From dental office manager to teacher.*

RESUME 69, CONTINUED

NANCY ADAMS continued…   732-477-5172 • nancyadams@hotmail.com

TRAINING INSTRUCTION & SUPERVISORY EXPERIENCE

Business Manager, Dental Office of Drs. Barklage & Neadeau, Brick Township, New Jersey • July 2002–Present

Receptionist, Dental Office of Susan Michaels, D.M.D., Lakewood, New Jersey • May 2001–July 2002

Assistant Manager, Dental Office of Dan Rogers, D.M.D., Brick Township, New Jersey • Sept. 2000–May 2001

Front Desk Coordinator, Dental Office of Drs. Rossi & Iooss, Howell, New Jersey • Aug. 1998–Sept. 2000

Receptionist, Dental Office of Dr. Zachary Jones, Brick Township, New Jersey • Aug. 1997–July 1998

- Currently supervise group activities of 14 office employees. As assistant manager, supervised 5.
- Assess individual performance, prepare written reviews, and assist in presenting results to each one.
- Provide one-on-one computer instruction in various software programs.
- Prepare written guidelines for patient/employee interactions, conduct role-playing, and give quizzes.
- Prepared for and conducted staff meetings/instruction to groups of 14–18 employees.

Accomplishments
- Created informational manual educating employees in job descriptions, policies, and procedures. Manual produced clarification of individual responsibilities resulting in less tension and greater teamwork (2002).

- Evaluated overall office performance by tracking each individual's performance and results and then organizing data into bar graphs and pie charts to demonstrate findings. Improved group performance by revising written informational lists, performing skits, and conducting one-on-one consultations.

COMPUTER SOFTWARE ABILITIES

Presentation, Word Processing & Financial: Print Shop, Photoshop, PowerPoint, Word, Excel, Lotus 1-2-3, Quicken

Communications & Operating Systems: Internet Explorer, Outlook Express, MSN Messenger, Windows, DOS

Page 2 of 2

Strategy: *Use the first page to highlight the information most relevant to her goal of teaching high school science. The Professional Experience section on page 2 includes only information that is transferable to her new career.*

Julia Flowers

15204 Caribou Road ◇ Staunton, Virginia 22587 ◇ 540.487.9586

*"Enhancing learning and providing an extraordinary environment
for students to recognize their full potential"*

Summary of Qualifications

Enthusiastic, dedicated, and adaptable; willing to experiment and adjust plans to the situation. Love to learn and make a difference in children's lives. Adept at finding root of problem and trying many options to help children reach potential.

Core Strengths

Problem-solving skills	Communication skills—verbal and written
Curriculum development	Community outreach and relations
Higher-level critical-thinking skills	Cultural diversity awareness

Education

- Accepted into **Master of Education** program, Radford University, Summer of 2004
- **Initial Teacher Licensure Program,** Maryland University, College Park, Maryland, 2003
- **Bachelor of Arts,** History, College of William and Mary, Williamsburg, Virginia, 1992
- **Associate of Arts,** Education, Northern Virginia Community College, Fairfax, Virginia, 1989

Professional Experience

Yorktown Elementary, Richmond, Virginia, April–June, 2003
Student Teacher

Taught 1st grade. Observed children for clues as to their needs and learning styles; adapted teaching methods to accommodate their needs. Identified a struggling reader and after consulting with parent, issued personal challenge for student. The child met challenge over summer and is doing well in 2nd grade this year.

- Parents related positive feedback from children.
- Received *A* for course.

Hecht's Department Stores, Fairfax, Virginia
Customer Service Representative 1999–Present
Personnel Manager 1994–1999
Cash Office Supervisor 1992–1994

Began in cash office; promoted to Personnel Manager; requested step-down to customer service position while completing education degree.

Extensive experience in **training, customer service,** and **management.** Good rapport with team members. Exceptional interpersonal skills. Use active listening, paraphrase problem to customer, remain calm, and provide options to resolve customer complaints and other issues. Interviewed and hired staff; recruited seasonal hires. Conducted three-hour new-employee training orientation. Encouraged questions and feedback from new hires. Practiced open-door policy.

- Instrumental in helping customer service desk receive rare score of 100 in internal audit.
- Received various awards and positive comments from customers.
- Developed creative merchandising methods; received positive comments from regional manager.

Career Change: *From retail salesperson and manager to teacher.*

Strategy: *Carefully match qualifications with the mission statement of the school district. Focus on her relevant people skills, customer service experience, and management and training background.*

STEPHANIE MCCALL

Page 1 of 2

8 Monahan Avenue · Staten Island, NY 10308 · Home: (718) 209–1129 · Cellular: (646) 692–2298

FOCUS AND QUALIFICATIONS

FOCUS: Career in college or university environment teaching graduate and undergraduate students.
Qualified to teach Criminal Justice, Political Science, Urban Affairs, History, and Public Administration.

QUALIFICATIONS: NYPD Sergeant with experience teaching graduate-level Criminal Justice and Public Administration courses at Baruch College, New York. Exemplary 20-year NYPD record, holding multiple awards. Talented instructor with New York State Police Instructor Certification (MOI) and a 10-year record of cross-level police instruction. Recognized by NYPD and educational institutions for outstanding academic performance, instructional skills, and community contributions. Extensive exposure to multicultural environments. Bilingual (English-German) with conversational skills in Spanish. Master's degree in Political Science.

EDUCATION, TRAINING, AND CERTIFICATION

- **MASTER OF ARTS DEGREE**—2002
  Major: **Political Science**
  Baruch College—New York, NY
  Graduated magna cum laude; G.P.A.: 3.90
  Recipient of Herbert Bienstock Research Award

- **BACHELOR OF SCIENCE DEGREE**—1995
  Major: **History**
  The College of Staten Island—Staten Island, NY
  Graduated magna cum laude—G.P.A.: 3.89

- **CERTIFIED SIMMUNITION TRAINING AND SAFETY SUPERVISOR**—2001
  Simmunition Division SNC Technologies, Inc.
  New York, NY

- **CERTIFIED VERBAL JUDO INSTRUCTOR**—1995
  Verbal Judo Institute—New York, NY

- **METHODS OF INSTRUCTION**—1992
  Division of Criminal Justice—New York State

PROFESSIONAL EXPERIENCE

TEACHING/INSTRUCTING

Solid 10 years of experience instructing recruits, in-service Police Officers, Sergeants, Lieutenants, and Captains. Selected in 2000 by Professor of Criminal Justice and Public Administration at Baruch College to serve as substitute lecturer while working toward master's degree. Average class size comprised 20 to 35 graduate and undergraduate students. Authored lesson plans, selected textbook readings, and assigned and graded homework. Received highly positive student feedback regarding methodology, professionalism, and personality.

- Authoring lesson plans for INTAC (In-Service Tactical Training Unit)—scenario-based training in a "live-fire" environment to reinforce proper tactics and firearms restraint to minimize escalation of incidents.
  Result: Sharp decline in shooting incidents since program's inception in 1996.
- Instructing NYPD Counter-Terrorism Program for INTAC Unit, teaching up to 30 people at a time.
- Transforming inexperienced recruits into street-ready Police Officers as Police Science Instructor, preparing recruits for NYPD career through familiarization with police administration and legal procedures.

Continued..

Career Change: *From police officer to teacher.*

Strategy: *Focus on her relevant teaching/training experience in her full-time job. Feature education prominently because it is recent and gives her an essential qualification for teaching at the college level.*

STEPHANIE MCCALL

Page 2 of 2

Home: (718) 209-1129

- Using outstanding classroom management skills and an interactive, animated teaching style, generated high level of student enthusiasm.
- Applying advanced communication and foreign-language skills to effectively interact with cross-cultural college students and international communities in New York City.

LAW ENFORCEMENT

Broad and successful background as Sergeant and Police Instructor. Challenged to patrol and supervise high-crime precincts, relying heavily on superior listening, communication, and negotiation skills to thwart potentially harmful incidents. Strongly committed to well-being of all parties involved.

- Special training in OSHA and hazmat regulations, suicide awareness.
- Consistent performance reviews ranking 4.5 to 5 out of 5 for excellence and professionalism.

CHRONOLOGY

Baruch College, New York, NY   2001 to 2003
Substitute Lecturer in Criminal Justice and Public Administration

New York Police Department (NYPD)   1983 to 2003
Retired June 2003

- INTAC Supervisor—In-Service Tactical Training Unit, Brooklyn/Queens   1996 to 2003
- Borough-based Training—Uniformed In-Service, Brooklyn   1994
- Recruit Instructor, Police Science—Police Academy, Manhattan   1992 to 1994
- Sergeant, Patrol Supervisor, and Desk Sergeant—Queens   1989 to 1992
- Police Officer—Brooklyn North   1983 to 1989

AWARDS AND HONORS

- **Education Achievement Citation**—NYPD, NY—2002
  Awarded for successfully balancing full-time work and six years of education.
- **Perfect Attendance Recognition Certificate**—NYPD, NY—2001
- **Herbert Bienstock Research Award**—Baruch College, New York, NY—2000
- **Greenpoint Community Service Award**—Greenpoint, NY—1989
  Awarded by community in recognition of effective volunteer youth efforts.
- **Commended for investigatory skills leading to homicide confession**—NYPD, NY—1988
- **EPD—Medal** (Excellent Police Duty)—NYPD, NY—1985
  Awarded for verbally disarming mentally disturbed person armed with knife.

RESUME 72: BY DON ORLANDO, MBA, CPRW, JCTC, CCM, CCMC

Curriculum Vitæ

Martin R. Kronfeld, B.A., M.S. (Statistics), M.B.A., PMP
2020 Northbeach Circle, Jefferson, Illinois 64100
mkr10000@jefflink.net ■ 630.765.5985

WHAT I OFFER **NORTON COMMUNITY COLLEGE** AS YOUR NEWEST INSTRUCTOR IN INFORMATION SCIENCES

- **Passion** to lead students to *want* to excel

- **Dedication** to help build interdisciplinary curricula

- **Skill** to "build in" quality measures my students and I use every day to maximize learning

- **Flexibility** to tailor media selection and teaching style to individual learners—on the fly, if necessary

- **Commitment** to continuing self-development so that what I teach has lasting value

- **Subject-matter expertise** to make courses "come alive" in the classroom

EDUCATION:

- M.B.A., University of Concord, Concord, Illinois   1992
  Earned this degree while working 40 hours a week. Funded by my employer. GPA 3.84.

- M.S., Statistics, Carlton Tech, Smithson, Illinois   1979
  Paid my own way. GPA 3.20.

- B.A., Psychology, Martin College, Shenleyville, South Carolina   1976

RECENT AND RELEVANT WORK HISTORY WITH SELECTED EXAMPLES OF SUCCESS AS AN EDUCATOR:

- Owner and **Practicing IT Consultant,** Kronsight Consulting, Jefferson, IL   2000–Present

  My company specializes in subcontract work touching on IT solutions for the telecommunications and e-mail industries. Companies engage me to analyze not only their business systems, but the data that underlies the information they need to prosper.

  EDUCATING TO EQUIP PEOPLE TO HANDLE PROBLEMS NOW AND IN THE FUTURE

  Completed a comprehensive "needs analysis" for a company that had to master new concepts to help it grow. Not only educated demanding, well-informed senior leadership, but gave their team members the skills they needed to educate their customers as well. *Outcomes:* Client's customer base grew significantly.

Career Change: *From computer programmer to college instructor.*

Strategy: *Show his performance as a teacher rather than from an IT perspective. An integral part of the strategy was a cover letter closely attuned to the needs of his target employer.*

Curriculum Vitæ (continued)

Martin R. Kronfeld	**Instructor in Information Sciences**	630.765.5985

■ *Hired away by the General Manager to be* **Senior Consulting Engineer,** Arista Technologies, Centerville, IL   1996 to 2002

This firm manufactured a line of high-speed data communications products. With sales approaching $200M, it served customers worldwide.

Served as a reporting official for five senior software and consulting engineers.

USING NEEDS ANALYSIS AS A FOUNDATION FOR LEARNING AND GROWTH

Transformed a group of well-intentioned strangers into a "learning machine" that got the answers to vital questions efficiently and effectively. Our customers and our engineers had "talked past each other" for 18 months when management called me in to troubleshoot. Used seminar techniques to help team members develop a clear vision of what they needed to learn to work together and value the process. *Outcomes:* Excellent solution in just six months.

■ **Director, Network Systems & Protocols,** Kronos Corp., Centerville, IL   1994 to 1996

This small, regional company provided data communications consulting.

Served as a reporting official for four programmers.

USING TECHNICAL SUBJECT MATTER EXPERTISE TO TEACH EFFECTIVE OUTCOMES

Gently guided a customer whose business model contained a faulty assumption. Did my homework to master the appropriate technologies and then asked the right questions of the right people. Using what we learned, I helped the customer develop a new business model. My instruction led him to adopt my suggestions as his own good ideas. *Outcomes:* Company had greater confidence in where to invest scarce resources and had trusted ways to estimate return on investment.

■ *Hired away by the Director to serve as* **Advisory Programmer,** Prodigy Services Company, White Plains, NY   1989 to 1994

PROVIDING DURABLE INSTRUCTION TO HELP LEARNERS BEYOND THE "CLASSROOM"

Showed a customer how to attack a complex problem—getting the most from three incompatible systems—in a consistent, logical fashion. Quickly found the native strengths of each team member; then used those strengths as a basis for mentoring. By documenting our approach, I built the "lesson plans" the company would later use to educate new employees. *Outcomes:* Went beyond solving the problem at hand to show employees how rigorous inquiry leads to excellence now and in the future.

■ Additional experience as a private consultant and **principal member of technical staffs** in software and network development groups for Unimation, Inc., and ITT.

RESUME 72, CONTINUED

Curriculum Vitæ (continued)

Martin R. Kronfeld   **Instructor in Information Sciences**   630.765.5985

CERTIFICATION:

- Project Management Professional, Project Management Institute   2003

COMPUTER LITERACY:

- **Networks and operating systems:**

  Expert: DOS, UNIX, Solaris, ESCON, Ethernet, and Giga-bit Ethernet

  Proficient: Windows NT, MVS, VM, DB 2, Linux SCSI, Fibre Channel, FICON, ATM, T1/E1, SONET, and ISDN

- **Programming languages:**

  Expert: C and SNMP
  Proficient: C++, MASM, Java, XML, MFC, WMI, SQL, CICS, and HTML
  Working knowledge: .NET, COM, IMS, IDMS, VTAM, PL/1, COBOL, CICS EXEC, Assembler, and ASP

- **Middleware:**

  Proficient: IBM MQ (Websphere)
  Working knowledge: TIBCO Rendezvous and MSMQ

- **Embedded systems development:**

  Proficient: CE and NT, RTX, C-EXEC, and VRTX
  Working knowledge: P-SOS

- **Protocols:**

  Expert: TCP/IP (sockets)
  Proficient: RS232 and RS422
  Working knowledge: NetBIOS, Novell IPX/SPX, ISO, and SS7

- **Wireless data protocols:**

  Working knowledge: GPRS, GSM, CDMA, TDMA, WAP, ANSI-41, and IS-95

- **Other:**

  Expert: Network device drivers and hardware support
  Proficient: Object-oriented design and programming (OOD/OOP), LAN/WAN installation and management, data networking protocols, telecommunications equipment ISO-9000, and computer-based project management

MEMBERSHIP IN PROFESSIONAL ORGANIZATON:

- Member, Project Management Institute   Since 2003

RESUME 73: BY JOHN O'CONNOR, MFA, CRW, CPRW, CCM, CECC

JOHN P. DALTON

897 Airborne Inn, Room 432   *(910) 958-8656—Phone*
Fort Bragg, North Carolina 28314   *Jdalton@cox.net*

University Program Director / Advisor / Training & Development Leader
Strategist and Management Leader—Greek Life Director—or Related University Roles

Strong management experience in a wide variety of roles within multiple high-pressure settings with skills that can be utilized to positively add value to programs/processes at the university administration level. Skill base summary includes but is not limited to the following:

- *Program Development/Facilitation*
- *Training Development*
- *Team Leadership*
- *Materials/Facility Management*

- *Operations Management*
- *Teaching, Mentoring, and Motivation*
- *Multi-Task Project Management*
- *Budget Management*

Education / Awards

NORTH CAROLINA STATE UNIVERSITY
Raleigh, NC
BS in Political Science, May 1996
- *ROTC Scholarship Winner*
- *Distinguished Military Graduate*
- *Who's Who Among Students in American Universities*
- *Inter-Fraternity*
- *Kappa Alpha Order, President*
- *Student Government Association*

UNIVERSITY OF GEORGIA
Athens, GA
- *Pursued MA in Counseling/Student Personnel Administration (1994–1997)*
- *Assistantship/Graduate Advisor, Men's Fraternities*

UNITED STATES ARMY/NATIONAL GUARD

Security Clearance
- *Top Secret Security Clearance*

Recognition
- *5 Army Commendation Medals—Desert Storm/Desert Shield and Operation Enduring Freedom*
- *Army Achievement Medal*
- *The National Defense Medal*
- *The Southwest Asia Service Medal*
- *Army Service Medal*
- *Airborne/Air Assault Schools, Maintenance Officer Course*
- *Officer Basic Leadership Course*

Summary of Qualifications

- Proven track record working with all levels of personnel and on projects in materials management, inventory control, shipping, logistics, and multiple distribution areas as well as highly disciplined military training through the U.S. Army, U.S. Army Reserves, and National Guard.
- Regarded by industry peers as a fair, knowledgeable, consistent, and trustworthy leader who strives for a high level of quality while meeting and exceeding quantity objectives.
- Excellent verbal and written communication skills; able to organize and present training or other materials to a group.
- Reputation as a team player and achiever who applies leadership skills to advanced managerial tasks.
- Team-based leadership philosophy and supervisory style; proven ability to successfully direct the integration of cross-functional teams, internal departments, and personnel to build organizations, develop ongoing training programs, and execute on-campus organizational plans.

Career Change: *From military officer to university administrator.*

Strategy: *Emphasize direct experience from positions in the military; emphasize advanced education.*

JOHN P. DALTON   *Page 2*

Professional Experience

UNITED STATES ARMY, Fort Bragg, NC
Plans & Operation Officer, United States Army Special Forces Command (Airborne) (12/2001–Present)

> From Recent Evaluations: *CPT Dalton is one of the best Captains I have served with in my 18 years of service...CPT Dalton has been my point man on my staff for Special Forces operations in Afghanistan, Uzbekistan, and Kuwait in support of Operation Enduring Freedom.*

- Position has included short international tours in addition to mission-critical responsibilities in support of Operation Enduring Freedom and PENTCOM AOR.
- Serve as National Guard Advisor—Plans and Operations Officer, Army National Guard at the U.S. Army Special Forces Command at Fort Bragg, NC. This critical coordination and high-profile position reports directly to senior/general staff and coordinates directly with the theater Special Operations Command, The National Guard Bureau, and others for planning and execution of exercises and major regional contingents.
- Selected key projects have included planning and operational support for the deployment of 1,600 Special Forces National Guard Personnel.
- Total responsibility for planning, supervising, and coordinating all actions for all Special Forces soldiers within the 79th and 89th Special Forces Group/Airborne Worldwide.
- Analyze and ensure logistics, strategic plans, training, and operational issues are coordinated and supported by the appropriate organization and resources.

CREE RESEARCH, Research Triangle Park, NC
Production Manager (6/1998–11/2001)
- In production management role, maintained readiness in a high-level, high-intensity production environment; responsibilities included setting, training, and enforcing quality standards within department.
- Supervised the production of chicken per production and safety specifications/standards.
- Provided daily scheduling and supervision of production employees; oversaw changing and proper functionality of production-line parts and materials.

PLANNING PARTNERS, Athens, GA
Sales Representative (6/1996–6/1998)
- Executed strategic marketing and sales plans; effectively utilized high levels of customer contact to drive sales and direct customer accountability as well as indirect through their sales managers and sales representatives.
- Managed existing customer relationships and developed new customer relationships in existing and new markets.
- Provided sales forecasts in their regions and closely monitored the attainment of the goals under their management.
- Developed tactical plans to ensure attainment of sales and profit goals for their customers and regions; attained gross margin and expense budget objectives to ensure that the budgeted profit was attained.

References Available upon Request

CHAPTER 9

Resumes for Career Changers Seeking Sports and Recreation, Cultural, and Creative and Performing Arts Positions

Many of the resumes in this chapter were written for people who wanted to make their avocation their vocation. Because these candidates are so passionate about their fields, they often have relevant (although perhaps unpaid) experience that they can highlight. You will also see some examples of personal statements and vision statements that convey the intangible yet important qualities that make these positions a great fit. The career transitions represented in this chapter include the following:

- Warehouse manager to sports/recreation director

- College teacher to manager of recreation programs in the hospitality industry

- Salesperson to professional sport fisher

- Military operations to fitness trainer

- Press-relations manager to wine and food promoter

- Telecommunications operator to broadcasting professional

- Landscaper to audio/video production assistant

- Fuels specialist in the military to film production apprentice

- College professor to interior designer

- Intelligence analyst in the U.S. military to architectural designer

- Attorney to cultural arts director

RODNEY ALLEN

213 Ashburn Farm Drive ♦ Ashburn, VA 20147
(703) 555-9576 ♦ sportsmanager@earthlink.net

GOAL

To advance 18+ years of management experience and an educational background in Recreation Administration and Intramural Sports into the career arena of sports administration, recreation programming, or facilities management.

♦ Senior manager offering extensive experience in purchasing and materials management; personnel training and supervision; and organizational development in both start-up and high-growth operations.

♦ Proven leadership and interpersonal skills; flexible in working with people of all ages and socioeconomic backgrounds.

♦ Performance-focused, intuitive coach; astute in recognizing individuals' strengths and assigning the right person for the right job.

♦ Highly effective in managing multiple priorities, with a propensity for minimizing problems through effective daily planning and scheduling.

♦ Noted by customers, management, and staff as ethical, intelligent, and hardworking.

♦ Committed to personal life-long learning and creating opportunities for individuals and teams to attain desired goals.

EDUCATION

Master of Intramural Sports and Recreation—Miami University, Oxford, OH
Bachelor of Arts, Recreation Administration—University of Maryland, College Park, MD

PROFESSIONAL RECORD

INDEPENDENT GLASS DISTRIBUTORS, Alexandria, VA   1997–present
(A full-service wholesale distributor of current-model and vintage automotive replacement glass.)

Facility Manager
Recruited to launch and manage a Baltimore-area start-up operation. Tasked with personnel recruitment, inventory stocking, and operations policy development. Oversee the day-to-day operation of an 18,500-sq.-ft. warehouse with annual gross sales of $2.5M. Direct the daily activities of a cross-functional team of sales representatives, warehouse workers, and delivery drivers servicing 75 customer accounts. Orchestrate long-range planning for operations, sales, and customer service.

♦ Established a formal materials management function to gain control of inventory and ensure purchasing of the best products at the most reasonable cost.

♦ Built and maintain a diverse and loyal customer base in a price-conscious, competitive consumer-products industry.

♦ Captured first-place standing for company-wide gross annual sales by strategically planning and executing targeted market development, maintaining comprehensive and up-to-date inventory, and enforcing dependable delivery schedules.

♦ Reduced employee turnover and improved morale and productivity by initiating flexible work schedules and pay for performance, and by providing access to the best tools and resources available.

Career Change: *From warehouse manager to sports/recreation director.*

Strategy: *Highlighted relevant degree along with transferable skills pulled from his unrelated experience as manager of warehouse operations.*

RODNEY ALLEN
(703) 555-9576
PAGE 2

PROFESSIONAL RECORD (continued)

SATELLITE GLASS, Bethesda, MD   1985–1997
    (An automotive glass retail installation company with 12 branches and an inventory warehouse.)

Warehouse Manager

Managed a 15,000-sq.-ft. warehousing and distribution operation during a period of accelerated industry growth, locally and nationwide. Responsible for the purchasing, receipt, and subsequent distribution of more than $2M merchandise annually.

- Focused efforts on identifying quality suppliers, reducing net purchasing costs, and managing inventory volumes while maintaining adequate and current stock to keep pace with new model releases and changing customer needs.

- Maintained strong vendor and customer relations while responding to numerous demands and shifts in work priorities.

- Established daily service goals; scheduled and dispatched drivers to ensure on-time delivery.

- Developed and delivered a safety management and training program for warehouse personnel.

Prior Experience   1982–1984

Managed the intramural sports program for GMI (Engineering and Management Institute), Flint, MI. Staffed and serviced a six-lane bowling alley; purchased and maintained all crib sporting equipment.

COMMUNITY INVOLVEMENT

ALEXANDRIA YOUTH ATHLETIC ASSOCIATION   1998–present

Youth Soccer Coach

Coach a team of youth, ages ten and under, developing and enhancing their individual and team skills and game strategies.

- Instrumental in drafting and implementing a Coaches Code of Conduct, which defines responsibilities and expectations for volunteer coaches and their interactions with players, parents, and other coaches.

- Plan and facilitate regular meetings to encourage parental involvement with the association and support of the Spectator Code of Conduct.

MIA ANDERSON

10/115 Constantine Avenue, Aspley Qld 4034 ♦ (04) 0233 3444 ♦ (07) 8888 9999 ♦ manderson@beonline.com

CAREER FOCUS

Hospitality Management...Recreation
Dynamic, results-driven manager seeking to capitalize on more than 9 years of sports and recreation experience utilizing exceptional leadership, customer relations, and sales and marketing skills.

"Mia has a deserved reputation as a positive leader who is skilled in leading teams to success in achieving organizational goals." (Current Employer)

PROFESSIONAL EXPERIENCE

Management and Administration
▶ Strategically planned, coordinated, and delivered multi-site sports and recreation training programs.
▶ Led team of 15 to achieve optimum results; hired, trained, motivated, and managed performance of staff.
▶ Oversaw development of effective policy and procedures for new department; implemented by deadline.
▶ Managed departmental budgets; consistently delivered initiatives on time and within budget.

Sales and Marketing
▶ Developed and implemented diverse range of innovative and highly customer-focused programs.
▶ Marketed services using cost-effective strategies; designed all advertising and promotional material.
▶ Coordinated events for 450+ people; secured nationally recognized guests and local media coverage.
▶ Delivered presentations to potential customers; displayed strong public speaking and networking skills.

Interpersonal and Communication
▶ Actively fostered relationships with existing and potential customers in industry and the wider community.
▶ Provided quick resolution to customer complaints; delivered win-win solutions and personalized service.
▶ Cultivated positive "can-do" spirit and culture of participation among diverse customers and staff.
▶ Multilingual; possess written and verbal fluency in English, Spanish, and Italian.

CAREER HIGHLIGHTS

♦ Built number of program participants from zero to 250 during initial 12 months; numbers now exceed 350 and still growing quarterly.
♦ Initiated quality improvement program for department; selected as winner of 2003 "Outstanding Individual Award" for contributions to continuous improvement.
♦ Secured senior management approval for numerous sports and recreation training programs; earned reputation for implementing "the right ideas at the right time."
♦ Set up, from scratch, two new fitness centers, including designing layout, ordering equipment, and training staff.
♦ Oversaw design and construction of new sports facilities for tennis, squash, and football.

EDUCATION & TRAINING

▶ **Certificate in Business Studies (Hospitality Management),** Cairns Technical College, Cairns, 2003
▶ **Bachelor of Applied Science (Human Movement),** University of Northern Queensland, Cairns, 1994
▶ **Advanced Open Water Diver and Rescue Diver,** Professional Association of Diving Instructors, Cairns
▶ **High Ropes Course Instructor,** YWCA, Townsville

EMPLOYMENT HISTORY

Manager (Sports, Recreation, and Fitness), Allanstown Private College, Allanstown, 2001–Current
Coordinator (Sports), North Sutherland Girls' School, North Sutherland, 1999–2001
Secondary Teacher (Sports), Sunshine Coast Girls' School, Buderim, 1995–1998

Career Change: *From college teacher to manager of recreation programs in the hospitality industry.*

Strategy: *Minimize references to teaching and play up ability to develop and implement sports and recreation programs, manage staff and budgets, develop sales and marketing strategies, and provide an exceptional level of customer service.*

BRENDON J. WALKER

AWARD-WINNING BASS FISHER

213 W. Belcrest ▶ Kewanee, IL 61614 ▶ (309) 852-0714 ▶ bassfish@aol.com

VISION STATEMENT

To utilize my professional sales and high-profile competition experience in effectively creating greater market exposure for my sponsors and their products / services; to provide vital sponsor support in penetrating new markets and expanding existing accounts; and to effectively use my sponsorships to catapult my professional competitor success to higher levels.

QUALIFICATIONS SUMMARY

Highly accomplished and enthusiastic professional bass fisher and sales professional with a proven track record of winning top-level competitions and increasing revenues by effectively promoting products. Polished communication, presentation, networking, and problem-solving skills; able to relate comfortably and effectively to people at all levels and develop long-term, professional, trusting relationships for repeat and referral business.

RECENT COMPETITIONS & AWARDS

CHAMPIONSHIP COMPETITION / CROSS LAKE—Shreveport, LA (September 11, 2002)
Placed 13th / Won $2,000

▶ **Placed 2nd / Won $20,000:** LAKE CHAMPLAIN—Plattsburgh, NY (July 19, 2002)
▶ **Placed 39th / Won $600:** LAKE WHEELER—Rogersville, AL (February 15, 2002)
▶ **Placed 50th / Won $500:** LAKE OUACHITA—Mt. Ida, AR (March 15, 2002)
▶ **Placed 64th / Won $400:** LAKE OKEECHOBEE—Clewiston, FL (January 23, 2002)
▶ **Placed 101st:** BEAVER LAKE—Rogers, AR (April 17, 2002)

PROFESSIONAL EMPLOYMENT

NORTHWEST WOOD PRODUCTS—Jefferson, IL   1994 to Present
Fast-track promotion through the following positions:

Sales Representative (2001 to Present): Recruited to promote a wide range of company fencing and deck products for the largest cedar fence and deck company in the state. Manage advertising, create flyers, directly pursue leads, utilize aggressive follow-up methods, design estimates, secure proposals, schedule jobs, and provide customer service.
▶ Successfully sold $600,000 of cedar fencing within a six-month period.
▶ Recognized as one of the company's top three sales representatives.

Supervisor (1995 to 2001): Directed, hired, trained, mentored, and motivated a staff of up to four workers in managing all aspects of fence installations for residential and commercial clients. Tracked footage installed weekly. Served as the central point of contact and client liaison in providing information and resolving issues at all levels.
▶ Reputation for providing excellent quality work with 100% of the jobs requiring no follow-up or additional repair.
▶ Routinely installed a record amount of fence footage weekly.
▶ Started as an installer and quickly was promoted to supervisory position.

RUSTIC PINES COMPANY—Madison Heights, IL   1989 to 1994

Foreman: Oversaw fence installations and supervised / trained crew members.
▶ Promoted from general laborer to foreman due to skill level and dedication.

EDUCATION AND TRAINING

Diploma, VICTOR J. MADISON HIGH SCHOOL—Fairview, IL

Career Change: From salesperson to professional sport fisher.

Strategy: Emphasize related experience and accomplishments from unpaid experience and part-time positions to support his goal of securing sponsorships and assuming a professional career in sport fishing.

RESUME 77: BY JAMES WALKER, MS

Fred Adams
316 Old Milford Road
Milford, KS 66514
Home: 785-237-1548
Work: 785-235-7200
Email: adamsf@hotmail.com

OBJECTIVE

Position as a physical fitness trainer helping others to improve their personal well-being, health, and physical fitness.

SUMMARY OF QUALIFICATIONS

Fitness Trainer Certification—International Sports Sciences Association. Well-conditioned athlete who has followed a rigorous personal fitness program for the past 15 years. Interviewed individuals to determine their interests in improving their physical condition. Helped others to develop personalized programs suited for their needs. Used diet planning, conditioning, aerobics, anaerobics, and supplemental programs. Familiar with various types of weight conditioning equipment.

FITNESS AWARDS

- 1st Place in Body Building, Lightweight Classification, Camp Red Cloud, South Korea

- Top 10, All-Services Fitness Competition, Osan, Korea

- Lightweight Wrestling Champion (3 years), Fort Hood, TX

- Army Physical Fitness Testing: minimum scores of 290 (out of 300) on all tests

INTERVIEWING

Met with prospective clients and discussed their interests in improving their physical condition. Secured information regarding their medical history, current state of physical conditioning, family medical history, and eating and sleeping habits. Also determined whether they were taking any medications that might have an adverse effect on training. Ascertained the extent of their commitment to goals for self-improvement.

DIET PLANNING

Asked individuals their personal likes and dislikes for beverages and food. Determined whether they had any particular adverse reactions to food and beverages. Identified their eating habits, schedules, and current weight. Established individualized goals for weight loss or gain. Created unique dietary plans that coincided with their training plans. Periodically checked their progress and altered plans as necessary.

CONDITIONING

Mapped out plans for phase training from beginning to advanced levels. Combined weight training with aerobics and anaerobics. Selected the right machines to develop each individual's program and conducted training in their proper use. Established cycle training with free weights and time schedules for aerobics combined with rest cycles. Also looked for long-term schedule changes concerning progress and relapse.

Career Change: *From military operations to fitness trainer.*

Strategy: *Use brief anecdotes to describe experiences that perfectly match the role he is seeking—even though these were secondary to his full-time job in the military.*

Fred Adams

SUPPLEMENTAL PROGRAMS

Developed programs and time schedules for vitamin intake and liquid supplements. Determined current status of each client before beginning planning for personal intake. Scheduled vitamin intakes and liquids to complement each training phase. Recommended general and specific content levels for each vitamin and liquid. Closely monitored each individual's attitudes, habits, and physical reactions.

CPR/FIRST AID AND SAFETY

Trained and certified in CPR and first aid. Attended basic health, safety, and physical fitness courses. Trained others how to make triage decisions for evacuation and treatment of personnel. Also taught the proper use of various types of weight training and aerobic equipment.

INTERPERSONAL SKILLS

Effectively communicated with people, demonstrating skill in assisting individuals to identify personal and professional goals. Quickly and easily adjusted to policies of many different supervisors of mixed racial, cultural, religious, and geographical backgrounds. Work well on my own with little or no supervision or as an effective member of a team. Seek added responsibility whenever possible. Frequently called upon by my superiors for special projects because they had the confidence in my ability to do them correctly and on time.

EMPLOYMENT HISTORY

- Physical Fitness Trainer, U.S. Army, Fort Hood, TX, and Fort Riley, KS, January 2000–December 2003

- Chemical Operations Supervisor, U.S. Army, Camp Red Cloud, South Korea, and Fort Hood, TX, January 1996–December 1999

- Chemical Operations Specialist, U.S. Army, Fort Bragg, NC, April 1993–December 1995

- Dental Assistant, U.S. Army, Fort Carson, CO, and Heidelberg, Germany, September 1988–December 1992

EDUCATION

- Certificate, Fitness Trainer, International Sports Sciences Association, Santa Barbara, CA, 2001

- Honor Graduate, Chemical Operations Specialist Course, 13 weeks, U.S. Army, Fort McClellan, AL, 1993

- Commandant's List, Primary Leadership Development Course, 4 weeks, U.S. Army, Fort Bragg, NC, 1995

- Diploma, Washington-Jefferson High School, Atlanta, GA, 1988

CHERI R. PIERRE

1434 Madison Boulevard   Residence: 954-555-1212
Orlando, FL 38917   Pierre2004@aol.com   Mobile: 954-555-1212

CAREER OBJECTIVE & SUMMARY

Passionate epicure seeking to transition to a career dedicated to the appreciation and promotion of wine and food. Particular interest and experience in the regional culinary and wine traditions of France. Able to write and speak expressively about the aesthetics that emerge at the nexus of wine, food, and culture.

Competencies in writing, editing, public relations, communications, management, strategy development, and marketing. Broad range of skills honed during a fast-track, 10-year public relations / communications career at industry-leading firms in the U.S. and France. Talented evangelist for products and concepts.

- Lived, Traveled, and Worked in France / Toured 50+ French Vineyards / Fluent French Speaker
- Earned a Diploma at Ecole Ritz Escoffier, School of French Gastronomy, Paris, France
- Authored Article: "From the Heart of France: The Undiscovered Culinary Traditions of Auvergne"
- Studied Principles of Vinification, Appellation, Winetasting, and Wine Serving
- Completed Coursework in Food Writing, Wines of France, and Wines of Bordeaux

TRANSFERABLE SKILL SET & SELECTED ACHIEVEMENTS

Writing—Wrote bylined magazine and newspaper articles, press releases, proposals, and presentations.

Editing—Established and maintained high standards for all written materials.

Public Relations & Communications—Achieved positive press coverage in top media in the U.S., the U.K., and France, including the *Wall Street Journal* and the *New York Times*.

Relationship Building—Gained access to and forged positive relationships with influential industry players.

Management—Coordinated and directed international teams to achieve consistent messaging.

Marketing—**Strategy Development, Positioning, Branding, Promotion**—Successfully managed a multimillion-dollar corporate positioning program for Big Four accounting firm and drove corporate image-building within the upper echelons of a Top-40 French company.

Events Management—Designed a seminar on new media attended by 300 people, including CEOs of top media companies and 30 key journalists.

PROFESSIONAL EXPERIENCE

SanteTechnologie, Paris, France
Multibillion-dollar medical software company. One of the top 40 companies in France.

Senior Manager, International Press Relations (2000–2003)

Managed business and trade press relations with U.S., U.K., and English-speaking media in Paris. Directed international media activities. Provided strategy-development consulting to senior executives. Coordinated and approved activities of 10 North American staff. Authorized to approve press materials and external communications for six divisions. Managed PR agencies in New York and London.

Career Change: *From press-relations manager to wine and food promoter.*

Strategy: *Describe unusual background and clearly relate to new goal; include a strong set of transferable skills along with the achievements to prove them.*

CHERI R. PIERRE (PAGE 2)

Professional Experience—(Continued)

- Secured positive press coverage on CNN and in the *Wall Street Journal,* the *New York Times, International Herald Tribune, Forbes, Fortune, Institutional Investor, Financial Times, Times of London,* and trade publications.
- Introduced American public relations standards, improving the company's ability to target U.S. markets with high growth potential.
- Introduced company to 100 key media targets, including 15 top-tier business publications.
- In a "first for the company," instituted policies and procedures to ensure that messaging was consistent company-wide. Incorporated personnel from communications, investor relations, and industry-analyst relations more fully into the PR process.
- Worked closely with the company's Secretary General and the Director of Government Affairs to achieve recognition for the company's CEO as a "player" in a global technology study group.
- Edited all announcements and print materials for high-profile events such as the *Fortune* Global Forum.
- Conceived, recommended, and sold a community outreach program to encourage grassroots innovation on the part of local Internet entrepreneurs.

BOWDITCH PUBLIC RELATIONS WORLDWIDE, New York, NY
Rapid promotion to VP at one of the world's largest independent PR agencies with 25 offices and $170 million in revenues.

Vice President, Corporate Affairs Group (1995–2000)

Managed major account relationships. Worked with the Executive Vice President and agency CEO to strategize and implement new-business initiatives. Liaised with senior executives in client organizations. Managed up to 10 direct reports. Supervised global account teams on the larger accounts. Managed crisis communications.

- Managed $3.2 million global positioning program for a Big Four accounting and consulting firm. Developed all strategic initiatives, including media activities; roundtables; high-level global seminars on financial transparency; and a book promotion in the U.S., Europe, and Asia.
- Played a key role in creating a Professional Services Group that tripled the number of clients for the firm. Assisted with the hiring of 20 cross-functional mid- and senior-level professionals.
- Credited by a *Wall Street Journal* reporter with rescuing a potentially damaging story about a client company by exercising skills in diplomacy, communication, and analysis.
- Instrumental in securing multimillion-dollar accounts and in developing and implementing global PR programs. High-profile clients included industry leaders in global management consulting, international law, financial services, human resources consulting, and corporate travel management.

PAINE & JONES, New York, NY
One of the top 60 law firms with 250 lawyers in six international offices.

Communications Manager (1992–1995)

Implemented marketing and communications program. Worked with partners and all 12 practice groups.

- Created all communication materials, including brochures for 12 practice areas.
- Instrumental in organizing a major three-day conference on energy with 200+ industry executives attending.

CHERI R. PIERRE (PAGE 3)

EDUCATION, AFFILIATIONS, AND SKILLS

UNIVERSITY OF CALIFORNIA AT BERKELEY
B.A. in English—Emphasis on literature and writing (1989)
Junior Year Abroad studying at the **British and European Studies Group, London, England**

NEW YORK UNIVERSITY, New York, NY
- International Business and Finance (1993)
- International Public Relations (1992)

ECOLE RITZ ESCOFFIER, SCHOOL OF FRENCH GASTRONOMY, PARIS, France (2002)
Diploma—Practical and Theoretical Training
Foundations of the French Culinary Tradition
- Techniques of food and pastry preparation
- Product selection
- Time management and organization
- Presentation and service
- History of French gastronomy
- Regional culinary customs and traditions

Foundations of French Wine
- Degustation (winetasting)
- Appellation (classification)
- Vinification (winemaking)
- Wine serving

BOSTON UNIVERSITY, Boston, MA
- Food Writing Seminar (2003)
- Careers in Food (2002)

THE NEW SCHOOL, New York, NY
- Basics of Wine Tasting (1998)
- Wines of France (1997)
- Wines of Bordeaux (1996)

PROFESSIONAL MEMBERSHIPS
- The Culinary Guild of the Southeast
- The French-American Chamber of Commerce
- The American Institute of Food and Wine

LANGUAGES: Fluent French speaker, proficient writer in the French language

COMPUTER SKILLS: Microsoft Word, Excel, PowerPoint; Internet research

Willing to relocate within the U.S. or internationally / Available to travel

GLENDA GULLIVER

1245 Corcoran Street NW, Apt. 15A, Washington, DC 20036
Home: (202) 833-4582, E-mail: glendagull@onlineamerica.com

GOAL	**Radio or Television Broadcaster / Announcer / On-Air Personality**

BROADCAST EXPERIENCE

Producer, *Daily Literary Theatre*, WWOW Radio, Washington, DC

➤ Collaborated with a six-person team to coordinate daily on-air performances of classic literature readings.

➤ Selected the works for the show, oversaw casting of roles, conducted rehearsals, and edited content of books selected.

➤ Received the following industry awards:

- **American Association of Female Broadcasters (AAFB) Broadcast Award** for the *Daily Literary Theatre*'s presentation of *The Howard Women* by Sally Skylar.

- **International Reading Organization Award for Broadcasting.**

- **National Radio Commission Broadcast Entertainment Award** for the *Morning Reading Theatre*'s presentation of *Long Road Traveled* by Mary Stephanie Stevens.

Producer, *Critic's Selections,* WWOW Radio, Washington, DC
Reader, *Permission to Dream,* WWOW Radio, Washington, DC

STAGE WORK

Performed dramatic and comedic roles in numerous productions at the following theatres: Washington Area Performing Arts Center, Impromptu Performance Theatre, and Broadway View Theatre.

Role	Production
Alison	*The Long Journey* by David T. Worley
Vera	*Abundance* by Thomas Shriver
Professor Callaghan	*The Course of Life* by Allen Griswold
Sarah Roberts	*Sarah Roberts* by Henri Connors
Judy Austin	*Weddings* by Alicia Sanders

POETRY READINGS

➤ *One Woman Show,* Community Spotlight Theatre, Washington, DC

➤ Black History Month presentation, U.S. Department of Labor, Washington, DC

➤ *Special Programs Featuring Young Producers,* Written Word Bookstore, Washington, DC

➤ *The Saturday Morning Series,* The Warner Theatre, Washington, DC

➤ *The Children's Literary Hour,* Novel Books, Washington, DC

➤ *Marathon Interpretive Reading of Epic Works,* Krandall Books & Café, Washington, DC

EDUCATION

BA, Performing Arts & Children's Literature, Howard University, Washington, DC

Career Change: *From telecommunications operator to broadcasting professional.*

Strategy: *Focus on diverse work in the performing arts, which she had pursued on a part-time and unpaid basis for many years. Dates are excluded to camouflage the exact number of years and thus disguise her age. Her unrelated work experience in telecom is not even mentioned.*

RESUME 80: BY LOUISE KURSMARK, MRW, CPRW, JCTC, CEIP, CCM

Alex Standish

4429 Del Mar Avenue, Chula Vista, CA 91915
Home 619-451-0904 ▶ Mobile 619-204-1121
audio-alex@aol.com

GOAL	**Audio/Video Production Assistant**
QUALIFICATION HIGHLIGHTS	▶ Current training in traditional and state-of-the-art audio and video production. ▶ History of bringing projects to successful conclusion, on time and on budget. ▶ Track record of leadership and achievement in customer-focused jobs. ▶ Proven ability to quickly learn and train others in new processes and systems. ▶ Positive attitude and strong work ethic.
EDUCATION	**Associate of Applied Science, Audio/Video Production** COASTAL COLLEGE OF TECHNOLOGY, San Diego, CA, December 2004

SKILLS

Production Management
- ▶ Script breakdowns
- ▶ Schedules
- ▶ Budgets
- ▶ Shot logs

Production
- ▶ DVC and DVCPro cameras
- ▶ AVID editing system
- ▶ Production aesthetics

Audio
- ▶ Microphone setup
- ▶ Location audio
- ▶ Pro Tools audio tools
- ▶ Analog recording
- ▶ Foley miking
- ▶ Foley editing
- ▶ Signal flow and patching on audio
- ▶ 24-track linear tape
- ▶ Non-linear Digital Audio Workstation

Lighting
- ▶ Studio, chroma-key & product lighting ▶ 3-point lighting ▶ Diffusion

PROJECTS

Repeatedly elected as **Production Manager** of 5–8 person project teams because of excellent organizational skills. Brought all projects in on time and within assigned budget without compromising quality. Highlights include

- ▶ **6 start-to-finish commercial filming projects.** Participated in hands-on project work (planning and setup of audio, camera, and microphones; studio filming; extensive editing). Prepared scripts, budgets, and timing sheets.
- ▶ **3 audio recording projects.** Prepared demo/marketing tapes for local bands via live studio sessions. Participated in studio hook-up, track mixing, level setting, CD burning.
- ▶ **Lighting, analog recording, Foley editing projects**—all facets of audio/video work.

ADDITIONAL EXPERIENCE

Project Manager/Landscaper: BAYSIDE NURSERIES, San Diego, CA, 1999–2000
- ▶ Independently managed assigned accounts, both residential and commercial; designed, installed, and maintained visually appealing landscape projects.
- ▶ Managed equipment, tools, and project schedules; quickly resolved on-site problems.
- ▶ Based on reliability and performance, selected to remain for year-round greenhouse position when seasonal work ended.

Customer Service Representative: AL'S GARDEN CENTER, Chula Vista, CA, 1998–1999
- ▶ Hired as first cashier prior to new store opening; rapidly promoted to customer-service desk based on ability to quickly and resourcefully resolve customer questions.
- ▶ Used computerized inventory program.
- ▶ Chosen to train new employees in store procedures and customer-service skills.

COMPUTER SKILLS
- ▶ Microsoft Word, Excel, and Publisher.
- ▶ Solid foundation of computer knowledge gained during 13 months of full-time studies in Computer Science (University of California at San Diego, 2000–2002).

Career Change: *From landscaper to audio/video production assistant.*

Strategy: *Highlight, in some detail, recent training, skills, and knowledge related to the field of audio/video production. Use the Additional Experience section as a differentiator from other new graduates.*

LaVonne J. Washington

123 Bayside Place, Middletown, RI 02840
401-235-1234 • ljwashington@earthlink.net

OBJECTIVE: Television, Video, and Motion Picture Production

Equipment:

Fill Lights	Boom Microphones	Lapel Microphones
VMS Editor	Graphics Creator	Sound Generator
Switchboard	CD Rewrite	VHS Camera
Camcorder	Studio Camera	

Software:

MS PowerPoint	MS Word	MS Excel
Internet communications	Studio 7	QuarkXPress

EXPERIENCE:

- Directed "The Last Man," semifinalist in The Universal Studios High School Competition, 1998.
- Directed and coordinated the production of television programs.
- As Producer, budgeted, procured equipment, cast talent, and composed and recorded music soundtracks.
- Coordinated production details to produce live television programs from locations distant from the station.
- Coordinated audio work, music, camera work, and script to produce show.
- Edited videos of television shows, music videos, commercials, documentaries, and short movies.
- Copied and edited graphics, voice, and music onto videotape.
- Read, interpreted, and edited script. Conducted rehearsals. Directed cast and technical crew.
- Auditioned and interviewed performers for specific parts, considering such factors as physical size and appearance, quality of voice, expressiveness, and experience.
- Scheduled sequences of scenes to be filmed for each day of shooting, grouping scenes together according to set and cast of characters to meet timeline requirements.
- Obtained costumes, props, music, or other equipment or personnel to complete production.
- Operated cameras, sound mixer, and videotape deck.
- Conferred with co-editor to ensure that music, sets, scenic effects, and costumes conformed to script.
- Conferred with cameramen to explain details of scene to be photographed. Utilized inserts, transparencies, backgrounds, and trick shots.
- Informed technicians of scenery, lights, props, and cameras required.
- Rehearsed live feed, music and commercials, and cast to elicit best possible performance.
- Met with directors, screenwriters, and other staff members to discuss production progress and results.
- Reviewed audiotape recordings. Verified that program, script, and sound effects conformed to broadcast standards.

TRAINING:

Television Production, Middletown High School, Middletown, RI, 1996–1999

Studies Included:

Beginning Studio	Basic Equipment	Studio Setup
Editing	Graphics	Sound Setup
Creating Talent	Audio Music	Switchboard Operations
Light Placement	Camera Operations	Computer Video Making

Laptop Computer Training	1999
Advanced Laptop Computer Training	2000

Career Change: *From fuels specialist in the military to film production apprentice.*

Strategy: *Ignore military experience and focus resume on real training and experience gained in high school.*

RESUME 82: BY ELLEN MULQUEEN, CRW

ANNE FITZPATRICK

PROFILE

- Highly motivated, creative, collaborative professional with diverse design credits.
- Gifted artist and skilled craftsperson, both imaginative and technically proficient.
- Strong leader with team spirit; organized, efficient, detail-oriented, and calm under pressure.
- Loyal, articulate, enthusiastic, supportive individual with good sense of humor.

DESIGN AND RELATED SKILLS

- Uniquely expressive in the manipulation of color, form, light, and texture.
- Sensitive to the interactive nature of space and flow as well as spatial relationships.
- Knowledgeable in historical periods/styles of architecture, art, and décor.
- Adept at eliciting concept and practical needs of client/director.
- Experienced in computer-aided drafting.
- Proficient at carpentry; technical drawing; painting; faux finishes; sewing; patterning; cutting; draping; and creation of window treatments, slipcovers, pillows, bedspreads, and shams.

TYPES OF DESIGN PROJECTS

- Decorated residential interiors.
- Remodeled historical homes.
- Created theatre costume shop with makeup/dressing rooms, laundry/dye facilities, and wardrobe storage.
- Designed and built theatrical scenery (professional and educational): commercial and residential interiors, hospitals, hotels, courtrooms, and exteriors that represented varied historical periods and social milieu.
- Fashioned stage costumes for dance, drama, musical theatre, and opera.
- Designed and executed stage lighting for dance, drama, musical theatre, and opera.

PERSONAL AND INTERPERSONAL SKILLS

- Proven leadership skills with capacity to empower individuals and promote teamwork.
- Excellent troubleshooting, problem-solving abilities.
- Aptitude for multitasking.
- Ability to create effective working relationship with client/director.
- Capacity for working independently or as part of group.
- Organized, disciplined, thorough, and reliable.
- Amiable, positive, and aware of needs of others.

489 Stratford Street ▪ New York, New York 10015 ▪ 212.987.1212 ▪ 212.689.3636 (cell) ▪ fitz205@the-spa.com

Career Change: *From college professor to interior designer.*

Strategy: *Emphasize design and related skills on page 1 but also include management experience and other facets of her academic background on page 2 to strengthen her overall credentials.*

ANNE FITZPATRICK—Page 2

EXPERIENCE

Interior designer/decorator and design consultant (freelance)   1990–Present

New York University, New York, NY
Chair of Theatre Department   1991–2003
- Recruited and evaluated students, faculty, and staff.
- Allocated and managed fiscal resources.
- Developed curriculum, scheduled courses, and reviewed academic programs.
- Managed theatre facilities.
- Coordinated/scheduled dance, drama, and music events.

SoHo Community Theatre, New York, NY
Production Manager   2000–Present
- Hired all technicians.
- Managed all production budgets.
- Created/maintained master calendar.
- Maintained costumes/properties/scenery during show runs.

EDUCATION

Yale University, New Haven, CT
Master of Fine Arts in Theatrical Design
Graduate Fellowship

University of Michigan, Ann Arbor, MI
Bachelor of Arts
Major: Theatre
Minor: Art

489 Stratford Street ▪ New York, New York 10015 ▪ 212.987.1212 ▪ 212.689.3636 (cell) ▪ fitz205@the-spa.com

DONALD D. CARPENTER

2307 Hillsborough Lane, Bradenton, FL 33901
(813) 671-1234 • doncarpenter@msn.com

Knowledge & Experience

Model Types:
- *Architectural models of single-family homes, apartment complexes, and commercial buildings.*
- *Diorama scale models, with historic accuracy and to appropriate scale with topographic detail:*

Industrial construction projects	*Furniture and cabinetry*	*Automobiles*
Model railroad accessories	*Dollhouses*	*Aircraft*

Materials:
- *Plastic, glass, balsa wood, foam, metal, paper, and papier-mâché.*
- *Cutting and gluing; painting and coloring with oil, acrylic, and enamel paint to produce finishing, weathering, and detailing.*

Tools:
- *In addition to the standard shop tools, such as table saws, bandsaws, and routers, utilize the following for working in miniature:*

Scroll saws	*Sanders*
Lathes, both woodworking and metal	*Miniature drills and drill presses*
Miniature welding and silver soldering equipment	*Airbrush to produce realistic finishes*

Memberships • Exhibitions • Education • Recognition

Associations / Memberships:

Cincinnati Railroad Club	*Plastic Modeler's Society*	*Victorian Society*
Louisville & Nashville Historical Society	*Surface Warship Association*	*Mid-America Modelers*

Published in:

How to Build Dioramas	Wooden Villages: Designs for 18 Miniature Buildings
How to Use an Airbrush	Encyclopedia of Military Modeling

Exhibitions:

North American Model Engineering	*Exposition Beaufort Ships Museum*
Mystic Seaport	*Cumberland Toy and Model Museum*

Education:
Bachelor of Science in Mechanical Engineering, *U.S. Naval Academy, Annapolis, MD, 1983*

Computer-Aided Design	*1996*	*From Idea to Blueprint*	*1997*
Architectural Modeling	*1997*	*Residential and Commercial Modeling*	*2001*
Instructor Training	*2000*	*Leadership / Management*	*2001*

Recognition:
- *Recognized as **"Modelmaker of the Year,"** Mid-America Modelers*   *2000*
- ***Navy Achievement Medal** for CAD Design Project*   *2002*

Career Change: From intelligence analyst in the U.S. military to architectural designer.

Strategy: Load the resume with diverse experiences that demonstrate his lifelong interest and extensive (although unpaid) experience.

Richard French

198 Jamison Boulevard
Orlando, Florida 32801

(407) 471-5195
rfrench@msn.com

ASSISTANT DIRECTOR OF CULTURAL AFFAIRS

QUALIFICATIONS SUMMARY

- Over 20 years of experience building and managing professional service organizations including Financial Planning / Staffing / Technology / Marketing / Planning & Forecasting / Administrative Management / Problem Resolution / Legal Affairs

- Experience in local government operations, systems, and legal compliance—accustomed to dealing with government policies, issues, and officials

- Accomplished public speaker: lecturer, seminar presenter, and radio and television talk-show host

- Strong cultural background inspired through family member, Graham French, a renowned American Abstract Expressionist displayed in museums worldwide

PROFESSIONAL EXPERIENCE

President	French Law Offices, CHTD; Lewiston, Florida	1996–Present
Managing Partner	Green, Hatfield & French, CHTD; Orlando, Florida Rated AV; Martindale-Hubbell Law Directory	1992–1996
Partner	French and Simon, P.A.; Orlando, Florida	1988–1992
Sole Practitioner	Richard French, Attorney at Law; Orlando, Florida	1982–1988

Established a general law practice in 1982; formed a partnership in 1988; merged with a larger firm in 1992; and returned to sole practitioner and business owner in 1996.

- Managed all phases of each practice, including financial management, administrative operations, staffing, technology, marketing, case management, and client relations. Built and managed a client base of 6,000+ clients encompassing a diverse range of industries.

- Created, produced, directed, and hosted an hour-long informative weekly talk-radio show, French's Legal Line (1987–2002), responding to callers' legal questions. Periodically invited guests included governors, mayors, Supreme Court justices, and other attorneys.

- Appointed by Lewiston City Mayor to Board of Directors of TVTV Channel 11 (2001). Worked as liaison between Lewiston City Council and TVTV. Assisted TVTV in obtaining funding/grants from Lewiston City Council 2001, 2002, and 2003. Managed yearly budget of more than $300,000; assisted with purchase of studio/office building, station management, program quality, and content.

- Created, produced, directed, and hosted weekly half-hour TV talk show. Oversaw production staff of nine people. Produced three hours of live programming every Monday night.

- Presented lectures and seminars on estate and financial planning for more than 15 years.

- Assisted in teaching a court-ordered bimonthly DUI school for offenders for 18 years.

Career Change: From attorney to cultural arts director.

Strategy: Highlight relevant key strengths, skills, experience, and accomplishments. Pull out arts- and culture-related activities he participated in during his many years as an attorney.

Richard French   Page 2

- As Managing Partner of Green, Hatfield & French, restructured operating, financial, and legal infrastructure for a group of six attorneys and eight staff members. Negotiated/renegotiated strategic partnerships, forged profitable new alliances, expanded market channels, and standardized contracts and business documentation. Achieved and honored with highest rating, AV, in Martindale-Hubbell law directory.

- Represented thousands of cases from initial interview through final hearing/judgment. Argued, petitioned, and tried cases in Magistrates Court, District Court, Florida Court of Appeals, Florida Supreme Court, and United States Supreme Court. Attended more than 1,500 pretrial conferences.

  – City Attorney, Downey, Florida, representing city in all legal matters. Attended all City Council meetings, providing advice and counsel on all matters. Provided civil representation for the city as well as prosecuting misdemeanor criminal cases.

  – Co-counsel for state of Florida United States presidential campaigns. Provided representation in state of Florida for two presidential elections.

  – As legal counsel to Textile Processors, AFL-CIO, negotiated contracts, assisted in employer/employee relations, and participated in collective-bargaining process.

  – Provided representation from trial through various appellate levels; argued, drafted, and prepared briefs for two published cases: Smith v. Hatter (Case No. 14721) and The State of Florida v. John Sherman (Case No. 15832).

  – Successfully defended a real estate developer/building contractor (High Ridge, Florida) in a high-profile, multimillion-dollar case.

Intake Counselor   Health and Rehabilitative Services, District 8, Orlando, Florida   1981 to 1982

As Intake Counselor/Child Advocate, represented the child in neglect and abuse cases. Participated in all court proceedings, including detention, emergency shelter placements, arraignments, adjudication, and disposition. Prepared reports and recommendations to the court.

EDUCATION

J.D.—South Texas College of Law, Houston, Texas

B.S.—University of Florida College of Journalism and Communications, Gainesville, Florida
        Major: Advertising—Minor: Theatre

Theatre—London Program, Florida State University

COMMUNITY WORK

Principal Civitan Club member since 1984 (a coed civic organization that assists in funding the Special Olympics)—Treasurer, 1985; Vice President, 1986; President, 1987; Judge Advocate for the 7-state Southeast District, 1988–89

Lewiston Chamber of Commerce member 1983–2000—participated in leadership training program

CHAPTER 10

Resumes for Career Changers Seeking Legal, Law Enforcement, Public Safety, and Investigator Positions

In response to changing world conditions, the growing field of public safety and security attracts people from all walks of life. To make their case, they must emphasize related skills drawn from their past experience, whether or not the experience is related directly to their new field. The resumes in this chapter focus on the following career transitions:

- Salesperson to public safety and security officer

- Correctional officer to police officer

- Welding foreman to police officer

- Police officer to corporate security professional

- Bank officer to fraud investigator

RESUME 85: BY KIRSTEN DIXSON, JCTC, CPRW, CEIP

SEAN MACBAIN

sbm67@rogers.com

895 King Street West, Apt. 1213
Toronto, Ontario, Canada M5V 3S1

home (416) 326-4109
mobile (647) 829-0426

"The world is a dangerous place to live, not because of the people who are evil, but because of the people who do not do anything about it." — Albert Einstein

OBJECTIVE

Public Safety and Security position where I can contribute my experience and education in health care, international relations, immigration, psychology, and creative problem solving. Areas of interest include community safety, crime prevention, emergency management, and counterterrorism.

RELEVANT AREAS OF EXPERTISE

Problem Solving

- Reduced hospital re-admittance rates and increased resources for new patients by instituting follow-up care processes for both patients and caregivers.
- Observed need for more communication after patient discharge and persuaded senior management to provide social workers with incentives for additional home visits.
- Initiated product line and service training for technicians who visited customer sites that led to increased profits.
- Investigated overseas shipping options and secured deals to minimize expenses.
- Successfully navigated through government bureaucracy to legally emigrate to the United States and then Canada.

Communication

- Built a productive network of contacts and cultivated relationships using presentation, delivery, cross-cultural, and interpersonal skills.
- Saved thousands of dollars through effective negotiation of supplier contracts and prices.
- Bilingual: English & Portuguese

Administration

- Managed RTR's New Jersey office and prepared detailed and timely reports for parent company that justified investment.
- Seamlessly expedited international sales process from acquisition to export.
- Incorporated RTR Import & Export, Inc., in the State of New Jersey.

Computer Applications

- Proficient with Windows applications: Microsoft Word, Excel, PowerPoint, Internet Explorer, and Outlook.

Career Change: *From salesperson to public safety and security officer.*

SEAN MACBAIN

PAGE TWO

(416) 326-4109

PROFESSIONAL EXPERIENCE

General Manager   1995–2002
RTR Import & Export, Inc., New Jersey, United States

Served as the sole United States territory representative for a large medical equipment supplier in Brazil. Challenged to establish U.S. market presence and broaden the sales portfolio by researching and pursuing profitable purchasing opportunities.

Sales General Supervisor   1993–1995
RTR Electronica Ltda., Uberlandia, Brazil

Recruited from medical school, for medical industry and product knowledge and fluency in English, to work for this major importer of critical-care medical equipment.

Medical Intern   1991–1992
Guadalupe Hospital, Uberlandia, Brazil

Successfully completed three internships with exposure to various specialties, including psychiatry, psychology, general clinics, social work, and emergency care. Worked directly with 15–17 patients at a time to explain therapy and provide family support.

After learning and analyzing operations of various departments, took initiative to develop and propose new action plans that enhanced the effectiveness of the system for the community. Served as a resource to diverse groups and collaborated in teams to realize positive outcomes.

EDUCATION

Medical Degree, State of Para Medical School, Uberlandia, Brazil   1993

PROFESSIONAL MEMBERSHIPS

Canadian Association for Security Intelligence Studies   Present

Strategy: *Use an objective statement to make the target clear and communicate how well the candidate's background and interests relate to his current goal. The functional approach on page 1 emphasizes relevant skills and achievements before revealing an unconnected work history on page 2.*

Peter M. Quinn

7509 Maple Drive
East Haven, Connecticut 06555
203-467-8585   peterquinn@snet.net

Law Enforcement Officer

- Graduate of Connecticut Police Officer Training; certified 2003.
- Proven ability to deal effectively with prisoners, establishing respect for authority while treating individuals fairly.
- Thorough, hard working, disciplined, and reliable, with a serious attitude and a career commitment to law enforcement.

Professional Experience

NEW HAVEN COUNTY SHERIFF'S DEPARTMENT   2002–Present
Corrections Officer • County Correctional Facility

Maintain inmate control over 100-plus prisoners in a dormitory-style jail. Supervise inmate behavior and respond to infractions. Count and lead prisoners to meals and recreation. Maintain detailed hourly logs and records of inmate transfers and other activities. Transport felons to higher-security jails. Assume responsibility in other areas of the jail on an occasional basis.

- Developed skills in dealing with individuals of all types.
- Gained experience in effectively handling tense situations.
- Consistently achieved excellent performance evaluations.
- Member of Sheriff's Power Lifting Team; hold an American record in bench press.

Other Experience

RYDER'S, New Haven, CT   2001–2002
Doorman/Bouncer

GRANT ASSOCIATES, New Haven, CT   1999–2001
Field Representative

Negotiated and sold the services of a collection firm to business clients such as mortgage companies, doctors, and other health-care providers.

Education

Connecticut Police Officer Training and Certification (2003), CONNECTICUT POLICE
    OFFICERS ACADEMY, Storrs, CT

Criminal Justice Degree Program (2002–Present), QUINNIPIAC COLLEGE, Hamden, CT

Graduate (1999), NORTH HAVEN HIGH SCHOOL, North Haven, CT
- Member of Wrestling Team

Career Change: *From correctional officer to police officer.*

Strategy: *Emphasize related experience from current job as a prison officer along with recent and ongoing education in the field of law enforcement.*

Charles Nelson
123 Winter Road • Willow Tree, Pennsylvania 17711 • 427.555.1761

SKILLS PROFILE

➢ Recognized for superior work ethic, productivity, and leading-by-example management style. Foster a sense of mutual respect among all department members. Exceptional verbal and written communication skills facilitate conveying objectives and delegating tasks.

➢ Prioritize and manage heavy workflow, seeing project through to completion. Take pride in producing precise, accurate work, following established procedures to reach goal. Excellent troubleshooter.

➢ Analyze situation before responding. Identify method, formula, procedure, or systems to solve problems. Take pride in ability to understand all facts of a situation before reaching conclusion. Display acute awareness of social, economic, and political implications of decisions.

➢ Thrive as leader in a team environment. Possess talent to motivate and work with people at all levels of a company through established credibility, trust, and respect. Promote commitment to high standards of excellence.

➢ Enjoy interaction with the public. Exercise tact and diplomacy; maintain confidentiality as needed.

EMPLOYMENT

Village Metal Fence Company—Summerville, Pennsylvania   *1994–Present*
FOREMAN (2002–Present); LABORER (1994–2002)
• Direct, coordinate, and schedule daily assignments for 2–3 weld shop crew members to produce orders for fence wholesaler with 25 employees. Operate forklift, piranha, cut-off saw, and chop saws.
• Ensure safety procedures are followed regarding work area and job performance. Selected to join safety committee.

East Jackson High School—East Jackson, Pennsylvania   *1995–2002*
BOYS BASKETBALL COACH: Elementary (1 yr.), **Jr. High** (4 yrs.), **JV** (3 yrs.)
• Instructed team members in rules of the game and proper play techniques. Promoted good sportsmanship, team values, and dedicated work habits.
• Produced teams that worked well together and attained several winning seasons, including one undefeated season and two tournament championships.

Midway Tube Company—Midway, Pennsylvania   *Summers 1997–1998*
DRAW BENCH OPERATOR / LABORER
• Commended for learning new skills rapidly and consistently producing quality work.

CERTIFICATIONS / LICENSES / TRAINING

• Act 33/34 Clearance in Pennsylvania, August 2002
• Firearm Permit (hunting, fishing, target, and protection permit)
• Target Range Shooting (bow as well as firearm)

• Archery League
• Basketball Referee, P.I.A.A.
• Little League Umpire

POLICE INTERNSHIP

Ride-along—400 hours—at Sharon Police Department. Observed and assisted with various police tasks and attended court hearings with officers.
• Wrote reports
• Learned laws
• Assisted with arrests and house searches
• Observed detective cases
• Served warrants
• Learned procedures

EDUCATION / CONTINUING EDUCATION

B.S., Criminal Justice and Sociology, 2000   Euclid State University—Euclid, Ohio
Sampling of law enforcement coursework / seminars:
• Police Operations
• Laws of Arrest
• Report Writing
• Legal Updates
• Use of Force / Defense Tactics
• Sensitivity and Communication Skills
• Informant Management
• Suicide Prevention with Persons in Custody
• Firearms and Related Topics
• DWI Detection Guide
• Juvenile Laws
• Search and Seizure

Career Change: *From welding foreman to police officer.*

Strategy: *Emphasize education and employment history that demonstrates longevity and physical fitness.*

RESUME 88: *BY* **MYRIAM-ROSE KOHN, CPRW, CEIP, JCTC, CCM, CCMC**

ALLEN JURGENS

3605 Red Barn Road
Agua Dulce, California 91350

661-859-3157
ajurgens@netzero.net

SECURITY PROFESSIONAL

More than ten years of increasingly responsible management experience as **Field Supervisor, Criminal Investigator,** and **Administrator.** Combination of strong field experience with excellent qualifications in departmental management, budgeting, resource allocation, reporting, and technology. Excellent performance in liaison affairs; negotiations; problem-solving, crisis management, and relationship management skills; investigations; and data analysis. Expert in law enforcement training and interagency relations. Good presentation and communication skills.

A dependable team player; relate well and work cooperatively with diverse personalities. Work well under pressure without losing control and with all levels of management in a professional, diplomatic, and tactful manner. Able to coordinate and focus efforts of others. Positive motivator, mentor, and delegator. Hardworking and dependable with a **strong work ethic.** Entrepreneurial attitude, energy, and style.

Well-versed in the use of advanced technologies for research, reporting / documentation, customer tracking, competitive intelligence, information management, and other applications. Knowledge of Internet search methods and online data sources. Hold direct responsibility for

- Asset and Personnel Protection
- Emergency Planning and Preparedness
- Crisis Response and Crowd Control
- Community Outreach and Education

- Interviewing and Investigations
- Fraud Investigation and Documentation
- Tactical Field Operations
- Discreet Surveillance

Appearances as **Expert Witness** in state and federal courts. Experience with special events: logistics, security, budget allocation, vendor sourcing, and contract negotiations.

AWARDS

- Unit Supervisor, **Team of the Quarter,** 2000
- **Employee of the Quarter,** 1998
- City of Torrance Proclamation for **Actions Above and Beyond the Call of Duty** (rescued people from fire), 1987
- City of Torrance Proclamation for **Actions Above and Beyond the Call of Duty,** 1985

PROFESSIONAL EXPERIENCE

LAGUNA NIGUEL POLICE DEPARTMENT, Oceanside, CA   1992–2004

Field Supervisor (1999–2004)
Watch Commander (1993–1999)
Field Training Officer (1991–1992)
Officer-in-Charge, Special Events (1995–2004 concurrently)

Rapidly promoted through a series of increasingly responsible law enforcement and management positions in this 125,000-resident community. Earned several commendations for outstanding service to the department and local residents.

Career Change: From police officer to corporate security professional.

Strategy: Spotlight safety expertise, knowledge of the law, and interpersonal skills.

ALLEN JURGENS–Page 2

LAGUNA NIGUEL POLICE DEPARTMENT   continued

- As **Field Supervisor,** held total responsibility for all tactical actions and daily activities. Directed management of personnel actions for 30 line officers. Ensured adherence to schedules in various projects. Executed major cost-reduction projects. Effectively listened and addressed citizens' complaints. Acted as community liaison: Designed, developed, and instructed a series of community outreach programs designed to increase resident knowledge of safety and security. Led multiple presentations to fraternal groups, business groups, schools, and non-profit organizations.

- As **Watch Commander,** handled all administrative work, ensured accuracy of reports, and resolved citizens' complaints. Mentored junior officers; provided remedial training for deficient officers and in-service training for field units.

- As **Field Training Officer,** trained, mentored, and evaluated rookies. Wrote performance reviews. Oversaw basic police patrol functions.

- The scope of responsibility as **Officer-in-Charge** was varied and encompassed staffing of auxiliary facility (scheduled shifts and served as **Consultant** on performance issues, among many other functions) and coordination of special events (such as the Employee of the Year Banquet), which entailed determining logistics and security, negotiating contracts, sourcing vendors, retaining master of ceremonies, selling tickets, and staying within budget.

- **Certified Drug Recognition Expert, Certified Drug Recognition Expert Instructor, Primary Response Team Member (SWAT):** Taught defensive tactics, instructed and trained new academy recruits, and monitored / evaluated unit performance. Administered drug tests.

- As **Unit Supervisor in Community Policing,** conducted surveys; analyzed results; and listened, dealt with, and resolved complaints.

TORRANCE POLICE DEPARTMENT, Torrance, CA   1984–1992

Narcotics Detective / Senior Officer / Police Officer
Provided patrol / undercover surveillance in this 75,000-resident community and regional drug trafficking center. Designed and led training for narcotics and the tactical unit. Initiated and coordinated narcotic investigations; selected and mentored new detectives for this special unit. Provided expert testimony in state and federal courts.

PROFESSIONAL AFFILIATIONS
Member, Board of Directors, Torrance Police Officers Association
California Narcotics Officers Association (CNOA)
Toastmasters

EDUCATION and CONTINUAL TRAINING

Master of Arts, Human Resources Management, California State University, Northridge, CA
Bachelor of Science, Criminal Justice Administration, Burlington State University, Burlington, SC

- 40-hour Basic Narcotics Investigator Course
- 40-hour Field Training Officer Course
- Various courses in narcotics investigations and drug recognition

- California POST, Advanced
- Drug Recognition Expert Course
- Drug Recognition Instructor's Course
- CPR

RESUME 89: BY ANNEMARIE CROSS, CPRW, CEIP, CRW, CCM

JANET BERENDS

5678 North Avenue ♦ Los Angeles, CA 92009 ♦ 619.222.9874 ♦ jberends@hotmail.com

INVESTIGATOR / FRAUD & LOSS MINIMIZATION SPECIALIST

Credit Card/Check Fraud ♦ Loss Aversion ♦ Fund Protection & Recovery ♦ Problem Resolution

<u>*15-year veteran in the banking & finance industry.*</u>

QUALIFICATIONS PROFILE

High-performance, results-focused professional with exceptional insight and experience into the investigation of credit card/check fraud, implementing initiatives to minimize loss while optimizing the recovery and protection of funds for bank and clientele. Possess extensive experience and outstanding accomplishments within the banking and finance industry, delivering customer service excellence to drive revenues, market growth, and overall bottom-line performance. Comprehensive insight into, and full compliance with, Code of Banking Practice, Privacy Act, and Discrimination and Harassment. Sound knowledge of banking products, policies, and procedures.

♦ Investigation & Arbitration Excellence	♦ Research & Analytical Excellence
♦ Loss & Fraud Minimization	♦ Credit Card Fraud Prevention
♦ Procedural Design & Execution	♦ Guideline & Protocol Compliance

Computer Expertise: CAPS, Control D, CICS, Vision, Microsoft Office Suite

QUALIFICATIONS & TRAINING

Code of Banking Practice ♦ Privacy Act ♦ Discrimination & Harassment
♦ Introduction to Legal Aspects of Banking ♦ Consumer Affairs & Trade Practices

Bachelor's Degree in Law ♦ Northeastern University, Massachusetts

SELECTED CAREER HIGHLIGHTS

Circumvented ombudsman/media involvement and averted losses through incisive investigative, negotiation, and arbitration competencies. Insightful in distinguishing genuine from fraudulent claims while executing strategic initiatives to secure successful outcomes without incident.

♦ Isolated and impeded numerous inaccurate claims for compensation against credit cards, merchant customers, and the bank by unscrupulous and often re-offending parties; investigated and interfaced with various departments/organizations to ascertain accurate occurrences; and executed strategic resolutions with full compliance to set guidelines and protocols.

♦ Prevented cashing of stolen checks; optimized bank's profile with large corporate client.

♦ Five years of experience in Fraud & Forgeries Department in a banking environment; gained exceptional understanding into operational methodologies/protocols and the establishment and maintenance of profiles for suspicious customers and account transactions.

Developed key alliances with law enforcement authorities, local community representatives, and cross-functional internal/external banking departments to facilitate achievement of goals and objectives in the prevention of fraudulent activities.

♦ Interfaced with local crime-prevention groups in the establishment and coordination of fraud profiles on suspicious entities, patterns, and behavior, with meticulous input into comprehensive database while remaining abreast of fraud activity trends.

♦ Provided pertinent credit card and other information to police to facilitate investigations and subsequent arrest of fraudulent credit card suspects.

♦ Collaborated with law enforcement authorities to ascertain and document associated crime statistics, enhancing and optimizing crime prevention within the local community.

Continued…

Career Change: *From bank officer to fraud investigator.*

Strategy: *Highlight transferable skills and experience to "repackage" her in line with her new goal.*

JANET BERENDS

Page 2

Problem-solved and defused numerous customer complaints and concerns without incident, executing strategic customer relationship management techniques to secure client satisfaction, retention, and repeat business; upheld the bank's reputation and professional profile.

♦ Arbitrated diverse cases, minimizing loss/claims through tactical investigation, sound judgment, and ability to devise and implement mutually acceptable solutions; renowned for expertise in resolving issues fairly, often being called by clients to mediate and offer advice concerning arising banking issues.

♦ Researched, advised, and arranged suitable banking products for customers unaware of best options to suit their needs; established rapport, trust, and recognition for banking products knowledge and expertise.

♦ Placated displeased client after they discovered double insurance premiums being deducted from their account over a two-year period; investigated and implemented corrective actions that successfully appeased and prevented customer from taking further action.

PROFESSIONAL EXPERIENCE

US BANKING CORPORATION   1991–Present
National Customer Liaison Officer (1995–Present)
Restore relationships with disgruntled customers over products/services or unresolved long-term issues to circumvent ombudsman involvement. Establish and maintain strategic alliances with cross-functional departments to facilitate speedy resolution of client complaints. Maintain scrupulous records and detailed accounts of customer contact, conversations, and reactions to impede possible future claims alleging improper handling of concerns. Minimize and reduce risks for customers and the bank by remaining current with credit risk procedures in order to identify trends in fraudulent activity and subsequently expedite necessary steps.

♦ Achieved stringent weekly targets of finalizing 24 cases requiring outstanding research, analysis, and resolution competencies to achieve realistic win-win outcomes, thus circumventing potential costly legal action.

♦ Frequently awarded Certificates of Recognition for exceeding 100% of targets.

♦ Distinguished from peers by receiving the majority of formal customer compliments for going above and beyond the call of duty.

♦ Entrusted by management to present induction training programs to new recruits due to extensive retail banking and credit card knowledge. Coaching encompassed standard protocols, role expectations, and methods to balance the art of customer service with diplomatic conflict resolution.

Customer Service Officer, Head Office Contact Center (1991–1995)
Fast-track appointment to Acting Team Leader role; supervised, trained, and mentored 30 staff to maximize team performance within a complex, high-pressure customer service environment.

♦ Recognized for outstanding performance, possessing a record of achievement that remains unbeaten to present day for exceeding call targets and selling most banking products.

♦ Enhanced and revitalized call center staff performance through provision of on-the-job training in product sales and customer needs analysis; crafted scripts of suggested responses to "brick walls" or rejection. Created environment that encouraged staff's continual knowledge growth.

♦ Pioneered comprehensive list of "*dos and don'ts*" to standardize telephone protocols, improve workflows, and drive revenues and market growth.

UNITED BANKERS NOMINEES   1988–1990
Data Entry Operator—Settlements Department
Meticulous data entry into computerized mainframe system, rapidly delivering output to achieve time-critical deadlines.

♦ Instrumental in capturing significant reduction in error rates, with virtual elimination of re-keying labor and overtime costs.

CHAPTER 11

Resumes for Career Changers Seeking Positions with Nonprofit Organizations

Whether fueled by passion for a cause or the desire to give back, there is a trend for experienced professionals to transition to nonprofit organizations. To show themselves as strong candidates for positions with these organizations, their resumes demonstrate both relevant skills/experience and some less-tangible but equally important assets that are highly pertinent to their target organizations. The resumes in this chapter represent the following transitions to nonprofit careers:

- Corporate administrative assistant to nonprofit researcher and administrator
- Clergy to nonprofit association manager
- Insurance sales agent to fund-raiser
- Engineering technician to Peace Corps volunteer
- Sales manager to town manager
- International consultant to association manager
- Attorney to association director

RESUME 90: BY NORINE DAGLIANO, CPRW

Annette Stiles Ollry

P.O. Box 52 ♦ Hagerstown, MD 21740   240.555.1815 ♦ aso@mindspring.com

Profile

Highly committed, intelligent career professional seeking to transfer 14+ years of corporate operational support experience to the non-profit arena.

Background exemplifies a proactive customer service orientation, computer proficiency, and exceptional written and verbal skills.

Recognized for strong reading comprehension and editorial abilities; excellent at synthesizing complex information to provide concise, streamlined responses to operational issues.

Naturally inquisitive; organized; detail oriented.

Exemplify a blend of creative and analytical abilities, which combine efficiency with innovation to produce bottom-line results.

Educational Background

BA, Interdisciplinary Studies, THE COLLEGE OF WILLIAM AND MARY, Williamsburg, VA   1998

Scholarship recipient for a summer study abroad, England

Knowledge of French, Spanish, German, and Italian

MAC and PC software applications and troubleshooting

Photography; graphics composition and layout

Professional Background

ABX GLOBAL EXPRESS, INC., Rockville, MD   1988–Present
(Internal transfers to Richmond, Springfield, and Vienna, VA)

Global market leader of the international air express industry serving more than 120,000 destinations in 228 countries and territories. Acquired a breadth of diverse experience within the company, which attests to ability to fully utilize resources and effect results that are profitable to the company and beneficial to the customer.

Positions Held

STATION ASSISTANT / SATURDAY OPERATIONS LEAD / COURIER / AIRFREIGHT ASSISTANT

♦ Demonstrate a thorough understanding of the complexities of international shipping and customs regulations; recognized as a key resource for compliance issues.

♦ Implement a consultative approach in assessing delivery problems and negotiating win-win resolutions with customers and staff.

♦ Utilize a worldwide corporate email, telephone, and fax network to communicate with customers and staff in processing international shipments.

♦ Assist in coordinating and planning most economical and efficient transport for bulk freight shipments.

♦ Plan and execute delivery and pick-up routes for time-sensitive materials.

♦ Consistently provide a level of service that meets or exceeds customer expectations.

Career Change: From corporate administrative assistant to nonprofit researcher and administrator.

Strategy: Identify and showcase skills in grant development and global affairs.

Annette Stiles Ollry
240.555.1815
aso@mindspring.com
Page 2

Professional Background (continued)

Highlights

- Assumed responsibility for supervising Saturday courier operations, delegating assignments to six employees, and providing oversight for the timely arrival and departure of shipments.

- Made key contributions to the successful implementation of a new computerized performance analysis system, conducting qualitative data assessment, analyzing reports, and making recommendations for performance improvements.

- Assisted in resolving complex handling of an international shipment; identified corporate, customer, and regulatory needs and requirements, and identified the appropriate existing guidelines and procedures to be followed to achieve the goal.

- Set up a company-standard email tracing system for the local office.

- Received numerous awards for service, innovation, and safety compliance.

RESEARCH ASSISTANT, SEARCH CORPORATION, Great Falls, VA   1985–1987

- Conducted research of American medical and technology companies and their products to provide information to international companies interested in investing in American high technology.

- Prepared comprehensive reports of findings and forwarded to client companies.

Technical Skills

MS Office	HTML
WordPerfect	Internet

Working knowledge of Adobe Photoshop, Illustrator, Java, JavaScript, and UNIX

Special Interests

COMPETITIVE HORSES, Middletown, VA   1970–Present
STABLE MANAGER / AMATEUR RIDER / TRAINER / INSTRUCTOR (personally and professionally)

- Managed stable operations for five farms in and around Great Falls, including budgeting; inventory; and employee supervision, training, and scheduling.

- Served as a liaison between the owners and borders, including clarifying business policies and procedures to mediate management and client misunderstandings.

- Provided comprehensive care to the horses; assisted with veterinary care and follow-up.

- Established proficiency goals and training objectives for instruction; gave one-on-one riding lessons to youth, ages four to ten years old.

- Worked as an assistant and groom to riders and trainers before and during competitions.

RESUME 91: BY JANICE SHEPHERD, CPRW, JCTC, CEIP

Tony J. Willows

7777 Altos Hill
Spokane, WA 99201

(509) 776-4560
email: tjw@email.com

PROFILE

Extensive **ADMINISTRATIVE** and **MANAGEMENT** experience with demonstrated strengths in **GUIDANCE** and **LEADERSHIP.**

Excellent presentation and communication skills—very good at bringing out the best in people.

Highly ethical, analytical, conscientious, diligent, and adaptable, with a great sense of humor and sense of drama.

Strong background in adult education and teaching, public relations, finance, and human resources management.

Successful consultant and trainer.

Proficient in program development and implementation.

Skilled in research and computer technology.

Willing to travel.

AREAS OF EXPERTISE

- Human Resources/Finance/ Real Estate Management
- Policies and Procedures Development and Implementation
- Volunteer Recruitment and Coordination
- Public Relations—Communication with Civic and Religious Leaders in Local and State Communities
- Public Speaking/Presentations—27 Years of Experience Presenting to Large Audiences
- Training Workshops—Office Personnel, Administrators, and Executives
- Teaching—Children and Adults
- Counseling—Premarital/Marital/Crisis/ Addiction Intervention/Bereavement
- Organist/Musician

"...interactions with people from diverse backgrounds and various ages are a definite advantage...sets goals, missions; knows how to attain them...stays current in methods of efficiency...."

"...his energy, his expertise, and his people skills are of the highest caliber...."

"...unusually bright, imaginative, possesses an orderly and logical mind, is both a critical thinker and curious, has excellent interpersonal skills, and is a 'natural' teacher...."

quotes from evaluators

"This instructor was the best teacher I have had...he made class fun and everyone understood what he was trying to teach...."

"...professor was always upbeat and knew his material...."

"...he is genuinely interested in the students' learning...can tell he is doing something he enjoys, which makes the best teacher...."

"Tony Willows is an excellent teacher, and I consider my time in his class invaluable...."

quotes from students

Career Change: *From clergy to nonprofit association manager.*

Strategy: *Downplay clergy title but highlight specific areas of expertise drawn from that background. Add punch with pertinent, positive endorsements.*

Tony J. Willows

page two of two

CAREER SUMMARY

Professor of Philosophy, 12/2001–present
Interdisciplinary Studies Department
Spokane Community College, Spokane, WA

- Instruct courses in Symbolic Logic.

Professor of Logic and Biomedical Ethics, 1990–2001
Arts and Sciences Department
Albuquerque Technical Institute, Albuquerque, NM

- Instructed courses in Biomedical Ethics and Philosophy to students of diverse cultural backgrounds. Tailored course materials and class activities to the context of students' life experiences and goals. Available for individual tutoring during and after office hours.

Organist, ongoing

- Provide service music and accompany congregational singing and professional vocal soloists. Prior to and following each service, perform concerts of recognized organ literature. Acted as Curator for the Allen Digital Organ. Elected to Board of Directors of American Guild of Organists (Albuquerque Chapter).

Pastor, 1971–1988 (retired)
Diocese of Halls, CA

- Performed ministry functions, public speaking, counseling, training, child and adult education, staff hiring and supervision, building maintenance, and budget management. Communicated with civic and religious leaders in local and statewide communities.

- Managed and oversaw design, construction, and repair of all corporate real estate holdings and buildings through Southern California—$100 million responsibility. Secured financial stability and debt reduction through member involvement.

Hospital Chaplain, 1990–1998
Bon Secours–St. Francis Xavier Hospital

- Provided spiritual care and counseling to patients, family members, and hospital staff.

Director of Recruitment, 1981–1984

- Supervised recruitment and training of candidates for religious leadership.

Judicial Vicar and Presiding Judge, 1973–1984

- Supervised and managed operations of judicial branch of Diocese of Charleston.

Chairperson, Personnel Commission, 1977–1978

- Advised CEO in placement of executive personnel.

EDUCATION AND CERTIFICATIONS

J.C.L.
University of St. Paul
Canon Law

M.C.L.
University of Ottawa
Canon Law

M.Ch.A.
Catholic University of America
Church Administration

M.A.
Catholic University of America
Theology

S.T.B.
Catholic University of America
Theology

B.A.
St. Mary's College
English, History, Philosophy

CPE, Certificate
Clinical Pastoral Education

JCL, Licensed Canon Lawyer,
European Civil Code

Joyce Melbourne, M.Ed.

11 Field Creek Court • Houston, Texas 77090 • Home (281) 681-1235 • Mobile (281) 818-6754
email: jmelbourne@sbcglobal.net

DIRECTOR OF PROGRAM DEVELOPMENT / FUND-RAISING EXPERT
Extensive Qualifications Within Higher Education Environments

Well qualified human services professional with 20 years of experience in program development, grant and proposal development, fund raising (federal, state, corporate, individual, alumni), and departmental management. Successful in the startup, management, and coordination of special services programs, family therapy operations, and political campaigns. Core competencies include

- Fund-raising Operations
- Public/Community Relations
- Volunteer Recruitment & Staffing
- Budget Development & Administration

- Program Development & Management
- Clinical & Business Data Analysis
- Clinical Service Operations
- Client/Program Advocacy

Nominated "Professional Woman of the Year," University of South Carolina.
Coordinated Fund-raising and Special Events for Democratic Senator Heyward E. McDonald's Campaign.
Served as Republican Delegate to Former Governor George Bush.
Active Member of the Texas Federation of Republican Women.

PROFESSIONAL EXPERIENCE

UNIVERSITY OF SOUTH CAROLINA, Columbia, South Carolina   1978–1984
Director of Special Programs
Recruited by the President of the University to spearhead the development of all special services programs for students with special needs. Assumed full leadership responsibility for program development to include research, grant and proposal development, staffing, volunteer recruitment, fund raising, budgeting, and political and community relations.

Identified federal programs and lobbied in South Carolina, Georgia, and Washington, D.C., to gain support from the federal and state governments. Presented educational programs to faculty, staff, and the local community to expand funding sources and enhance public awareness. Authored and submitted grant proposals; secured funding through political, business, community, charitable, and civic associations. Pioneered the nation's first special-needs program for a particular target group. **Successfully raised more than $1 million.**

FAMILY THERAPY ASSOCIATES, Columbia, South Carolina   1984–1996
Founder/General Manager
Established and built a well-respected family services practice from the ground floor. Full P&L and management responsibility for business development, program and service development, individual and group counseling, billing, marketing, and public/community relations. **Cultivated a high-profile clientele in South Carolina and a large referral network of influential politicians in Washington, D.C.**

Career Change: From insurance sales agent to fund-raiser.

Strategy: Bring earlier (relevant) experience to the forefront; highlight political and fund-raising connections.

Joyce Melbourne, M.Ed.   Page Two

PROFESSIONAL EXPERIENCE *(Continued)*

HARPER INSURANCE AGENCY, Columbia, South Carolina   1984–1996
Director of Marketing/Partner
Challenged by this commercial insurance agency to expand existing operations to include the startup and development of a life, health, and disability program. Led the evaluation and computerization of agency operations. Built a large network of insurance products, recruited and trained staff, and built a highly successful new division. **Ranked within the "Top 12 Agents Nationwide" for Standard Life Insurance Company.**

INDEPENDENT INSURANCE AGENT, Houston, Texas   1997–Present
Market/sell commercial insurance and employee benefits to businesses. Evaluate client needs, research appropriate products and/or services, and manage sales presentations. Services address gifting, wealth creation and preservation, and estate planning.

Earlier career as a Rehabilitation Counselor for the South Carolina Department of Vocational Rehabilitation, Columbia, South Carolina (1971–1974), and a Substitute Teacher for the Searcy Independent School District, Searcy, Arkansas (1974–1978).

EDUCATION & PROFESSIONAL CREDENTIALS

University of South Carolina, Columbia, South Carolina, **M.Ed., Rehabilitation Counseling**—1976
Erskine College, Due West, South Carolina, **BS, Psychology**—1971
American Association of Marriage & Family Therapy, (AAMFT), Washington, D.C., **Clinical Certification**—1986
Society of Neuro-Linguistic Programming, Tampa, Florida, **Business Applications Certification**—1988
Licensed Insurance Agent, State of Texas & South Carolina
Life Underwriter Training Council Fellows **(LUTCF),** Houston, Texas—2000

RESUME 93: BY JUDIT PRICE, MS, CDFI, IJCTC, CCM

Mark Kejanian

6 Wentworth Drive
Middleton, MA 01949

(978) 372-7779

mkej@yahoo.com

PEACE CORPS / SOCIAL ACTION / NGO OR INTERNATIONAL ASSISTANCE PROGRAMS

Experienced, highly motivated engineer with a strong desire to help people and make a difference. Combine social action with engineering and management skills to support sustainable projects in developing countries. Ability to create and manage programs that generate a focused commitment to measurable results. Successfully built relationships, established effective interaction among diverse communities, and developed a high degree of mutual loyalty and trust at all levels. Socially active, interacting directly to help people function the best that they can in their environment. An excellent record of positive outcomes and attention to cost with sensitivity to the complexities in meeting the needs of multiple constituencies. Recognized talent in balancing conflicting priorities and creating a clear direction to improve people's lives. Qualified by:

- Direct Service
- Operations Management
- Client Advocacy
- Communication
- ESL Training

- Program Planning/Implementation
- Community Outreach
- Needs Assessment
- Community Resources Integration
- Alliance and Team Building

SUMMARY OF ACCOMPLISHMENTS

- Collaborated on major engineering contributions for the development of products in medical instrumentation, surgical technology, and genome research.

- Awarded six patents.

- Managed numerous multi-discipline technical teams challenged to create state-of-the-art products with fixed budgets and critical schedules.

- Applied engineering skills pro bono to several municipal projects involving facilities construction, qualification of vendors, lobbying for funding, site selection, and project oversight.

- Provided ongoing assistance to immigrant co-workers and their families with immigration assistance administration, ESL and GED prep training, house hunting, and home-construction projects.

- Assisted family business in managing environmental compliance.

- Assisted Tanzanian students via the Internet in obtaining books and other materials for a local college, developed Internet content material for a Tanzanian-owned tour company, and tutored students in computer use and Internet search skills.

- Taught beginning through advanced snowboarding techniques to children and adults, 22 hours per week during the winter.

- Provided help and inspiration over many years to a person afflicted with Muscular Dystrophy.

Career Change: *From engineering technician to Peace Corps volunteer.*

Strategy: *Emphasize public-service activities that have been largely voluntary but are substantial and relevant.*

Mark Kejanian   Page 2

PROFESSIONAL EXPERIENCE

Farmington Technologies, Dover, MA   2001–Present
Project Manager
Responsible for managing the mechanical/optical development of an advanced technology compact laser-marker system. Additional responsibility for delivery of custom-design solutions for laser scanner systems.

Dorchester Products, Medfield, MA   1997–2001
Manufacturing Engineering/Facilities Manager
Responsible for product design transitioning to manufacturing, budgeting, tooling, supplies, and facilities maintenance for a metal-fabrication job shop that manufactures made-to-order retail display fixtures. Managed 7 professionals and staff.

American Controls, Newbury, MA   1995–1997
Product Development Engineer
Responsible for integrating mechanical and industrial airflow control systems and clean-room HVAC valves for critical environments (e.g., temperature, moisture, cleanliness).

TKG, Franklin, NH   1994–1995
Principal Mechanical/Industrial Design Engineer
Collaborated on a multidisciplinary engineering team to develop affordable electronic fingerprint-acquisition technology.

International Transfer Technologies, Billerica, MA   1991–1994
Mechanical/Industrial Design Engineer
Design engineer developing 3-D laparoscopic technology for increased surgical accuracy.

Museum of Arts and Science, Beijing, China   1990–1991
Mechanical Engineer
Contract position designing 31 unique interactive museum displays to exhibit scientific principles. The project was completed on time and within budget.

EDUCATION

MS, Finance—Boston University, Boston, MA
BS, Mechanical Engineering—University of Michigan, Ann Arbor, MI
Entrepreneurship and Intrapreneurship Program—Worcester Polytechnic Institute, Worcester, MA
Fine Arts Studies—New Boston School of Arts, Boston, MA
Alternative Energy Opportunities Forum, Lowell, MA

FRED ANDERSON

89 Lawrence Street • North Granby, CT 00000 • (860) 595-2091 • fredanderson@aol.com

TOWN MANAGER

Over 10 years of leadership experience in town government as an elected chief administrative and fiscal officer. Key contributor impacting operational, budgetary, staffing, and resource needs throughout the municipality.

Extensive human resources and public speaking background. Effective communicator and team builder with planning, organizational, and negotiation strengths, as well as the ability to lead, reach consensus, establish goals, and attain results. Additional business management experience in the private sector. Competencies include

- **Management/Administration**
- **Fiscal Management/Budgeting**
- **Project/Program Management**
- **Public/Private Sector Alliances**
- **Economic Development**
- **Staff Development/Empowerment**

PROFESSIONAL QUALIFICATIONS

TOWN OF NORTH GRANBY, North Granby, CT   1993 to Present
SELECTMAN (part-time elected position)

Administration/Management—Proactive executive providing strategic planning and leadership direction to diverse municipal departments as one of 3 elected board members governing the Town of North Granby. As board member, direct multiple open town meetings, develop and oversee $10 million budget, and administer various projects. Experience includes chairing Board of Selectmen for 3 years. Serve as a Police Commissioner.

Human Resources—Authority for recruitment, promotion, and supervision of town administrator and 10 department heads with up to 214 full- and part-time staff, as well as Department of Public Works and Police Department. Personnel functions also encompass recruitment, contract negotiations, benefits administration, employee relations, and policy development and implementation.

Economic Development—Support strong public/private partnership toward diversified growth and prosperity. Source and negotiate with businesses, as well as secure agreements to retain and attract new businesses. Develop financial vehicles for public improvements.

Regulatory Affairs—Develop and manage relationships, as well as advocate for municipal affairs, with federal and state regulatory agencies, local business executives, congressional members, and other legislators.

Public/Community Relations—Instrumental in enhancing Town's image and building consensus with all boards. Active participant in numerous annual community events; act as spokesperson with the media.

Contributions

- Turned around employee morale and productivity, instituted training and employee recognition programs, and fostered interdepartmental cooperation, creating a positive work environment while restoring accountability and confidence in the administration. Municipality is recognized for having the "most responsive and best-managed administration statewide."
- Leader in the execution of several town revitalization projects following failed attempts by prior boards:
  - $2.9 million renovations to Town Hall, Senior Center, and Council on Aging
  - $5 million public safety complex
  - $1.3 million public library project with state library grant of $200,000
  - $15 million sewer project with more than $5 million secured in federal grant funding
- Personally negotiated Tax Incentive Financing (TIF) Agreements to retain and attract businesses.
- Effectively negotiated with the presidents of local companies to relocate their businesses back to North Granby. Results led to construction of new manufacturing facility for 4 companies employing 550 people and an agreement to expand employee base.
- Spearheaded search for new providers and negotiated improved employee benefits program while avoiding any rate increase.

Career Change: *From sales manager to town manager.*

Strategy: *Focus on his 10 years of municipal leadership experience and accomplishments rather than his "real" job as a district sales manager.*

FRED ANDERSON - Page 2

BUSINESS MANAGEMENT EXPERIENCE

MONROE & COMPANY, New York, NY · 1992 to present
(Global multibillion-dollar manufacturer)

District Manager · 1999 to present
Account Manager · 1993 to 1999

Promoted to develop business plan and manage $23 million district that extends from the Northeast to Florida. Supervise 5 broker sales organizations.

Manage budgets; oversee and motivate the sales team; deliver sales presentations; and provide training on sales strategies, product knowledge, marketing programs, and administrative policies/procedures.

Develop and implement sales and marketing programs. Interface with executives of multimillion-dollar corporations. Manage $3 million annual marketing/advertising budget, providing support to major customers.

Contributions

- Implemented successful sales/marketing programs that contributed to the district's growth and exceeded sales plan during last two trimesters in 2003 despite declining sales trend company-wide.
- Single-handedly transitioned the district from a direct sales force to a successful food broker network; efforts represent an entirely new direction for the company.
- Elected to the Leadership Club in 1999 for consistently ranking among the top 10% in overall sales performance throughout company.
- Renegotiated marketing programs with major customers that increased sales and profits while achieving acceptable dollar spends.
- Succeeded in securing new authorizations and expanding existing accounts while opening key accounts generating substantial business volume.

EDUCATION / PROFESSIONAL DEVELOPMENT

BENTLEY COLLEGE, Bentley, VT
M.B.A., Finance, 1999
B.S., Business Administration, 1995

Additional: Several seminars on municipal administration sponsored by Connecticut Municipal Association and Selectmen's Association

COMMUNITY AFFILIATIONS / LEADERSHIP

Selectmen's Association
Vice President, North Granby Rotary Club
Chairman, Conservation Commission

RESUME 95: BY GEORGE DUTCH, CMF, CCM, JCTC

MONIQUE OUTREMOUNT

6821 rue Agincourt
Orléans, Ontario, Canada K1P 4R9
Tel.: 613 286-9648 (day) / 286-6735 (evening)
Fax: 613 286-3370
mfco@internet.ca

"Integrity, purpose, and the right to opportunity"

Dedicated professional committed to strengthening institutional capacity to design and implement policies and programs that reflect the needs, interests, and aspirations of the poor and marginalized groups in developing countries. More than 20 years of experience providing strategic direction and optimizing organisational and human resources. Highly effective working within international environments. Specialized in good governance, social responsibility, poverty reduction, and gender equality. Skilled cross-cultural negotiator with excellent interpersonal, problem-solving, and communication skills in French, English, and Spanish. Additional capabilities include

- Leadership & Team Management
- Strategic Planning
- Policy Analysis & Development
- Social Auditing, Reporting & Accounting
- Coaching
- Program/Project Design, Implementation, Monitoring & Evaluation

- Civil Society & Government Linkages
- Community Development & Outreach
- Capacity Building & Institutional Strengthening
- Gender Mainstreaming
- Facilitation
- Results-based Management & Outcome Mapping

PROFESSIONAL ACCOMPLISHMENTS

- Championed improved access to and use of social services for the poor through $6M capacity development initiative in social communication (CIDA—Pakistan).

- Set strategic direction for $5.5M capacity-building project to mainstream gender equality considerations in the policies and programs of the Government of Bangladesh and sectors of civil society.

- Implemented complex analytical needs assessment of CIDA/partners' capacity to integrate gender equality considerations within 20 new/ongoing projects through review of concept papers, PADs, PIPs, AWPs, and RBM frameworks. (The Commonwealth Caribbean/Canada).

- Designed evaluation methodology/survey instruments to analyse perceptions for Inter-American Development Bank (IDB). Results utilised to revise gender training program.

- Designed methodology and led impact evaluation of a rural water supply and sanitation project.

- Led review of South American and Central American Gender Equity funds evaluating institutional development, HRD, sustainability, and gender equality strategies.

- Set organisational policy direction impacting overall management of firm, human/financial administration, implementation of all assignments, and launch of corporate marketing plans.

EMPLOYMENT HISTORY

MFCO Consulting, Inc., 2002–Present
President/Management & International Development Consultant
Colabour International, 1997–2002
Vice-President, Social Development Group and Corporate Marketing, 1999–2002
Project Manager/Gender Equality and Institutional Specialist, 1997–1999

Career Change: *From international consultant to association manager.*

Strategy: *Highlight her relevant professional accomplishments while clearly conveying her passion and commitment to nonprofit causes.*

Service-Growth Consultants, 1993–1995
Management Consultant
WATCH International Centre, 1990–1992
Executive Director, 1991–1992
Management Coordinator, 1990–1991
Conference Board of Canada, 1988–1990
Corporate Secretary, 1989–1990
Development Manager, 1988–1989
Berlitz Language Centers, 1976–1988
Director, 1979–1988
Language Instructor, 1976–1979

BOARDS OF DIRECTORS

Canadian Association of International Development Consultants, 1998–2000
Canadian Council for International Cooperation, 1990–1992
WATCH International Centre, 1989–1990

PROFESSIONAL AFFILIATIONS

Canadian Association of Management Consultants
Ethics Practitioners' Association of Canada
Association for Women's Rights in Development (AWID)
Society for International Development

EDUCATION/PROFESSIONAL DEVELOPMENT

Master of Business Administration (1998)
University of Ottawa, Ottawa, ON
International Strategy Certificate (1997)
École Supérieure de Commerce, Reims, France
Bachelor of Social Science—Political Science (1979)
University of Ottawa, Ottawa, ON

*Various specialized training modules: Corporate Director Certificate (Schulich School of Business);
Social/Ethics Auditing, Reporting & Accounting, (EthicScan); Organisational Effectiveness (Universalia);
Outcome Mapping (IDRC); Results-Based Management Training (CIDA); Social Gender Analysis Training
(CIDA); Project Management Certification (Bates Project Management, Inc.); Media Training (Conference
Board of Canada)*

PRESENTATIONS/PUBLICATIONS

Violence Against Women: A Human Rights & Development Issue—OECD DAC/WID Working
Group (1993)
Human Rights and Cultural Pluralism from a Gender Perspective—Canadian Foreign Service (1993)
Women's Rights as Human Rights—Presentation to Ford Foundation (1993)
Canadian Council for International Co-operation—Position paper to Foreign Affairs Parliamentary
Committee

EXPERIENCE IN & KNOWLEDGE OF DEVELOPING COUNTRIES

Commonwealth Caribbean, Costa Rica, El Salvador, Guatemala, Honduras, Nicaragua, Panama, Bolivia,
Brazil, Colombia, Ecuador, Paraguay, Peru, Rwanda, Tanzania, Zimbabwe, Bangladesh, Pakistan, and
Vietnam.

- 2 -

Joseph M. Ramirez, Sr.

825 West Jackson #215 • Chicago, Illinois 60661
ramirezlawoffice@aol.com   Home: 312-466-5321 • Cell: 312-606-1112

EXECUTIVE DIRECTOR

‣ Proactive legal professional with 25+ years of day-to-day and strategic experience in entrepreneurial, public service, advertising, and general management positions. Accomplished public speaker with early acting career in local markets.

‣ Strong desire to transition a "gift of persuasion" and 30-year passion for motorcycles into a career building membership for the Indian Riders Group. Avid motorcycle enthusiast averaging 6,000–8,000 miles each year.

‣ Background working with boards of directors, fund-raising committees, legal teams, and a diverse public to ensure actions reflect organizational values and goals. Experience managing budgets up to $16 million.

‣ Technical skills include Microsoft Word and Excel and knowledge of records/membership database management.

Notable Skills:

Start-up Ventures	Alliance Development	Board of Directors Interface	Budget Management
Fund-raising Efforts	Organizational Development	Analytical/Financial Analysis	Advertising Production
Media Relations	Long-Range Planning	Customer-Driven Management	Persuasive Selling
Public Outreach	Strategic Planning/Leadership	P&L Management	Customer Loyalty

CAREER PATH

LAW OFFICE OF JOSEPH M. RAMIREZ, SR., Chicago, Illinois   1989–Present

Principal
Hold full P&L responsibility and manage strategic administration of day-to-day operations while practicing law as a Criminal Defense Attorney. Handle family law, real property law, collections, Uniform Commercial Code issues, and bankruptcy cases. Supervise a three-member administrative team.

‣ Increased revenue 10–15% year-over-year, with 75% of business built on referrals. Began business by relying on court appointments and quickly developed private clientele.

FRONT-TIER CORPORATION, Omaha, Nebraska   1988–1989

General Counsel/Board Secretary
Led four-member legal team and held strategic responsibility for legal business concerns of time-share property/resort property corporation. Managed securities regulation, taxation, employee benefits, termination issues, real property concerns, and other corporate issues.

‣ Reported to six-member Board of Directors and served as Board Secretary.

WOODBURY COUNTY, IOWA, Sioux City, IA   1987–1988

Interim County Attorney (7/88–11/88)
Managed $16 million budget and directed staff of ten attorneys and eight support/clerical personnel. Continued to maintain heavy caseload of trial work while advising various county entities on legal matters. Prepared and drafted legal documents pertinent to county suits.

‣ Selected from a pool of five applicants to serve out term of former County Attorney.

Assistant County Attorney (8/87–7/88)
Conducted in-depth research and prepared/drafted legal documents (motions, orders, and trial briefs) for felony prosecutions. Maintained heavy caseload with concomitant plea negotiations and other necessary tasks.

‣ Elevated status of position and office by prosecuting the first Class A felony in the county.

Page 1 of 2

Career Change: *From attorney to association director.*

Strategy: *Pull out accomplishments directly related to the position of executive director of a motorcycle association.*

Joseph M. Ramirez, Sr. *Page 2 of 2*

CAREER PATH *(continued)*

LAW OFFICES OF BAKER AND RAMIREZ, Des Moines, Iowa 1986–1987

Partner
Managed administrative and financial duties, including case and status updating. Represented clients in areas of family law, real property law, collections, and bankruptcy. Participated in court-appointed public service work.

UNION COUNTY, Cresco, Iowa 1984–1985

Assistant County Attorney
Managed a heavy caseload to provide legal counsel to county residents. Supervised a four-member administrative support team.

EARLY CAREER

TRIAD STUDIOS INCORPORATED, Omaha, Nebraska

Advertising Promotion
Hired as a method actor for TV and radio commercials. Negotiated advertising contracts with small- to large-size companies, including Radio Shack, Bankers Trust, and Aetna. Prepared and presented promotional advertising copy.

▸ Won 11 Addie Acting Awards for interpretations of various characters. Played a key role in winning two additional Addie Awards for the company.

EDUCATION

DRAKE UNIVERSITY, Des Moines, IA

Doctor of Jurisprudence, Drake School of Law—1982
Bachelor of Arts, History & Political Science—1979

LEADERSHIP / MEMBERSHIPS

Memberships:
Illinois Bar Association
American Bar Association
Alpha Kappa Gamma Law Fraternity
Veterans of Foreign Wars

Leadership:
Boy Scouts of America:
Steering Committee, Mid-Iowa Council 1998–1999
Eagle Scout Leader / Scoutmaster, Boy Scouts of America 1986–2001
Fund-raising Committee 1996–2001
(Solicited $40,000–$50,000 annually for Camp Mitigua)
Eagle Scout Aeronautical Achievement Committee
(Raised $210,000–best year in history)

825 West Jackson #215 • Chicago, Illinois 60661 • ramirezlawoffice@aol.com • Phone: 312-606-1112

CHAPTER 12

Resumes for Senior Executives Seeking Lower-Level Business Positions

The typical career progression is upward, from one position to a more challenging and responsible role. But sometimes, for a variety of reasons, business leaders who have reached the top decide to step back just a bit. They want to be involved in important business challenges but prefer not hold the most senior role in the company. Just as with other career-changer resumes, the key is to highlight just those skills and achievements that relate to the current goal without distracting or overwhelming the reader with career information that might be true but is not relevant at this career stage. The example transitions in this chapter include the following:

- Senior manager to mechanic

- IT manager to hands-on technologist

- Company president to sales/operations manager

- CEO to marketing manager

- CEO to human resources executive

TOM W. MURRAY

301-555-5616   103 Mason Place ♦ Cascade, MD 21719   twmurray@aol.com

PROFILE

- High-energy self-starter with a broad scope of experience in the manufacturing, purchasing, product development, and quality inspection of electromechanical and electronic devices.
- Committed to the continuous improvement process, with total team participation.
- Proven ability to meet all delivery, quality, and cost-savings objectives.
- Exceptional interpersonal skills; diplomatic and effective with customers, managers, and production teams.
- Detail oriented; competent in managing paperwork and written communication.
- Strong mechanical aptitude.
- Computer proficient with Word, Excel, and PowerPoint.

PROFESSIONAL EXPERIENCE

Electronics Corporation, Frederick, MD   1975–2000
Completed a successful career with a world leader in the design, manufacturing, marketing, and sales of power protection, thermal sensing, and electronic packaging products. Strong record of achievement in the following areas:

Technical & Mechanical Applications

- Developed an expertise in reading and interpreting blueprints and technical drawings.
- Established a CNC department, showing comprehensive knowledge of machine setup, operation, and SPC.
- Implemented a completely automatic assembly line that produced 30K subminiature thermostat units daily.
- Developed and implemented a scheduled preventative maintenance program that reduced breakdowns and improved equipment longevity.
- Led teams operating injection-molding machines, die-casting and screw machines, cut-off and band saws, vertical milling machines, vertical CNC machining centers, lathes, and high-speed drill presses.

Quality Assurance

- Skilled in the use of all precision-measuring instruments, including calipers, micrometers, and dial indicators.
- Monitored manufacturing processes and tested products for compliance with industry specifications; proficient in using SPC methods for process control.
- Involved in ISO 9001 certification process for Thermal Products Group Division; qualified as ISO auditor.

Inventory & People Management

- Planned and scheduled people and materials; shortened product flow distance through the manufacturing areas by more than 55%.
- Converted a manual MRP system to a fully automated system; directed the installation of MAPICS/DB.
- Excelled in organizing and coaching personnel to work effectively in teams.
- Oversaw team operations in Manufacturing Engineering, Facilities Engineering, Purchasing, Materials, Scheduling, and Shipping & Receiving.
- Diagnosed and rectified production needs and problems.

Purchasing

- More than 15 years of experience managing supplier relations, purchasing, cost control, and supplier quality; directed a +95% improvement in OTD.
- Developed a total working knowledge of indented bill of materials as well as shop-floor routings.
- Managed the bid process for all purchased materials/components, tooling orders, and MRO supplies; established a vendor rating system; negotiated contracts.
- Worked with engineering and QA to develop sources and track national/international marketing trends.
- Dealt in various commodities such as stampings, turned assemblies, molded plastics, magnets, die-cast components, and electronics components.

MECHANICAL HOBBY

Build custom Harley-Davidson motorcycles.

Career Change: *From senior manager to mechanic.*

Strategy: *Use a skills-based format and delete his high-powered job title.*

SASHA SAMPSON

1699 Hillsdale, San Jose, CA 95124
Ph: 408.333.2221 ▪ Cell: 408.999.2221
email: sasha@tech.net

SOFTWARE ENGINEER

➢ Hands-on project-management and software-development strengths.
➢ Solid record of contributions to project success, business growth, and technology advancement.
➢ Reputation for strong work ethic, commitment to customers, industry knowledge, and ability to thrive in challenging situations.

SALES & TECHNICAL EXPERTISE

▪ Relationship Building	▪ Startup / Turnaround	▪ Vendor Relations / Negotiations
▪ Customer Service / Support	▪ IT Needs Assessment	▪ Technical Training
▪ Technical Troubleshooting	▪ IT Infrastructure Development	▪ System Security / Disaster Planning
▪ Project Development	▪ Systems Implementation	▪ Productivity Improvement

CAREER & ACHIEVEMENT SUMMARY

ALPHORIM, INC.—Santa Clara, CA
(Startup technology company engaged in providing proprietary hardware/software solutions with capacity to deliver voice, data, and video over DSL, PONs, and regular POTs circuits)
MANAGER, INFORMATION TECHNOLOGY (2001 to Present)

Overview: Initially hired as company's sole IT staff member with responsibility for establishing internal 24×7 IT infrastructure to support community of more than 120 local/remote users over a 2-year period. Specifically responsible for all networking, data storage, remote access, and telephony operations, as well as installations, maintenance and upgrades, budgeting, purchasing, and negotiations for services and equipment. Charged with creating stable and scalable environment while maintaining low costs without compromising quality. Upgraded and maintained Windows networking and UNIX environments; ensured 100% backup of information; selected vendor for off-site storage; oversaw internal voice, data, and support contracts; and served as key contact for all software/hardware purchasing. Provided technical leadership, technical troubleshooting, and performance improvement for all IT operations. *Assumed greater responsibilities as company grew from initial staff of 20 to more than 120 employees.*

<u>**Key Projects & Contributions**</u>

- **Successfully led move of entire IT infrastructure,** including servers, networking, and telephony over single weekend with successful "opening" by start of business Monday.
- **Captured significant telecommunication savings** by selecting outsourced VOIP phone system with contract that included equipment, training, installation, and PRI circuits for 120+ users (initially 50, grew to 120). Consolidated bandwidth, local, and long-distance expenses.
- **Consistently boosted system functionality and performance** by upgrading backup system and implementing VPN (and enhancing when necessary). Performed ongoing monitoring of network and firewall, and closed performance issues with Network Appliance Filers.
- **Delivered $1,000 monthly savings while improving support and overhead** by researching/selecting new phone system for customer service group.
- **Saved more than $100K in IT equipment purchases in 2003** (recognized as "one of the lowest-spending departments in the company").
- **Sustained cost-effective IT operations** by cultivating excellent vendor relationships, expertly negotiating pricing, and utilizing alternative technologies to solve problems.
- **Impacted profitability results** by hiring one Desktop Support Administrator to support all IT efforts; work in tandem to ensure smooth operations and high productivity despite rapid growth of company.
- **Enhanced overall IT operations and productivity** by authoring and implementing formal security usage (policy and procedures) and IT disaster recovery plan.

Career Change: *From IT manager to hands-on technologist.*

Strategy: *Emphasize strong technical experience and omit mention of senior-level leadership activities.*

RESUME 98, CONTINUED

SASHA SAMPSON
Ph: 408.333.2221 ▪ Cell: 408.999.2221
email: sasha@tech.net

JOURNEY TECH—Santa Clara, CA
(Technology company engaged in bringing video to home market via broadband [DSL] connection using proprietary hardware and video compression software)
SENIOR LAN ADMINISTRATOR (2000 to 2001)

Overview: Charged with managing network and client workstations and administering internal functions including email, adds, moves, and changes for voice and data operations. Supported users and managed backups and VPN usage. Provided research for new equipment, led purchasing decisions, and performed general system administration of all Windows NT and 2000 servers. *Note: Company was not able to generate profits and closed shortly after launching.*

Key Projects & Contributions

- **Introduced productivity improvements,** including testing and documentation of bug-tracking system (DreamApps) and ERM (FirstWave).
- **Facilitated user training on several technology applications,** including new bug-tracking system.

SOLUTION CENTRAL—San Mateo, CA
(Startup web portal company; initial products included a database of technical training courses)
SITE ADMINISTRATOR (1999 to 2000)

Overview: Accountable for all systems administration and desktop support of Windows NT Network for ecommerce portal; essentially functioned as Information Architect. Assisted development staff with transfer of data to production environment and provided ongoing maintenance and troubleshooting.

- **Reduced monthly expenses** by leading transition from company mail with external hosting to in-house Exchange 5.5 within one week (including all setup and user training).
- **Managed site transfer from in-house servers to off-site servers.** Created duplicate set of servers in-house that matched that of hosted production site and led staging/test area for code.
- **Improved security** by managing company firewall; halted unauthorized network infiltration.

NEW YORK UNIVERSITY—New York, NY
PROGRAMMER ANALYST (1997 to 1999)

Overview: Hired to support email and dial-up accounts for 10,000 end-users; quickly earned promotion to Programmer Analyst. Authored technical notes and procedure documents related to changes in network architecture, services, and software. Monitored system logs and backups. Performed troubleshooting for campus-wide networking and SMTP issues as well as individual accounts.

- **Developed numerous well-received classes, including** "You, Your Computer, and the Internet," "E-mail Tips and Tricks for Windows 95/98," "Advanced Eudora Tips and Tricks for Windows 95/98," and "Linux Dial-in Pitfalls: How to Avoid Them."
- **Generated high levels of productivity for staff of 13;** trained new network operations staff members in troubleshooting methods and customer service while fielding all escalated calls.
- **Designed and implemented ACD system** to help route calls and generate reports related to hosted website that held training materials, scheduling, and software downloads.

EDUCATION & CERTIFICATION

BA, English Literature—New York University, New York, NY

UNIX Systems Administration Certification, valid through 2006—U.C. Extension
Numerous seminars, including USENIX and technical writing and editing

RYAN EDISON

Home 781-944-1063 • Mobile 781-709-2401
292 Pearl Street, Reading, MA 01867
ryan_edison@verizon.net

Sales & Operations Management Professional

Invigorating Growth • Improving Performance • Surpassing Expectations

Strategic and tactical leader of both sales and operations, with a track record of consistent growth, continuous improvement, and turnaround leadership. Effective manager of sales organizations, production teams, and key business initiatives, combining customer and process focus with authentic leadership style that creates a collaborative teamwork environment.

Sales Qualifications: Consultative/needs-based/solution sales expert. Repeatedly satisfied customers by developing solutions that save time, cut costs, and ensure consistent quality. Restored dormant accounts and gained preferred/exclusive provider status. Drove rapid sales growth.

Operations Expertise: Leader in introducing technologies, methodologies, and processes that streamline operations and achieve stringent quality, production, and profit goals. TQM/Production Cells/Quality Manuals/Performance Incentive Plans/Team Building/Cost Control.

Experience and Achievements

EASTERN RUBBER & PLASTICS, Lynn, MA   2001–Present
Distributor of industrial rubber products to MRO buyers in multiple diverse industries

BRANCH MANAGER, SOUTHERN NEW HAMPSHIRE, 2002–Present

Provided turnaround leadership for faltering branch suffering sliding revenues and 7 years of unprofitable performance. Developed and executed strategic plan for rapid improvement and sales growth.

Scope of responsibility is diverse and includes all operations as well as sales and business development for $1M+ branch. Hire, train, and manage sales associates in target markets; train and manage warehouse employees in compliance with company ISO 9002 procedures.

- Rejuvenated sales performance: Grew sales 30% in one year and was the only company branch to achieve sales growth in 2003.
- Successfully launched OEM sales for the company and grew to 20% of branch revenues. Secured the company's first OEM account ($50K annual sales) and created the operational and administrative processes for efficient management of this line of business.
- Transformed "order taking" to needs-based consultative selling/customer problem-solving that resulted in key wins with new and existing customers:
  - Became preferred supplier to a key target account and grew that business from zero to $20K.
  - Converted a product trial to $10K in new business with annual savings of $10K to the customer.
  - Rebuilt relationships with former accounts, translating their needs to product solutions that generated $20K sales revenue.

OPERATIONS MANAGER, HEADQUARTERS, 2001–2002

Created a high-performance organization—refocused and recharged the team, instilled customer orientation, and put in place metrics and benchmarks to guide continuous improvement. Brought on board to drive performance improvements and expand the business to new markets and sales channels. Managed operations team of 5, with full responsibility for timely, accurate, cost-effective shipments of 5 core product groups to customers nationwide.

- Led warehouse team from lackluster performance to consistent achievement of defined goals for productivity, inventory management, and housekeeping. Bonus attainment skyrocketed from 62% to 93%.
- Led a cost-cutting initiative, analyzing all operational expenses to find ways to drive cost from the operation without affecting quality, performance, or strategic growth:
  - Cut utility consumption by 60%.
  - Eliminated $8K annually in customer gifts that delivered little return on investment.

Career Change: From company president to sales/operations manager.

Strategy: Emphasize his recent interim role as branch manager without mentioning his concurrent title and responsibilities as president of the company.

RYAN EDISON   Home 781-944-1063 • Mobile 781-709-2401 • ryan_edison@verizon.net

- Created a collaborative work environment where customer service was the focus and the team knew precisely what was expected and how to achieve it. Initiated monthly team meetings and invited staff input.
- Improved efficiency by defining standards, developing operating procedures, and creating processes:
  - Matched product surplus with shipment status through inventory analysis.
  - Monitored orders through the entire workflow; pinpointed and eliminated bottlenecks.

EDISON CERTIFIED HOSE, Saugus, MA   2001
Start-up OEM supplier, acquired by Eastern Rubber & Plastics

GENERAL MANAGER

Launched start-up and, within 3 months, became an approved OEM supplier of certified hydraulic hose assemblies. Secured investment capital, developed business plan, put in place processes and equipment, wrote a quality manual, and gained production authorization.

- Negotiated profitable sale of the business to Eastern Rubber & Plastics; joined new organization as Operations Manager of its headquarters location.

BAY STATE INDUSTRIAL HOSE/REVERE RUBBER COMPANY, Revere, MA   1989–2001
Suppliers of certified industrial hoses through both OEM and distributor sales channels

GENERAL MANAGER/DIRECTOR OF SALES

Spearheaded both sales and operations for jointly owned industrial sales companies, one concentrating in the OEM market and the other in distributor sales; combined revenues exceeded $3M annually. Managed finance, P&L, human resources, production and shipping, purchasing/vendor relations, sales, and marketing. Used first-rate organizational and time-management skills to juggle diverse responsibilities for the 2 companies.

Operational Achievements

- Improved productivity 75% by introducing state-of-the-art methodologies (e.g., production cells).
- Instituted TQM meetings, wrote the firm's first quality manual, and built a culture of quality and teamwork.
- Eliminated $20K in unnecessary cost by analyzing expenditures and matching investment to ROI.
- Problem-solved customer production processes and recommended solutions that cut costs, streamlined production, and resulted in substantial sales opportunities.
  - Grew a $140K account to $700K by supplying quality (99%) and on-time delivery (99.99%) that could not be matched by the competition.
  - Gained exclusive account status with a key OEM customer by suggesting solutions that cut their costs and improved their profitability—while generating $250K in annual sales to our company.

Sales Performance

- Personally achieved 30% of company sales, topping 3 other producers while concurrently managing company operations.
- Realigned sales territories to better match resources with market opportunities. Equipped sales staff with technology to improve territory management and proposal processes.
- Developed and continuously refined marketing and sales strategies to drive profitable growth. Aligned sales initiatives with strategic growth opportunities; motivated and evaluated sales staff; performed sales/market analysis; created account plans; and trained sales staff in strategic, consultative selling.

Education

Bachelor of Business Administration/Major in Finance   Salem State University, Salem, MA

Professional Development: Sandler Sales Institute and President's Club
                          University of Industrial Distribution: Key Account Selling and Territory Planning;
                          Selling and Building the Sales Team; Sales and Market Planning

RESUME 100: BY ROMONA CAMARATA, BS ED., MS ED., GCDF

AMY M. CROW

812 Vermillion Street
La Porte, Indiana 46404

219-939-1415
E-mail: crow@insightbb.com

EXECUTIVE MARKETING MANAGEMENT ▪ STRATEGIC BUSINESS EXPANSION

Professional career reflects more than 12 years of results-oriented senior marketing expertise focused on enhancing comprehensive marketing strategies, developing advertising and public relations programs, and initiating brand recognition programs for established and start-up companies. Demonstrated history of creative problem solving in research and communications to develop and launch innovative campaigns earning recognition in mass media. Successful record of building, mentoring, and motivating teams to achieve goals and ensure full client satisfaction. These leadership abilities led to 45% revenue growth and substantial market-share increase over a 12-month period.

CREDENTIALS AND OBJECTIVES

In progress, **Master of Business** degree in **Marketing and Healthcare Administration.** Supported by **Bachelor of Science** degree in **Business** and **Bachelor of Arts** degree in **Psychology,** both from Purdue University. Have enhanced academic and professional credentials with additional training in leadership development, project management, corporate finance, healthcare management, and national and divisional accounts supervision.

These skills and experiences would enable me to serve your organization in a variety of leadership capacities. I believe my abilities could be maximized as **Vice President of Business Development, Vice President of Marketing, or Director of National Business Planning.** Given the opportunity to represent myself to you in person, I am confident you will find me to be a worthy addition to your marketing leadership team.

SELECTED ACCOMPLISHMENTS

Marketing

➤ Conducted daily competitive research and managed multiple ongoing projects, including corporate campaign development, company-wide product branding, national public relations, and presentation packets.
➤ Designed innovative visual aids impacting successful branding and campaign launch.
➤ Developed training manuals and documented new product designs using new troubleshooting processes.
➤ Created numerous media, investor, and marketing communications packages, including press releases for TV and radio announcement, ad copy, speeches, direct-mail campaigns, billboards, Web pages, PowerPoint presentations, and annual reports for Fortune 500 companies bringing in billions of dollars of revenues.
➤ Substantially improved internal communications by supplying clients with strong marketing displays for trade shows.
➤ Supplied clients with high-impact product branding to include packaging and launch services, logo and identity development, point-of-sale programs, and kiosks for national and international exposure.
➤ Authored how-to marketing articles for *Texas Lawyer* and *The Dallas Business Journal,* resulting in millions of dollars of increased revenues.

Business Management & Expansion

➤ Led teams in analyzing properties, developing competitive market forecasts, and creating expansion plans.
➤ Streamlined the market analysis methodology and efficiently managed multiple projects in tight time constraints.
➤ Implemented a successful acquisition group that yielded $40M in revenue and 82% increase in market share.
➤ Developed and implemented requirements, recommendations, and operations strategies for hundreds of customer-requested projects.

Career Change: *From CEO to marketing manager.*

Strategy: *Begin with a strong marketing-related positioning statement and support this with an extensive list of marketing-related career achievements.*

AMY M. CROW   PAGE 2

CAREER HISTORY

CEO/Co-Owner   **Party & The Game Room**   **2002–Present**
- Took lead role in family-owned business and developed a marketing plan that increased revenue by 35%.
- Redesigned logo, Web site, and all marketing communications to create new brand image aligned with strategic business focus.

Vice President, Marketing   **E3M**   **5/01–10/01**
- Point person for subsidiary of Concentra Healthcare, focused on providing Internet software to Workers' Compensation industry. Developed the entire marketing and public relations plan and product branding from conception to launch.
- Implemented very successful marketing campaigns to capture business.
    - Collaborated with technical, product, and sales staffs.
    - Interacted with advertising agencies, printers, and other vendors to achieve goals and timelines.
    - Exhibited at domestic and international conventions.
    - Managed a five-member team consisting of a graphic designer, content manager, PR writer, field sales person, and marketing assistant.
- Negotiated distribution contracts with 200+ vendors.
- Established A1 credit lines with all suppliers within first year.

Executive Vice President   **JPI**   **1/99–5/01**
- Developed a market analysis to complete an in-depth assessment of key markets across 17 states for the nation's largest real estate investment (REIT) firm.
- Led three staff to finalize all communications and plans of conventional and student properties.
- Provided accurate assessment of current customers' emerging needs and predictions of overall market trends.
- Conducted national focus groups in each market over four-month period and presented results to board of directors and acquisition groups.
- Prepared extensive marketing materials, trade magazine ads, annual catalogs, and brochures for the California market.
- Organized and prepared an accurate assessment of current customers, emerging needs, and predictions resulting in unprecedented new business developments with 20% increase in revenues.

President/Founder   **C.E.O. spa**   **1998–2001**
- Established company focused on enhancing leadership abilities of CEOs of small companies to Fortune 100 institutions. Received extensive media coverage from publications: the *Wall Street Journal, Fortune* magazine, *Forbes*, etc.

Principal, President/CEO   **LedgeCOM/LedgeMARK**   **1995–1999**
- Founded and grew successful advertising, marketing, and public relations agency providing a wide range of services to Fortune 500 companies including Nokia, Cisco, and EmCare. Hired and managed team of six.

Consultant   **EmCare**
- Contracted to evaluate and integrate all marketing and advertising campaigns to create a unified message for the nation's largest emergency medicine physician provider.

Product Consultant   **Nokia**   **1997–1999**
- Guided the product management group of a cellular phone manufacturer through a complex medical and technical information plan incorporating the Americans With Disabilities Act.

Director of Marketing   **Cardiovascular Physicians Resources**   **1995–1997**
- Directed the activities of 18 personnel to create an unprecedented marketing campaign and implementation program.

JOHN GREGORY
gregoryjohnjr@mindspring.com
789 Craigmont Avenue, Duluth, MN 33383
(218) 333-3726

SENIOR EXECUTIVE PROFILE
Strategic Human Resources Leadership / Organizational Development / Change Management
Performance Optimization / Leadership Training & Development / P&L Management
Harvard MBA

Distinguished management career leading organizations through start-up, change, revitalization, turnaround, and accelerated growth. Cross-functional expertise with proven success in optimizing organizational growth, productivity, and efficiency. HR Generalist experience in benefits, compensation, recruitment, training, and HRIS technology. Expert team building, team leadership, communication, and interpersonal relations skills.

PROFESSIONAL EXPERIENCE

Chief Executive Officer / HR Director   1999 to Present
MED HEALTH SOLUTIONS, Duluth, Minnesota

CHALLENGE: *Lead the organization through a comprehensive organizational development and change management program to support corporate-wide diversification strategy.*

Senior Executive recruited to plan and orchestrate a complete redesign of strategic planning, HR/OD, administrative, information technology, marketing, and operating functions to increase revenues and bottom-line profitability. Manage within a tightly regulated and competitive industry.

- One of two senior executives credited with transitioning Med Health Solutions from 1999 revenues of $700,000 to current revenues of $1.8 million. Drove profit growth by more than 45%.
- Built a best-in-class HR organization; implemented advanced HRIS technology; designed benefit and compensation programs; established a formal salary structure; and introduced employee training, counseling, and coaching programs.
- Revitalized all core financial functions, implemented client/server architecture to optimize technology performance, and created a team-based/customer-based corporate culture.
- Negotiated $2.8 million acquisition of competitive company and facilitated seamless integration of personnel, technology, and product lines.

President / General Manager / HR Director   1990 to 1999
DYNAMIC SOLUTIONS, INC., Tampa, Florida

CHALLENGE: *Launch entrepreneurial venture in an intensely competitive consumer market and create strong infrastructure to support continued growth and market penetration.*

Senior Executive with full responsibility for strategic planning, business development, all HR functions (particular emphasis on staffing), operations, marketing, and P&L performance of an independent venture.

- Built new venture from concept to more than $1 million in annual sales with a 23% profit margin.
- Created performance-based training programs for all hourly and management personnel.
- Achieved and maintained a stable workforce with less than 5% turnover in an industry with average turnover of better than 20%.

Career Change: *From CEO to human resources executive.*

Strategy: *Emphasize only the challenges and results that relate to his target of human resources leadership.*

JOHN GREGORY – Page Two

gregoryjohnjr@mindspring.com
(218) 333-3726

Human Resources Director / CEO   1983 to 1990
LSI SOCIEDAD, S.A., Santo Domingo, Dominican Republic

CHALLENGE: *Orchestrate growth of new international venture within the financial services industry and transition through organizational change and market repositioning.*

Senior Management Executive and HR Director building a new professional services organization. Created organizational infrastructure, recruited/trained personnel, designed marketing and business development programs, and created all administrative and internal reporting systems.

- Built new company from concept into a $12 million annual revenue producer with EBIT of $1 million annually. Achieved/surpassed all corporate revenue and profit objectives.
- Led the organization through a successful internal transition and recreated core business processes to support massive change and recreate corporate image.
- Recruited and trained a team of more than 60. Introduced incentives linked to performance and focused on customer development, retention, and growth.
- Negotiated health and insurance benefit contracts for the corporation. Designed salary structures, incentive programs, and executive compensation plans.

Personal Assistant to CEO   1981 to 1983
BANCO DEL COMBRERO, Santo Domingo, Dominican Republic

CHALLENGE: *Facilitate market and revenue growth for a specialty import/export company.*

Recruited by CEO to assist with building a profitable international business venture. Scope of responsibility spanned all core executive functions, with particular emphasis on organizational design, policy/procedure development, recruitment and training, sales, and marketing.

- Instrumental in driving growth from $2.5 million to $5.5 million in annual revenues.
- Recruited former Procter & Gamble executive to the organization to provide critical industry and market leadership. Recruited sales producers from leading Latin American companies.
- Created organizational infrastructure and HR support to facilitate diversification and expansion into both emerging and established consumer markets.
- Designed HR policies, compensation plans, and performance review schedules.

EDUCATION

Executive MBA—Harvard University—1989 *(Distinguished Alumnus Award)*

BS—Business Administration—Lillymount University—1981

PROFESSIONAL AFFILIATIONS

Society for Human Resource Management (SHRM)

American Society for Training & Development (ASTD)

APPENDIX

Internet Career Resources

With the emergence of the Internet has come a huge collection of job search resources for individuals who are changing careers. Here are some of our favorites.

Dictionaries and Glossaries

Outstanding information on keywords and acronyms.

Acronym Finder	www.acronymfinder.com
Babelfish Foreign-Language Translation	http://babelfish.altavista.com/
ComputerUser High-Tech Dictionary	www.computeruser.com/resources/dictionary/dictionary.html
Dave's Truly Canadian Dictionary of Canadian Spelling	www.luther.ca/~dave7cnv/cdnspelling/cdnspelling.html
Dictionary of Investment Terms	www.county.com.au/web/webdict.nsf/pages/index?open
Duhaime's Legal Dictionary	www.duhaime.org
High-Tech Dictionary Chat Symbols	www.computeruser.com/resources/dictionary/chat.html
InvestorWords.com	www.investorwords.com
Law.com Legal Industry Glossary	www.law.com
Legal Dictionary	www.nolo.com/lawcenter/dictionary/wordindex.cfm
Merriam-Webster Collegiate Dictionary & Thesaurus	www.m-w.com/home.htm
National Restaurant Association Restaurant Industry Glossary	www.nraef.org/pdf_files/IndustryAcronymsDefinitions-edited-2-23.pdf

Refdesk	www.refdesk.com
Technology Terms Dictionary	www.computeruser.com/
TechWeb TechEncyclopedia	www.techweb.com/encyclopedia/
Verizon Glossary of Telecom Terms	www22.verizon.com/wholesale/ glossary/0,2624,P_Q,00.html
Washington Post Business Glossary	www.washingtonpost.com/ wp-srv/business/longterm/ glossary/index.htm
Webopedia: Online Dictionary for Computer and Internet Terms	www.webopedia.com
Whatis?com Technology Terms	http://whatis.techtarget.com
Wordsmyth: The Educational Dictionary/Thesaurus	www.wordsmyth.net

Job Search Sites

You'll find thousands and thousands of current professional employment opportunities on these sites.

GENERAL SITES

6FigureJobs	www.6figurejobs.com
AllStar Jobs	www.allstarjobs.com
America's CareerInfoNet	www.acinet.org/acinet
America's Job Bank	www.ajb.dni.us
BestJobsUSA	www.bestjobsusa.com/index-jsk-ns.asp
BlackWorld Careers	www.blackworld.com
Canada WorkInfo Net	www.workinfonet.ca
CareerAge	www.careerage.com
CareerBuilder	www.careerbuilder.com
Career.com	www.career.com
CareerExchange.com	www.careerexchange.com
Career Exposure	www.careerexposure.com
The Career Key	www.careerkey.org/english
Careermag.com	www.careermag.com
CareerShop	www.careershop.com
CareerSite.com	www.careersite.com
Contract Employment Weekly	www.ceweekly.com

Digital City (jobs by location)	home.digitalcity.com
EmploymentGuide.com	www.employmentguide.com
Excite	http://careers.excite.com
FlipDog	www.flipdog.com
Futurestep	www.futurestep.com
GETAJOB!	www.getajob.com
Help Wanted	www.helpwanted.com
HotJobs.com	www.hotjobs.com
The Internet Job Locator	www.joblocator.com
It's Your Job Now	www.ItsYourJobNow.com
JobBankUSA	www.jobbankusa.com
Job-Hunt.org	www.job-hunt.org
JobHuntersBible.com	www.jobhuntersbible.com
JOBNET.com	www.jobnet.com/philly
JobOptions	www.joboptions.com
Job Source	www.jobsource.com
JobWeb	www.jobweb.com
Kiwi Careers (New Zealand)	www.careers.co.nz
Monster.com	www.monster.com
MonsterTRAK	www.jobtrak.com
NationJob Network	www.nationjob.com
NCOA MaturityWorks	www.maturityworks.org
Net Temps	www.net-temps.com
Online-Jobs.Com	www.online-jobs.com
The Riley Guide	www.rileyguide.com
Saludos Hispanos	www.saludos.com
TrueCareers	www.careercity.com
Wages.com	www.wages.com.au
WorkTree	www.worktree.com

ACCOUNTING CAREERS

American Association of Finance and Accounting	www.aafa.com
CPAnet	www.CPAnet.com
SmartPros Accounting	www.accountingnet.com

ARTS AND MEDIA CAREERS

Airwaves MediaWeb	www.airwaves.com
Auditions.com	www.auditions.com
Fashion Career Center	www.fashioncareercenter.com
Playbill (Theatre Jobs)	www.playbill.com/jobs/find/
TVJobs.com	www.tvjobs.com

EDUCATION CAREERS

Academic360.com	www.academic360.com
Chronicle of Higher Education Career Network	www.chronicle.com/jobs
Council for Advancement and Support of Education	www.case.org
Education Jobs.com	www.educationjobs.com
Education Week's Marketplace Jobs Online	www.edweek.org/jobs
Education World	www.education-world.com/jobs
Jobs.EduFind.com	www.jobs.edunet.com
Teaching Jobs	www.teaching-jobs.org/index.htm
University Job Bank	www.ujobbank.com

ENTRY-LEVEL CAREERS

CampusCareerCenter.com	www.campuscareercenter.com
College Grad Job Hunter	www.collegegrad.com
College Job Board	www.collegejobboard.com/?1100
MonsterTRAK	www.jobtrak.com

GOVERNMENT AND MILITARY CAREERS

Federal Jobs Net	www.federaljobs.net
FedWorld	www.fedworld.gov
FRS Federal Jobs Central	www.fedjobs.com
GetaGovJob.com	www.getagovjob.com
GovExec.com	www.govexec.com
HRS Federal Job Search	www.hrsjobs.com
Military Career Guide Online	www.militarycareers.com

| PLANETGOV | www.planetgov.com |
| USAJOBS | www.usajobs.opm.gov |

HEALTH CARE/MEDICAL/PHARMACEUTICAL CAREERS

Great Valley Publishing	www.gvpub.com
HealthJobSite.com	www.healthjobsite.com
Health Leaders	www.HealthLeaders.com
J. Allen & Associates (physician jobs)	www.NHRphysician.com
MedHunters.com	www.medhunters.com
Medzilla	www.medzilla.com
Monster Healthcare	http://healthcare.monster.com/
Nursing Spectrum	www.nursingspectrum.com
Pharmaceutical Company Database	www.coreynahman.com/ pharmaceutical_company_database.html
Physicians Employment	www.physemp.com
RehabJobsOnline	www.rehabjobs.com
Rx Career Center	www.rxcareercenter.com

HUMAN RESOURCES CAREERS

HR Connections	www.hrjobs.com
HR Hub	www.hrhub.com
Human Resources Development Canada	www.hrdc-drhc.gc.ca/common/ home.shtml
Jobs4HR	www.jobs4hr.com

INTERNATIONAL CAREERS

EscapeArtist.com	www.escapeartist.com
International Career Employment Center	www.internationaljobs.org
LatPro	www.latpro.com
OverseasJobs.com	www.overseasjobs.com

LEGAL CAREERS

FindLaw	www.findlaw.com
Greedy Associates	www.greedyassociates.com
Legal Career Center	www.attorneyjobs.com

SALES AND MARKETING CAREERS

American Marketing Association	www.marketingpower.com
Job.com	www.job.com/jobsearch/index.cfm? tid=search.cfm&us=226&catbox=53
MarketingJobs.com	www.marketingjobs.com
Rollins Search Group	www.rollinssearch.com

SERVICE CAREERS

Chefs Job Network	www.chefsjobnetwork.com
Culinary Jobs	www.pastrywiz.com/talk/job.htm
Escoffier On Line	www.escoffier.com
Foodservice.com	www.foodservice.com

TECHNOLOGY/ENGINEERING CAREERS

American Institute of Architects	www.aia.org
American Society for Quality	www.asq.org
Brainbuzz.com IT Career Network	www.brainbuzz.com
CareerShop	www.careershop.com
Chancellor & Chancellor Resources for Careers	www.chancellor.com/fr_careers.html
ComputerWork.com	www.computerwork.com
Computerworld Careers Knowledge Center	www.computerworld.com/ careertopics/careers?from=left
Dice	www.dice.com
IDEAS Job Network	www.ideasjn.com
IEEE-USA Job Service	jobs.ieeeusa.org/jobs/services/
Jobserve	www.jobserve.com
National Society of Professional Engineers	www.nspe.org
National Technical Employment Services	www.ntes.com
Quality Resources Online	www.quality.org
Resulte Universal	www.psisearch.com
Techies.com	www.techies.com

SITES FOR MISCELLANEOUS SPECIFIC FIELDS

AG Careers/Farms.com	www.agricareers.com
American Public Works Association	www.pubworks.org
AutoCareers.com	www.autocareers.com
BrilliantPeople.com	www.brilliantpeople.com
CareerBank.com	www.careerbank.com
CEOExpress	www.ceoexpress.com
CFO.com	www.cfonet.com
Environmental Career Opportunities	www.ecojobs.com
Environmentalcareer.com	www.environmental-jobs.com
Find A Pilot	www.findapilot.com
International Seafarers Exchange	www.jobxchange.com
Logistics Jobs	www.jobsinlogistics.com
MBACareers.com	www.mbacareers.com
Social Work Jobs	www.socialservice.com
Vault	www.vault.com

Company Information

Outstanding resources for researching specific companies.

555-1212.com	www.555-1212.com
Brint.com	www.brint.com
EDGAR Online	www.edgar-online.com
Experience	www.experiencenetwork.com
Fortune Magazine	www.fortune.com
Hoover's Business Profiles	www.hoovers.com
infoUSA (small business information)	www.infousa.com
Intellifact.com	www.igiweb.com/intellifact/
OneSource CorpTech	www.corptech.com
SuperPages.com	www.bigbook.com
U.S. Chamber of Commerce	www.uschamber.com/

| Vault Company Research | www.vault.com/companies/ searchcompanies.jsp |
| Wetfeet.com Company Research | www.wetfeet.com/asp/ companyresource_home.asp |

Interviewing Tips and Techniques

Expert guidance to sharpen and strengthen your interviewing skills.

About.com Interviewing	www.jobsearch.about.com/business/ jobsearch/msubinterv.htm
Bradley CVs Introduction to Job Interviews	www.bradleycvs.demon.co.uk/ interview/index.htm
Dress for Success	www.dressforsuccess.org
Job-Interview.net	www.job-interview.net
Northeastern University Career Services	www.dac.neu.edu/coop.careerservices/ interview.html

Salary and Compensation Information

Learn from the experts to strengthen your negotiating skills and increase your salary.

Abbott, Langer & Associates	www.abbott-langer.com
America's Career InfoNet	www.acinet.org/acinet/select_ occupation.asp?stfips=&next=occ_rep
Bureau of Labor Statistics	www.bls.gov/bls/wages.htm
Clayton Wallis Co.	www.claytonwallis.com
Economic Research Institute	www.erieri.com
Health Care Salary Surveys	www.pohly.com/salary.shtml
Janco Associates MIS Salary Survey	www.psrinc.com/salary.htm
JobStar	www.jobstar.org/tools/salary/index.htm
Monster.com Salary Info	salary.monster.com/
Salary and Crime Calculator	www.homefair.com/homefair/ cmr/salcalc.html
Salary Expert	www.salaryexpert.com

Salarysurvey.com	www.salarysurvey.com
Wageweb	www.wageweb.com
WorldatWork (formerly American Compensation Association)	www.worldatwork.org

INDEX OF CONTRIBUTORS

The sample resumes in chapters 4 through 12 were written by professional resume and cover letter writers. If you need help with your resume and job search correspondence, you can use the following list to locate a career professional. Many, if not all, of these resume professionals work with clients long-distance as well as in their local areas.

You will notice that most of the writers have one or more credentials listed after their names. In fact, some have half a dozen or more! The careers industry offers extensive opportunities for ongoing training, and most career professionals take advantage of these opportunities to build their skills and keep their knowledge current. If you are curious about what any one of these credentials means, we suggest that you contact the resume writer directly. He or she will be glad to discuss certifications and other qualifications as well as information about services that can help you in your career transition.

Trish Allen, CPRW, CEIP
Resumes at Work
P.O. Box 1416
Stafford, Queensland 4053
Australia
E-mail: resumesatwork
@optusnet.com.au
www.resumesatwork.com.au

Ann Baehr, CPRW
Best Resumes
122 Sheridan St.
Brentwood, NY 11717
Phone: (631) 435-1879
Fax: (631) 977-2821
E-mail: resumesbest@earthlink.net
www.ebestresumes.com

Jacqui D. Barrett, MRW, CPRW, CEIP
Career Trend
11613 W. 113th St.
Overland Park, KS 66210
Phone: (913) 451-1313
Fax: (801) 382-5842
E-mail: Jacqui@careertrend.net
www.careertrend.net

Janet Beckstrom, CPRW
Word Crafter
1717 Montclair Ave.
Flint, MI 48503
Phone: (800) 351-9818
Fax: (810) 232-9257
E-mail: wordcrafter@voyager.net

Carolyn Braden, CPRW
Braden Resume Solutions
108 La Plaza Dr.
Hendersonville, TN 37075
Phone: (615) 822-3317
Fax: (615) 826-9611
E-mail: bradenresume@comcast.net

Tracy Bumpus, CPRW, JCTC
President, RezAMAZE.com
P.O. Box 515
Waverly, TN 37185
Phone: (931) 296-6949
Fax: (877) 887-9590
E-mail: tracy_bumpus@yahoo.com
www.rezamaze.com

Diane Burns, CPRW, CCMC, CCM, CEIP, JCTC
Career Marketing Techniques
Phone: 011-49 (0) 9335-997647
E-mail: diane@polishedresumes.com
www.polishedresumes.com

Romona Camarata, BS Ed., MS Ed., GCDF
Area Director, RL Stevens & Associates
707 Skokie Blvd. #555
Northbrook, IL 60063
Phone: (847) 509-0054
Fax: (847) 509-1004
E-mail: rcamarata@rlstevens.com

Annemarie Cross, CPRW, CEIP, CRW, CCM
Advanced Employment Concepts
P.O. Box 91
Hallam, Victoria 3803
Australia
Phone: + 613 9708 6930
Fax: + 613 9796 4479
E-mail: success@aresumewriter.net
www.aresumewriter.net

Jean Cummings, MAT, CPRW, CEIP
A Resume For Today
123 Minot Ct.
Concord, MA 01742
Phone: (978) 371-9266
Fax: (978) 964-0529
E-mail: jc@AResumeForToday.com
www.AResumeForToday.com

Norine Dagliano, CPRW
ekm Inspirations
616 Highland Way
Hagerstown, MD 21740
Phone: (310) 766-2032
Fax: (310) 745-5700
E-mail: ndagliano@yahoo.com
www.ekminspirations.com

Kirsten Dixson, JCTC, CPRW, CEIP
President, New Leaf Career Solutions
P.O. Box 963
Exeter, NH 03833
Phone: (866) 639-5323
E-mail: kirsten@newleafcareer.com
www.newleafcareer.com

George Dutch, CMF, CCM, JCTC
JOBJOY
130 Slater St., Ste. 750
Ottawa, ON K1P 6E2 Canada
Toll-free: (800) 798-2696
Fax: (613) 594-8700
E-mail: george@georgedutch.com
www.georgedutch.com

Debbie Ellis, MRW, CPRW
Phoenix Career Group
Phone: (800) 876-5506
Fax: (859) 236-3900
E-mail: debbie@phoenixcareergroup.com
www.phoenixcareergroup.com

Wendy S. Enelow, CCM, MRW, JCTC, CPRW
2265 Walker Rd.
Coleman Falls, VA 24536
Phone: (434) 299-5600
Fax: (434) 299-7150
wendyenelow@wendyenelow.com
www.wendyenelow.com

Donna Farrise, JCTC
Dynamic Resumes of Long Island, Inc.
300 Motor Pkwy., Ste. 200
Hauppauge, NY 11788
Phone: (631) 951-4120
Fax: (631) 952-1817
E-mail: donna@dynamicresumes.com
www.dynamicresumes.com

Dayna Feist, CPRW, CEIP, JCTC
President, Gatehouse Business Services
265 Charlotte St.
Asheville, NC 28801
Phone: (828) 254-7893
Fax: (828) 254-7894
E-mail: gatehous@aol.com
www.BestJobEver.com

Louise Fletcher, CPRW
Blue Sky Resumes
15 Merriam Ave.
Bronxville, NY 10708
Phone: (914) 337-5742
Fax: (914) 337-1943
E-mail: lfletcher@blueskyresumes.com
www.blueskyresumes.com

Art Frank, MBA
Resumes "R" Us
334 Eastlake Rd. #200
Palm Harbor, FL 34677
Phone: (727) 787-6885
Toll-free: (866) 600-4300
Fax: (727) 786-9228
E-mail:
AF@PowerResumesAndCoaching.com
www.PowerResumesAndCoaching.com

Louise Garver, CPRW, CMP, JCTC, CEIP, MCDP
Career Directions, LLC
115 Elm St., Ste. 203
Enfield, CT 06082
Phone: (860) 623-9476
Toll-free: (888) 222-9476
Fax: (860) 623-9473
E-mail: TheCareerPro@aol.com
www.CareerEdgeCoach.com and
www.ResumeImpact.com

Sharon Green, M.A., LPC
Ace Resume
3040 E. Shea #2182
Phoenix, AZ 85028
Phone and fax: (602) 494-1688
E-mail: resource56@cox.net

Susan Guarneri, NCC, NCCC, CPRW, CCMC, CEIP, MCC
President, Guarneri Associates
1905 Fern Ln.
Wausau, WI 54401
Toll-free: (866) 881-4055
Fax: (715) 355-1936
E-mail: Resumagic@aol.com
www.resume-magic.com

Cheryl Ann Harland, CPRW, JCTC
Career Source, Inc./Resumes by Design
25227 Grogan's Mill Rd., Ste. 125
The Woodlands, TX 77380
Phone: (281) 296-1659
Fax: (281) 296-1657
E-mail: cah@ResumesByDesign.com
www.ResumesByDesign.com

Beverly Harvey, CPRW, JCTC, CCM, CCMC
Beverly Harvey Resume and Career Services
P.O. Box 750
Pierson, FL 32180

Phone: (386) 749-3111
Toll-free: (888) 775-0916
Fax: (386) 749-4881
E-mail: beverly@harveycareers.com
www.harveycareers.com

Diana Holdsworth, CPRW
Action Communications Resume Services
P.O. Box 234
Rowayton, CT 06853
Phone: (203) 831-0070
Fax: (203) 831-0541
E-mail: hold@optonline.net

Jan Holliday, NCRW
Arbridge Communications
Harleysville, PA 19438
Phone: (215) 513-7420
E-mail: info@arbridge.com
www.arbridge.com

Gayle Howard, CERW, CCM, CPRW, CRW
Top Margin Resumes Online
P.O. Box 74
Chirnside Park, Melbourne 3116
Australia
Phone: 613 9726 6694
Fax: 613 9726 5316
E-mail: getinterviews@topmargin.com
www.topmargin.com

Marcy Johnson, NCRW, CPRW, CEIP
President, First Impression Resume & Job Readiness
11805 U.S. Hwy. 69
Story City, IA 50248
Fax: (515) 733-9296
E-mail: success@resume-job-readiness.com
www.resume-job-readiness.com

Bill Kinser, MRW, CPRW, JCTC, CEIP, CCM
To The Point Resumes
4117 Kentmere Sq.
Fairfax, VA 22030
Phone: (703) 352-8969
Fax: (703) 991-2372
E-mail: bkinser@tothepointresumes.com
www.tothepointresumes.com

Myriam-Rose Kohn, CPRW, CEIP, JCTC, CCM, CCMC
JEDA Enterprises
27201 Tourney Rd., Ste. 201
Valencia, CA 91355
Phone: (661) 253-0801
Fax: (661) 253-0744
E-mail: myriam-rose@jedaenterprises.com
www.jedaenterprises.com

Cindy Kraft, CCMC, CCM, JCTC, CPRW
Executive Essentials
P.O. Box 336
Valrico, FL 33595
Phone: (813) 655-0658
Fax: (813) 354-3483
E-mail: cindy@career-management-coach.com
www.career-management-coach.com

Bonnie Kurka, CPRW, JCTC, FJST
Resume Suite
Tulsa, OK
Phone: (918) 494-4630
Fax: (877) 570-2573
E-mail: bonnie@ResumeSuite.com
www.resumesuite.com

Louise Kursmark, MRW, CPRW, JCTC, CEIP, CCM
Executive Master Team—Career Masters Institute
President, Best Impression Career Services, Inc.
9847 Catalpa Woods Ct.
Cincinnati, OH 45242
Phone: (513) 792-0030
Fax: (877) 791-7127
E-mail: LK@yourbestimpression.com
www.yourbestimpression.com

Lorie Lebert
The Loriel Group/Resumes For Results
P.O. Box 267
Novi, MI 48376
Phone: (248) 380-6100
Toll-free: (800) 870-9059
Fax: (248) 380-0169
E-mail: Lorie@DoMyResume.com and
Info@CoachingROI.com
www.DoMyResume.com and
www.CoachingROI.com

Michael S. Levy, CPRW, CEIP, MCDP, PHR, GCDFI
Career Designers Services, LLC
P.O. Box 626
Brandon, FL 33509-0626
Phone and fax: (813) 655-1461
E-mail: careers@careerdesigners.com
www.careerdesigners.com

Kim Little, JCTC
President, Fast Track Resumes
1281 Courtney Dr.
Victor, NY 14564
Phone: (585) 742-2467
Fax: (585) 742-1907
E-mail: info@fast-trackresumes.com
www.fast-trackresumes.com

Peter S. Marx, JCTC
3208 Wallace Ave.
Tampa, FL 33611
Phone and fax: (813) 832-5133
E-mail: marxps@aol.com

Linda Matias, CEIP, JCTC
Executive Director, CareerStrides
37 E. Hill Dr.
Smithtown, NY 11787
Phone: (631) 382-2425
Fax: (631) 382-2425
E-mail: linda@careerstrides.com
www.careerstrides.com

Sharon McCormick, MS, NCC, NCCC, CPRW
Sharon McCormick Career and Vocational Consulting Services
1061 85th Terrace N., Ste. D
St. Petersburg, FL 33702
Phone: (727) 824-7805
E-mail: career1@ij.net

Eva Mullen, CPRW
A+ Resumes/A+ Business Services
3000 Pearl St., Ste. 111
Boulder, CO 80301
Phone and fax: (303) 444-3438
E-mail: info@ABSonline.biz
www.ABSonline.biz

Ellen Mulqueen, CRW
The Institute of Living
Campus Lodge, 200 Retreat Ave.
Hartford, CT 06106
Phone: (860) 545-7000, ext. 77678
Fax: (860) 545-7140
E-mail: emulque@harthosp.org
www.instituteofliving.com/Programs/
rehab.htm

Carol Nason, CPRW
Career Advantage
95 Flavell Rd.
Groton, MA 01450
Phone: (978) 448-3319
Fax: (978) 448-8948
E-mail: nason1046@aol.com
www.acareeradvantageresume.com

**John O'Connor, MFA, CRW, CPRW,
CCM, CECC**
CareerPro Resumes
3301 Women's Club Dr., Ste. 125
Raleigh, NC 27612
Phone: (919) 787-2400
Fax: (866) 447-9599
E-mail: john@careerproresumes.com
www.CareerProResumes.com

**Debra O'Reilly, CPRW, CEIP, JCTC,
FRWC**
A First Impression
16 Terryville Ave.
Bristol, CT 06010
Phone: (860) 583-7500
Fax: (860) 585-9611
E-mail: debra@resumewriter.com
www.resumewriter.com

**Don Orlando, MBA, CPRW, JCTC, CCM,
CCMC**
The McLean Group
640 S. McDonough
Montgomery, AL 36104
Phone: (334) 264-2020
Fax: (334) 264-9227
E-mail: yourcareercoach@aol.com

Tracy M. Parish, CPRW
Career*Plan*, Inc.
P.O. Box 507
Kewanee, IL 61443
Toll-free: (888) 449-2200
Fax: (309) 856-7710
E-mail: resume@CareerPlan.org
www.CareerPlan.org

Sharon Pierce-Williams, M.Ed., CPRW
The Resume Doc
609 Lincolnshire Lane
Findlay, OH 45840
Phone: (419) 422-0228
Fax: (419) 425-1185
E-mail: Sharon@TheResumeDoc.com
www.TheResumeDoc.com

Barbara Poole, CPRW, CRW, CCMC
Hire Imaging
1812 Red Fox Rd.
St. Cloud, MN 56301
Phone: (320) 253-0975
Fax: (320) 253-1790
E-mail: barb@hireimaging.com
www.hireimaging.com

Judit Price, MS, CCM, IJCTC, CDFI
Principal, Berke & Price Associates
6 Newtowne Way
Chelmsford, MA 01824
Phone: (978) 256-0482
Fax: (978) 250-0787
E-mail: Judit.Price@comcast.net
www.careercampaign.com

Michelle Mastruserio Reitz, CPRW
Printed Pages
3985 Race Rd.
Cincinnati, OH 45211
Phone: (513) 598-9100
Fax: (513) 598-9220
E-mail: michelle@printedpages.com
www.printedpages.com

Jane Roqueplot, CPBA, CWDP
JaneCo's Sensible Solutions
194 N. Oakland Ave.
Sharon, PA 16146
Phone: (724) 342-0100
Fax: (724) 346-5263
E-mail: jane@janecos.com
www.janecos.com

Teena Rose, CPRW, CEIP, CCM
President, Resume to Referral
1824 Rebert Pike
Springfield, OH 45506
Phone: (937) 325-2149
E-mail: admin@resumetoreferral.com
www.resumebycprw.com

Carol J. Rossi, CPRW
Computerized Documents
4 Baywood Blvd.
Brick, NJ 08723
Phone and fax: (732) 477-5172
E-mail: info@powerfulresumes.com
www.powerfulresumes.com

Jennifer Rushton, CRW
Keraijen
Level 14, 309 Kent St.
Sydney, NSW 2000 Australia
Phone: 612 9994 8050
E-mail: info@keraijen.com.au
www.keraijen.com.au

Igor Shpudejko, BSIE, MBA, CPRW, JCTC
Career Focus
23 Parsons Ct.
Mahwah, NJ 07430
Phone: (201) 825-2865
Fax: (201) 825-7711
E-mail: Ishpudejko@aol.com

Janice M. Shepherd, CPRW, JCTC, CEIP
Write On Career Keys
Bellingham, WA 98226
Phone: (360) 738-7958
Fax: (360) 738-1189
E-mail: janice@writeoncareerkeys.com
www.writeoncareerkeys.com

Gail Taylor, CPRW, CEIP
A Hire Power Resume
21213-B Hawthorne Blvd. #5224
Torrance, CA 90503

Phone: (310) 793-4122
Fax: (310) 793-7481
E-mail: hirepower@yahoo.com
www.call4hirepower.com

Ilona Vanderwoude, CPRW, CEIP, CCMC, CJST
Career Branches
P.O. Box 330
Riverdale, NY 10471
Phone: (718) 884-2213
Fax: (646) 349-2218
E-mail: ilona@careerbranches.com
www.careerbranches.com

Vivian VanLier, CPRW, JCTC, CEIP, CCMC
Advantage Resume and Career Services
6701 Murietta Ave.
Valley Glen (Los Angeles), CA 91405
Phone: (818) 994-6655
Fax: (818) 994-6620
E-mail: vvanlier@aol.com
www.CuttingEdgeResumes.com

James Walker, MS
Counselor—ACAP Center
Bldg. 219, Rm. 206, Custer Ave.
Ft. Riley, KS 66442
Phone: (785) 239-2278
Fax: (785) 239-2251

Pearl White, CEIP
A 1st Impression Resume
41 Tangerine
Irvine, CA 92618
Phone: (949) 651-1068
Fax: (949) 651-9415
E-mail: pearlwhite@cox.net
www.a1stimpression.com

Paul Willis, CECC
Career Pro
3301 Woman's Club Dr. #125
Raleigh, NC 27612
Phone: (919) 787-2400
Fax: (919) 787-2411
E-mail: pwillis@bww.com
www.careerproinc.com

INDEX